HELPING SKILLS FOR
HUMAN SERVICE WORKERS

ABOUT THE AUTHORS

Kenneth France grew up in Jacksonville, Florida, attended Davidson College, and then transferred to Wake Forest University, graduating two years later with honors in psychology. In the clinical psychology program at Florida State University, he earned his master's and doctoral degrees, and he did his internship in the clinical psychology department at the University of Florida. For three years he taught at Francis Marion College in South Carolina, and for the last twenty-seven years he has been at Shippensburg University of Pennsylvania, where he was the first recipient of the university's Salute to Teaching. He was the second recipient of the state's Suzanne Brown Excellence in Teaching Award. He is the training coordinator for Warm Line in Carlisle, and he serves as the lead mentor with the online service of the New Hope Crisis Counseling Center. In Pennsylvania, South Carolina, California, and Florida, he has worked with a variety of human service programs. Besides his contributions to *Helping Skills*, he has written several other books.

Kim Weikel graduated from Lycoming College with honors in psychology. She earned a master's degree at the University of Dayton and a Ph.D. at Kent State University, both in clinical psychology. Prior to achieving licensure as a psychologist in Pennsylvania, she completed her predoctoral internship at the Cleveland Department of Veterans Affairs Medical Center and gained postdoctoral experience in a rural Pennsylvania mental health agency. For the last eleven years, she has been teaching in the Psychology Department at Shippensburg University, as well as providing pro bono clinical services and training workshops for local mental health programs.

Michelle Kish is from San Jose, California. She completed her college education at Shippensburg University as an honors student earning a B.A. in Psychology and a minor in English. Following graduation she was employed as a Crisis Intervention Worker at Holy Spirit Hospital's Community Mental Health Center where she had done her pre-graduate internship. Later, Michelle moved her employment to the Stevens Mental Health Center where she again served as a Crisis Intervention Clinician until moving to Auburn, Washington. In Washington, Michelle was a Life Skills Counselor at The Elizabeth House, a foster care group home for pregnant or parenting teens. In addition to her paid employment, Michelle has been an actively involved Youth and Senior Pastor's wife since 1989. Recently, she helped her husband establish a Police Chaplaincy program that integrates pastoral care with crisis intervention services.

Second Edition

HELPING SKILLS FOR HUMAN SERVICE WORKERS

Building Relationships and Encouraging Productive Change

By

KENNETH FRANCE, PH.D. *and* **KIM WEIKEL, PH.D.**

Department of Psychology
Shippensburg University
Shippensburg, Pennsylvania

and

MICHELLE KISH

CHARLES C THOMAS • PUBLISHER, LTD.
Springfield • Illinois • U.S.A.

Published and Distributed Throughout the World by

CHARLES C THOMAS • PUBLISHER, LTD.
2600 South First Street
Springfield, Illinois 62704

ISBN 0-398-07630-8 (hard)
ISBN 0-398-07631-6 (paper)

Library of Congress Catalog Card Number: 2005052976

With THOMAS BOOKS *careful attention is given to all details of manufacturing and design. It is the Publisher's desire to present books that are satisfactory as to their physical qualities and artistic possibilities and appropriate for their particular use.* THOMAS BOOKS *will be true to those laws of quality that assure a good name and good will.*

Printed in the United States of America
CR-R-3

Library of Congress Cataloging-in-Publication Data

France, Kenneth, 1949-
    Helping skills for human service workers : building relationships
and encouraging productive change / Kenneth France and Kim
Weikel and Michelle Kish.--2nd ed.
        p. cm.
    Updated. ed. of: Supportive interviewing in human service
organizations. 1995.
    Includes bibliographical references and index.
    ISBN 0-398-07630-8 -- ISBN 0-398-07631-6 (pbk.)
    1. Helping behavior--Textbooks. 2. Interpersonal communication--
Programmed instruction. I. Weikel, Kim, II. Kish, Michelle. III.
Title.

HV43.F68 2006
361.3'2--dc22

                                                        2005052976

To
The Warm Line workers of the STAR program
Carlisle, Pennsylvania

PREFACE

If building relationships and encouraging productive change are enterprises you wish to learn, this book is for you. Perhaps you aspire to work in crisis intervention, mental health, case management, or social services. You may be a staff member at a group home, rehab center, youth facility, or partial hospitalization program. You may have a job that involves pastoral duties, triage, death notifications, patient care, or working with consumers. Performance in any of those arenas, and a host of others, can be enhanced by the communication skills taught in this book.

In order to introduce you to relevant concepts, we arranged the chapters in the following manner. Chapter 1 discusses several basic issues regarding the development and use of helping skills. Chapter 2 explores common modes of response. In Chapter 3 you will encounter several ingredients that foster positive relationships. Chapter 4 presents a step-by-step approach to problem solving. Chapter 5 examines responses that can detract from your efforts. In Chapter 6 you will find a straightforward approach to establishing goals, objectives, and plans. Chapter 7 describes channels of nonverbal information and commonly encountered nonverbal messages. Chapter 8 highlights endeavors that take center stage before, during, and after scheduled appointments. And Chapter 9 considers the needs of several groups: children, older persons, clients having low socioeconomic status, psychotic individuals, and persons experiencing long-standing issues.

In the second edition, all of that material has been updated with regard to supporting research. In addition, there are several new features. Those include a list of feeling words in Chapter 2, expanded discussion of the factors that characterize positive relationships in Chapter 3 and problem solving in Chapter 4, the addition of objectives and plans to Chapter 6, and inclusion of considerations relating to long-standing maladaptive behavior in Chapter 9.

Chapters 2-9 provide you with opportunities to try out the content being presented. There are multiple-choice questions, as well as short-answer and fill-in-the-response items.

You will discover a progression as you read the practice items in the text. Early chapters include topics such as being away from home and making a career transition—circumstances commonly encountered by undergraduate and graduate students, and by new staff members of human service organizations. Since you probably are in one or more of those categories yourself, you may find you have experienced issues similar to the ones being portrayed. In later chapters, the examples become more diverse in their content, as we demonstrate how helping skills can be used with a wide variety of issues.

There are two complete interviews in the book. One is in Chapter 4 and the other is in Chapter 6. In both interactions the *client* is going to school and is a newly employed staff member of a human service organization. As with the early practice items, our hope is that you will readily identify with the person being interviewed. From the client's perspective, we want you to appreciate the value of the skills being demonstrated.

Throughout the book we write as though you are interacting with one person. But all of the material also applies to interactions with two or more individuals.

Some authors of counseling, interviewing, and helping texts praise naturalness, spontaneity, flexibility, and individual creativity, then go on to present complex sets of tactics or overwhelming amounts of information that are impossible to keep in mind. In this book the basic system we present is simple and straightforward. Consequently, it *will* become possible for you to keep in mind the fundamental concepts, thereby giving you the freedom to be flexible, spontaneous, creative, and natural.

As an introductory treatment of helping skills, simplicity and the building of foundation abilities are guiding principles for what follows. Consequently, there are many topics that are beyond the scope of this book. Examples of such areas include more specialized endeavors (such as humor and paradoxical intention) and various theoretical perspectives (such as psychodynamic and cognitive-behavioral).

Other topics on which you will find limited information are habits associated with gender, affectional orientation, cultural heritage, and ethnicity. We believe that each client brings to the interaction a host of individual preferences, some of which are based on the factors just named. In our opinion, it is beyond the scope of this book, or any single book, to address the thousands of possible backgrounds possessed by clients. Whatever a client's background, we believe workers should be respectful of the person's values and beliefs. (At the same time, we agree that it may be appropriate for staff members to help clients explore the consequences of problematic values and beliefs that become topics of discussion.) When many of your clients share a common background, you may wish to do additional research on central influences affecting your client base. This can help you more effectively mesh your own efforts with the expectations of those you serve.

Because of the traditions of some client groups, it is possible for discussion of feelings and encouragement of independent problem solving to be inappropriate activities. When that is the case, you will need to learn relationship-building and change-promoting practices that are in tune with the backgrounds of those persons.

Although the approaches we advocate in this book are in agreement with many of the ideas discussed by other authors, it appears that our style of helping does have some unique aspects. We emphasize being natural, *demonstrating* understanding of the client's thoughts and feelings, avoiding repetitive phrasing, and choosing responses with an eye toward the interaction's ultimate purpose.

We hope the book aids in your development of helping skills appropriate for use by human service workers. If you have any feedback or comments you would like to pass along, please contact K.F. at the Department of Psychology, Shippensburg University, Shippensburg, PA, 17257.

K.F.
K.W.
M.K.

ACKNOWLEDGMENTS

The book exists today because of the support provided by Michael Thomas of Charles C Thomas, Publisher. There is content taken from previous collaborations with Charles C Thomas, Publisher. Some information appears in *Crisis Intervention: A Handbook of Immediate Person-to-Person Help, Fourth Edition*, Copyright 2002.

CONTENTS

HELPING SKILLS FOR
HUMAN SERVICE WORKERS

Chapter 1

INTRODUCTION

Clients in helping relationships make progress when they feel understood and actively work toward goals that they care about, as documented by extensive empirical research (e.g., Lambert & Barley, 2002; Tryon & Winograd, 2002). This book applies those findings by presenting ways for promoting rapport and facilitating desired change. We describe ways to create positive relationships and engage clients in joint efforts that focus on developing adaptive targets to work toward and achieving productive outcomes. Effective coping is the ultimate goal, and encouraging movement in that direction is the reason for all of the techniques we discuss.

There are many approaches one can take when working with clients. Empirical research indicates, however, that factors which are common to most helping strategies are some of the best predictors of client improvement (Lambert & Ogles, 2004). Compared to techniques associated with particular approaches, common factors account for twice as much client improvement, and, regardless of the approach taken, clients improve more when they experience a strong therapeutic bond with the human service worker (Lambert & Barley, 2002). To better understand that bond, the American Psychological Association's Division of Psychotherapy developed a task force to investigate specific relationship factors associated with productive client change. The task force concluded that strong and consistent research findings document the effectiveness of three factors in person-to-person human-service relationships: developing a therapeutic alliance, demonstrating empathy, and focusing on goal consensus and collaboration (Norcross, 2002). Those three factors are important components of the helping skills discussed in this book. We address ways of developing a therapeutic relationship in Chapter 3, with emphasis on conveying empathy. Promoting consensus and collaboration is a central focus of both the material on problem solving in Chapter 4 and the techniques in Chapter 6 for establishing goals, objectives, and plans. In the remaining chapters we discuss ways to enhance those fundamental skills.

Now that we have looked at the worker's perspective, let's consider the client's point of view. Clients requesting assistance from human service workers often are feeling anxious, low, or combinations of both emotions. There are essential commonalities among anxiety and depressive disorders according to empirical evidence reviewed by Barlow, Allen, and Choate (2004). They assert that at the core of those disorders is a sense of being unable to control events, which results in negative emotions. Emotional disorders can arise out of biological pre-dispositions and early learning experiences, and then intensify during challenging situations in which individuals perceive a lack of control.

According to Barlow and his colleagues, successful therapeutic interventions focus on building a basic sense of being able to influence events. The development of such confidence can be supported in a number of ways. Possibilities include the following three strategies: (1) logically thinking through things prior to taking on challenging situations (such as realistically estimating both the likelihood of negative events happening and the true nature of negative consequences that actually might occur), (2) actively exploring ways of confronting and dealing with challenging situations, and (3) accepting emotions rather than expending effort trying to avoid them.

Consistent with the ideas of Barlow and his associates, the problem-solving approach described in Chapter 4 can be used to help clients control what they are able to influence. We support the following: (1) logically thinking through challenging situations in advance, (2) active-ly exploring ways of confronting those situations and dealing with them adaptively, and (3) accepting negative emotions and then addressing their causes via realistic problem solving to bring about environmental change and/or by adaptively modifying the way one views the circumstances.

ENCOURAGING CLIENT AUTONOMY AND SELF-EFFICACY

Throughout the book we emphasize providing a supportive relationship in which clients can explore their thoughts and feelings, consider options, and make their own decisions regarding changes they might like to implement. In other words, we support client *autonomy*. Empirical research has demonstrated that individuals try harder and perform better when changes are more internally motivated and are developed in a nonauthoritarian context, than when change is motivated by the expectations of others (e.g., Sheldon & Elliot, 1999; Vansteenkiste, Simons, Sheldon, Lens, & Deci, 2004). Consequently, we discourage advice giving and encourage active client involvement in problem solving and in the establishment of targets for change.

Clients who actively participate in setting targets for behavior change may experience greater self-confidence or, more specifically, greater self-efficacy regarding their abilities. Albert Bandura (1997) defined *self-efficacy* as belief in one's ability to successfully execute a particular behavior. He noted that self-efficacy predicts how much effort and persistence one puts into changing a behavior. Clients with higher self-efficacy regarding coping and behavior change (in other words, clients who believe they actually will be able to cope with difficulties and accomplish desired change) are more likely to persist when faced with obstacles and are, consequently, more likely to successfully bring about desired change. Empirical research confirms that stronger belief in one's ability to accomplish change is associated with greater success. This effect has been demonstrated in a variety of areas, including the following: overcoming phobias, achieving and maintaining weight loss, improving athletic performance, increasing activity level, and coping with anxiety (Bandura, 1997; Bandura & Locke, 2003; Evon & Burns, 2004; Rejeski et al., 2003).

Research has also investigated interactions between internal motivation and self-efficacy. For example, one study (Senecal, Nouwen, & White, 2000) looked at dietary self-care among adults with diabetes. Adherence to dietary plans was associated with both internal motivation to regulate diet and higher self-efficacy for controlling one's diet.

Given the links among autonomy, self-efficacy, and successful coping, efforts to foster autonomy and self-efficacy seem important. Bandura (1997) identified a number of ways to enhance self-efficacy, including receiving credible verbal encouragement and successfully accomplishing what you set out to do. He suggested that performance success, or what he called mastery experience, is a primary way of increasing self-efficacy. From our perspective, both self-efficacy and autonomy are enhanced when the worker encourages productive change by helping clients engage in adaptive coping efforts that foster success in areas which are important to them.

REWARDS AND COSTS OF USING HELPING SKILLS

Let's consider some of what you do as an effective human service worker. Since the ultimate goal is for *clients* to develop insights and to cope more adaptively, you encourage their input and foster their initiative. Using the least amount of authority necessary, you seek to understand feelings, and you encourage the expression of ideas. By sharing responsibility for determining the subject matter and the pacing of interactions, you put clients in position to take credit for progress they make, thereby enhancing their self-efficacy and autonomy.

The preceding considerations imply both rewards and costs for you. Costs include:

- as a student, trainee, or new employee, you must make the effort to learn the art of helping;
- as a skilled worker, you will need to allot sufficient time for problem-solving interactions with clients (with about 20 minutes being the minimum for an initial problem-solving discussion).

Rewards include:

- knowing you can flexibly deal in-depth with a wide range of topics;
- possessing the skills to create and maintain a productive alliance in which the client eventually emerges as being responsible for positive change.

In addition to rewards within the worker-client relationship, learning helping skills has other advantages, including both relationship-building and career-enhancing benefits. Let's consider some of those, starting with the career side.

When CEOs of human service organizations are asked to name the skills they would most like to see in an entry-level staff member, effective interpersonal communication often tops their lists. Consequently, developing the skills discussed in this book will give you very marketable abilities.

With regard to relationship building, one of the most universally helpful forms of assistance is appraisal support. This form of assistance means aiding others in understanding and coping with problems. Since facilitating problem solving is a key skill that we will address, learning the material that follows will enhance your ability to provide one of the most valued forms of social support.

Of course, when you are with friends, you aren't always talking about problems, and lighthearted exchanges often have an unfocused quality. But in this book we are concentrating on something different. Compared to social conversation with acquaintances, discussions with clients can be distinguished in several ways. First, the interactions are planned. Second, the focus is on *clients'* thoughts and feelings. And third, human service workers do not avoid unpleasant topics.

MAKING PROGRESS

Since you are reading this book, it's likely that communicating effectively is important to you. And because of your interest, you probably already possess a good set of abilities.

But you may be in for a surprise.

When trying helping strategies for the first time, individuals often feel awkward and uneasy. And it is common to find that the quality of your skills actually declines during the initial phase of training. Although it is not unusual for students and new workers to doubt their abilities, results of empirical studies suggest that self-efficacy increases and stress decreases with education and experience (e.g., Levitt, 2001).

Wrestling with the material that follows will be demanding and frequently will require a fair amount of trial and error. On the other hand, perseverance probably will lead to an ability level that is far better than your present one. In order to reach that higher plane, you must develop ways of combining your current skills with what you are about to learn.

If you are in a class that teaches helping principles, you will see that students progress at different rates. For those who hit their stride a bit later than some of their classmates, seeing others excel can be exasperating. But such frustration actually can be productive, if it helps one become more effective in using feedback to make adjustments. When you are responsive to feedback and subsequently are able to improve your performance a bit, your self-efficacy for learning helping skills should increase, and you should feel more motivated to continue practicing the skills.

Another way of gaining motivation for sticking with the material is to see how productive it is when used in professional settings. If there are opportunities for you to observe skilled human services workers, take advantage of those possibilities. Such experiences can energize you and can help you perceive the value of the techniques you are learning. Another benefit of such observations is that you can see the professional manner in which veteran human service workers do their jobs. Observing staff members calmly handle difficult situations may help you realize that the pressure of being a novice eventually dissipates. Bandura (1997) refers to such observation as vicarious experience, and he notes that it can increase self-efficacy.

Unfortunately, you may also observe veteran staff members who display inappropriate behavior. Some persons fail to use the helping techniques in which they have been trained. When bad performance is what you encounter, pay attention to the effects it has on clients. And remember that you can learn how to do a better job than the one you are seeing.

THE ROLE OF PRACTICE

This book presents essential content and provides realistic scenarios in which you can apply helping principles. Studying the material and completing the exercises will be useful, but we believe the most important learning will take place when you practice with another person, record the interaction, receive feedback from knowledgeable observers, and then use what you have learned the next time you do a role play.

Learning from your critiqued performances may be easier if you maintain your own library of recorded role plays you do. Having your personal copy of interactions allows you to review them at your convenience and also provides evidence of your improvement over time.

If you are a student in a helping skills class, you probably will do role-play interactions as part of the course. But it is also possible to arrange role plays yourself. Such efforts can be worthwhile if you record the interactions and have them critiqued by a person who appreciates what you are trying to learn.

Doing recorded role plays and being evaluated by others can be nerve-wracking. As we have noted, however, such nervousness usually decreases with time and experience.

During the interaction try to stay calm. You will feel more relaxed as the novelty wears off.

Once you are a veteran with several practice role plays under your belt, the learning cycle will be more familiar. You will become accustomed to the process that involves (1) identifying areas needing improvement, and (2) making appropriate adjustments.

It is natural to regret having behaved in ways that led to corrective feedback. But the goal is to learn from your miscues, rather than to become anxious about the fact that you are not perfect.

Instead of worrying about your own imperfections, during a role play you should focus on the client. As a worker who is supposed to be assisting that person, the number one priority in your practice interactions is to concentrate on the client's words and nonverbal behavior. Keep your focus on the other person. Pay attention to what the individual is saying. While the person is talking, do not think about what you are going to say next. Simply listen. When there is an opportunity for you to speak, gather your thoughts and make an appropriate response. Immediately prior to your comment, a few moments of relaxed silence are perfectly acceptable.

You may need to read the preceding paragraph again. As information from a client begins to accumulate, most novices feel a great temptation to begin planning a response, in order to be ready with a comment when the opportunity arrives. But if you start thinking about yourself, you stop listening to the client. Consequently, the response you make is likely to be out of touch with the totality of what the client has communicated. On the other hand, accomplished human service workers rarely make such gaffs, because they focus on their clients rather than on themselves.

In order to assist your efforts at becoming a skilled human service worker, this book presents a number of useful techniques. In general, a set of techniques has value if it provides effective ways of thinking and behaving. Much of the power of these adaptive strategies comes from the self-efficacy you experience once you become proficient with them. When armed with a set of methods that you feel comfortable using, you expend less effort on thinking about your abilities, and you focus more energy on actually getting the job done.

Although techniques can be beneficial, it is also possible for them to be counterproductive if they are applied in a rigid or artificial manner. Consequently, when employing the strategies described in the chapters that follow, you should always use them with flexibility and common sense.

INTRODUCTIONS

If you are learning helping skills in a group setting, how you get along with others in the group is more important than interpersonal relationships in traditional lecture-discussion environments. Since most skill-development formats involve giving feedback to one another, participants and leaders need to feel comfortable with each other and need to share a certain amount of trust. One approach to laying a foundation for group cohesiveness is to begin with an introductions exercise. The activity we recommend is found in Appendix A. If you are in a class that will be using it, you should *not* read Appendix A before participating in the exercise.

YOUR CURRENT SKILLS

In preparation for the next chapter, it is worthwhile to take a baseline measure of your current helping style. A good way to sample your skills is for you to do a role play. If you are in a course, one option is for the instructor to conduct a baseline exercise, which can be structured in the following manner. The class divides into three-person groups. In each group there is an observer, a client, and a worker. The task of the observer is to write what the *worker* says. (It probably will be impossible to write everything, so just be sure to jot down the first few words of each comment and as much of the rest of it as you can.) The task of the client is to portray a person in need of problem-solving assistance. (Your instructor may provide you with a scenario to role play.) And the task of the worker is to do what you think is appropriate in such an interaction. The role play need not be long. Generally, three to five minutes is sufficient.

The reason for the baseline exercise is to get an indication of your group's current skills. Consequently, these role plays probably will differ from later ones in two ways. First, there is no feedback after the role play. The intent is to get a sample of everyone's skills, rather than to change those skills. Second, the observer keeps the observation notes rather than giving them to the worker. Observers retaining their own observer notes allows the workers to remain anonymous as the baseline measures are discussed in the class.

When processing baseline role plays, remember *not* to identify the individuals who made worker comments that come up for discussion. The purpose of the exercise is not to identify who said what. Instead, the objective is to discover the kinds of responses made by members of the group.

Another way of measuring your current skills is to do the dialog exercise in Appendix B. Your instructor may give you directions with regard to the exercise. If that is not the case, you should do it on your own prior to reading Chapter 2.

FEEDBACK

Although you will not have any individual feedback if you do the baseline role plays, all subsequent role plays should involve detailed feedback. The purpose of such critiques is for participants to consider their efforts and to modify behaviors that show room for improvement. But, as results of empirical research have demonstrated (e.g., Daniels & Larson, 2001), being told that one has made mistakes can evoke strong reactions. Since feedback is helpful only if the recipient uses it, here are some guidelines for productive evaluations.

• ***Focus on what the worker actually did.*** To the best of your ability, describe what the worker said or did, then state what you liked or didn't like about it. Since there are many correct ways of handling any situation, it generally is not productive to concentrate on "should haves," "would haves," or "could haves." Wide-ranging discussion of alternative responses can take place after feedback to the worker is over, but not as part of commentary on his or her performance.

- *Be succinct.* We all have limits on how much criticism we can absorb. Oversaturation is not productive. Consequently, think about the points you want to make, communicate them to the person, and then stop.

If there is an instructor or trainer who gives feedback, pay attention to how that person delivers both positive and corrective feedback. Over time, feedback you give will become increasingly more like that of the leader.

As we have said, for all but the baseline role plays, there should be written feedback on every training interaction you do. There are a variety of formats for arranging written comments; Appendix C contains the approach we use.

Just as there are different ways of providing written feedback, there also are various approaches to structuring a helping skills course. In Appendix D you will find one set of possibilities regarding class organization.

SUMMARY

When used effectively, helping skills engage clients in an alliance intended to promote effective coping. Once you become a skilled worker who schedules sufficient time for interactions, you will be able to facilitate flexible contacts that leave clients feeling responsible for productive changes that take place. In addition, learning the art of helping can increase your professional marketability, as well as enhance your effectiveness in offering social support.

Learning helping skills typically involves practicing, making mistakes, and using feedback to do better the next time. The trauma of role playing usually lessens with repetition, and performance generally improves when workers focus on their clients rather than on themselves.

Initial tasks in a helping skills course include taking measures of your current skills and becoming comfortable with the persons who will be giving you feedback. When you are the one providing feedback, you should succinctly focus on actual behavior displayed by the worker.

Chapter 2

FIVE WAYS OF RESPONDING

Take a look at the dialog exercise (Appendix B) and see where your slash mark is for option A. Since the dread being felt by the client is discounted by that response, it is an insensitive comment. Hopefully, you were dissatisfied with the statement and placed your mark toward the left end of the line. But if your mark is on the right portion of the line, and you still believe the comment is a good one, you should discuss the item with a knowledgeable person, such as your instructor or your supervisor.

Option A functions as a litmus test. Its purpose is to verify that we share a common starting point for viewing responses as being helpful or detrimental.

Now let's begin to make some finer distinctions.

David Johnson (2003) has asserted that when one person is trying to be supportive of another, most comments from the would-be helper can be categorized according to five modes of response. Each of these modes has a different objective, and each has its own effects on the interaction.

ADVICE

The purpose of advice is to tell others what to do. Results of empirical research suggest that such direct guidance is often associated with interactions that workers subsequently view as being shallow and of little value, and that clients subsequently see as being rough and unpleasant (Friedlander, Thibodeau, & Ward, 1985).

Advice provides ready-made courses of action, rather than encouraging individuals to generate their own solutions. When you bypass others' own decision-making capabilities, you communicate the belief that you are in a better position than them to decide what should be done, and you may damage their self-esteem by implying that your ideas are superior to theirs. Your clients' agreement or disagreement with your high opinion of yourself will be reflected in one or more of the following basic consequences that can follow advice giving.

- *Rejected.* If you tell a client what to do, the person may reject the advice. When that happens, the individual may also have come to believe that you do not really understand the problem, since you made such an inappropriate suggestion. Consequently, rejected advice often is a sign of poor rapport, which can hinder subsequent efforts at relationship building.
- *Accepted.* The client may accept the advice. That probably is what you wanted when you made the suggestion. But there still may be trouble ahead, since there are two remaining possibilities.
- *Failed.* Having accepted your advice, the client later tries it. The result, however, is a miserable failure. Circumstances now may be worse than they were before, and the client may blame you for the mess. Such finger pointing can occur even if the advice was good and the problem actually was with the client's implementation of your recommendations.
- *Worked.* This is the best possible outcome. You give advice, it is accepted, and it works. When faced with a new and equally difficult decision, what is the client going to do? Having successfully implemented your advice in the past, the person may again turn to you for guidance. If that happens, you may be fostering dependency, rather than encouraging independent problem-solving abilities.

Recognizing the risks of advice, there are times when it is appropriate. The most crucial occasion for advice-giving is during life-threatening situations. For example, with a suicidal person it is always appropriate to say (if you mean it), "I don't want you to kill yourself." Although this is telling the individual what not to do, preserving life is worth the risk of dependency.

In the dialog exercise, option B is an example of advice. Take a look at where your slash mark is. Next, if you did the baseline role plays, check your observer notes for examples of advice. Compare what you and your peers thought of advice before, to what you think of it now.

ANALYSIS

When you analyze, you describe your opinion of how things got to be the way they are. As with advice, the emphasis is on what *you* believe, instead of on what the client thinks.

Sometimes analysis comes in the form of general observations about life. These are truisms that you think are applicable. For instance, you might say, "Most people feel uneasy at first. It takes time to get to know someone." Clients may or may not see such pronouncements as being relevant to their situations. And, as with all analysis, general observations about life put the focus on your beliefs rather than on your clients' thoughts. Consequently, it is best to avoid such comments.

There are occasions when analysis is appropriate. For example, during initial interviews with new clients, psychotherapists often negotiate goals for the intervention, and then provide a rationale for how counseling can facilitate progress toward those objectives. By identifying potential therapeutic strategies, therapists also imply the existence of certain causative factors, as in the following scenario. "You have selected 'understand my children better' as one of your goals. In order to improve that understanding, we will do some role playing exercises, and eventually you will have homework assignments in which you try out communication skills that we develop in our sessions." The analysis implied in this rationale is that the client's lack of communication skills has contributed to the problem.

Although there are some situations that call for your analysis, such as when providing a rationale for a recommendation you make, we encourage you to use this response sparingly. As much as possible, the focus should be on the *client's* interpretation and understanding of events.

In the dialog exercise, option C is an example of analysis. Look at the location of your slash mark. Also check your observer notes for the baseline role plays and see if you find any examples of analysis. Now consider whether you have changed your opinion of this response mode.

SYMPATHY/REASSURANCE

When laypersons try to be supportive, two of the most commonly used responses are sympathy and reassurance. Sympathy seeks to communicate concern by saying how you feel about the other person's difficulties, and reassurance is intended to calm the individual by offering some type of guarantee.

If you are in a relationship that typically involves self-disclosure of personal information about yourself, it may be entirely appropriate to say how you feel about the other person's difficulties. But if the relationship does not involve you regularly revealing your personal thoughts and emotions, then sympathy probably is inappropriate. When communicated in a professional relationship, sympathy can be perceived as pity or can be seen as being insincere. In either case, it is likely to hinder rather than to enhance rapport.

The appropriateness of reassurance depends on the worth of its guarantee. In order for a statement of reassurance to be believable, there must be evidence to support it. For example, an auto accident victim goes to the emergency room with an injured arm and has X-rays taken. The E.R. physician receives the report of the radiology consult and then says to the patient, "The X-rays show no signs of any broken bones." Such a statement is an example of appropriate reassurance because the speaker has evidence to back up the assertion.

In order to consider another kind of reassurance, let's continue the hospital scenario. Imagine the accident victim is a friend, and you are with her in the E.R. examining room. While waiting for the radiology report, you say, "I'm sure everything will be fine." Although you are seeking to calm her, this statement may have the opposite effect. She may believe that you don't appreciate the severity of the situation, and she may belittle your future efforts to be helpful.

There is no value in false reassurance. Its guarantee is worthless.

(Rather than signifying a response mode, the term "reassurance" can also mean an emotion experienced by the client. Used in this manner, reassurance might describe unpleasant feelings being relieved or positive expectations being strengthened.)

In the dialog exercise, look at where your slash mark is for option D. In addition, check your observer notes for examples of sympathy and reassurance. Think about the appropriateness of these two frequently encountered responses.

INTERROGATION

If you ask questions or specify the topic to be discussed, you are interrogating–a mode of response that has been the focus of several classic empirical studies. When evaluating interactions that contain high levels of such information seeking, workers subsequently have viewed them as being shallow and of little value, and clients subsequently have seen them as being rough and unpleasant (Friedlander et al., 1985). Ongoing clients have been shown to feel less understood and less supported when the intent of the worker was to interrogate (Hill, Helms, Spiegel, & Tichenor, 1988). And for both brief interactions and ongoing contacts, questioning has been found to be negatively related to clients feeling understood (Elliott, James, Reimschuessel, Cislo, & Sack, 1985). Given those findings, it is not surprising that trainees tend to ask their clients fewer questions at the end of their training than they did at the beginning (Kivlighan, 1989).

As this research implies, interrogation is a powerful and directive technique. But there are degrees of control you can use, as we will see.

Open Probes and Questions

One area of worker control in interrogation is whether an inquiry is open or closed. Open probes (statements that specify the area to be discussed) and questions give the client considerable freedom in choosing what to say. Open questions usually begin with the word "What" or with the word "How." Open probes often start with phrases such as "Tell me" or "Describe." Here are several examples of open interrogation.

- How are things going?
- What is on your mind?
- Tell me about your efforts since our last meeting.
- Describe some of the feelings you've been having.

A number of researchers have compared the effects of open and closed questions. (Closed questions are discussed below.) Hargie (1984) summarized the findings and noted the following research conclusions. When responding to open questions as opposed to closed questions, individuals engage in higher levels of self-disclosure, convey information that is more accurate, and provide longer replies. In addition, they perceive the worker to be more empathic.

Most open questions provide some degree of direction. When that is the case, it generally is more effective for the initial focus to be on current issues. If you want to explore other topics, such as experiences from the past, that can come later.

In the dialog exercise, take a look at where your mark is for option E. Also examine your observer notes for examples of open interrogation. We believe that, "How have you tried to deal with your fears?" is an example of a productive open question. Likewise, the open probes and questions you find in your observer notes may have had positive effects on the interaction.

Closed Probes and Questions

Closed questions and probes can be answered with a small bit of information or with a simple "Yes" or "No." There are many phrases that can begin closed questions, including "Do you," "Are you," "Is it," and "Have you." The following responses are examples of closed interrogation.

- Did you talk to Mr. Richards?
- Have you told him what you think?
- When did you go to see him?
- Tell me his phone number.

Closed questions and probes are appropriate when you would be satisfied with receiving just the specified information. But, in reality, clients often ignore the fact that the question is closed, especially if you are working with cooperative middle-class adults. For instance, "Have you told Mr. Richards what you think?" may result in a long description of interactions between the client and Mr. Richards.

Sometimes, though, clients take you at your word and only answer the question you actually asked. If that is the case, the reply to, "Have you told Mr. Richards what you think?" is only a "Yes" or "No." Such minimal responses are most likely to come from children, uncooperative individuals, persons highly respectful of your authority, and members of lower socioeconomic classes.

With uncooperative clients, there is one particularly problematic question format that can help you paint yourself into a corner. This sticky form of interrogation begins with phrases such as "Would you," "Could you," "Will you," and "Can you." When asking one of these questions you usually are seeking agreement or cooperation, but the phrasing of your request sets you up for a different answer: "No." Consequently, if you are looking for an affirmative reply, do not ask "Would you," "Could you," "Will you," or "Can you" unless you are certain of getting a positive response.

Let's say you are working with a teenager who is viewed as a discipline problem. You say to the young person, "Could you tell me what happened yesterday?" And the reply is "No." You can cope with that response in a number of ways, but they all are time consuming and all require some backtracking on your part. It would have been better to have asked, "What happened yesterday?" Since a "What" question does not invite a "Yes" or "No" answer, you may get a fuller response.

Ill-conceived closed questions can also lead to inefficient communication that simply generates unusable responses. For example, when inner-city case workers ask clients, "Do you know your Social Security number?" a common reply is "Yes." Consequently, staff members learn to be more precise in phrasing questions. They generally drop the "Do you" question and replace it with "What is your Social Security number?"

In the development of your own abilities, you can adopt one helping style that you will use with cooperative middle-class adult clients and another style that you will use with children, uncooperative individuals, persons highly respectful of your authority, and members of lower socioeconomic classes. But an alternative strategy is to build a solid foundation of skills that are effective in a broad range of circumstances. The latter approach is the one we advocate. Consequently, our view is that closed probes and questions generally should be avoided, unless you would be perfectly satisfied with the brief response you are requesting.

Where is your mark for option F in the dialog exercise? We believe, "Will you be with him tomorrow?" is an unnecessary closed question. But let's say, for some reason, you really must know the answer. If that is the case, you will get a more informative response if you ask, "What are your plans for tomorrow?"

Look for examples of closed probes and questions in your observer notes. As with option F, most of the closed questions you find probably could have been deleted, with some being replaced by more productive open questions.

Questions to Avoid

You should simply stay away from some forms of interrogation. We will examine three sorts of questions to avoid.

Leading questions seek agreement rather than an honest response. With leading questions the reply you want is communicated by your biased phrasing. Here are several examples.

- You've been in this situation before, haven't you?
- You talked to her, didn't you?
- You're still unsure, aren't you?

Clients' responses to such questions often have more to do with their opinion of your authority than with the actual answers. Although the truth may be considerably different, you generally get affirmative replies from clients who respect you and who want to please you. Conversely, leading questions may generate negative responses from clients who do not respect you or who want to displease you.

Examine your mark for option G in the dialog exercise. Also look for examples of leading questions in your observer notes. In the future, remember that this is one style of interrogation to avoid.

Multiple questions are another flawed form of interrogation. This type of response involves asking two or more questions before giving the person a chance to answer. When the reply does come, you may not know what it means, especially if you have asked multiple closed questions. For example, you ask, "Did you speak with her or did you decide to wait?" and the client says, "I did." Although you have an answer, you still don't know whether the client spoke with her or decided to wait.

The replies to multiple closed questions tend to be confusing to workers. On the other hand, any multiple question can be confusing to clients. For instance, "What might you say to her? How could you approach her?" may be perceived as difficult to answer.

Multiple questions can come about in a couple of ways. Sometimes while asking a question you think of additional ideas, and you inadvertently incorporate them into what you are saying. The problem here is one of pacing. Rather than trying to cover too much at once, it is better to be patient. The result will be communication that is understandable and effective.

A second way in which multiple questions can come about is when you ask a question, realize you could have phrased it better, and then immediately ask another version of it. Wanting to rephrase an awkwardly asked question is a natural desire, but it is better to stop after one question and wait for the client's response. Usually the person will understand what you wanted to ask and will give you the sort of reply you are seeking. When that is not the case, you eventually can clarify your intent and try again.

Take a look at your mark for option H in the dialog exercise. You can also scan your observer notes for examples of multiple questions, but you probably won't find any. That may be because the worker did not ask any multiple questions, or it may be because you could not write fast enough to get them down.

Why questions are a third style of interrogating that you should avoid. Whatever your purpose in asking them, "Why" questions often are perceived as accusations. And when clients feel threatened, they tend to respond defensively. In order to justify themselves, they may distort information, or they may fabricate answers.

If you absolutely must know "Why," you can start your question with a phrase such as, "What might be some of the reasons for. . . ." For instance, "Why are you waiting to make a decision?" could become, "What might be some reasons for waiting to make a decision?" We believe the latter question is less likely to be perceived as a challenge.

Where is your mark for option I? Check your observer notes for sentences that begin with "Why." In the future, remember to stay away from such questions.

REFLECTION

Reflection is using fresh words to summarize important thoughts and feelings expressed by another person. This definition has several implications.

- *Fresh words.* The key terms in your comment are different from the ones used by the client. Repeating what the person said is not reflection.
- *Summarize.* Reflection is selective. You do not try to include everything the person communicated.
- *Thoughts AND feelings.* Reflection can involve both ideas and emotions. Continually focusing on one, to the exclusion of the other, does not constitute good reflection.
- *Expressed.* You are focusing on the client's message. The communication you receive can involve nonverbal as well as verbal behavior, but the basis for your comment can be found in what has just transpired.

Is reflection a new mode of response for you? If it is, you may feel as though you aren't doing anything when you reflect. But we contend, for two reasons, that you *are* doing something.

First, you are doing something when you reflect because there usually are positive effects on the interaction. The other person typically perceives that you have been paying attention and that you are attempting to understand. Consequently, the individual is likely to continue discussing appropriate information.

Second, you are doing something when you reflect because reflection is hard work. You must hear the person's words, understand them, remember essential themes, wait for an opportunity to speak, choose your own words to describe important messages, and then concisely make your comment to the person.

Fortunately, reflection is a fairly forgiving response. If you occasionally make a mistake and reflect inaccurately, the most likely event is that the client will correct you. So, even if you are off target once in a while, you can still be fostering good communication.

Nevertheless, you do not *want* to be incorrect and to miss the point. With regard to brief contacts, the results of one empirical study indicated such misperception to be the most common way in which workers hindered interactions (Elliott et al., 1985). And in an empirical investigation that focused on continuing contacts, the more misunderstood clients felt, the less value they assigned to the session (Hill et al., 1988).

Other researchers (Gallagher & Hargie, 1989) compared a group of experienced counselors who had recently completed a helping skills program to another group of experienced counselors who had not been through the program. In terms of their helping behaviors, the greatest difference between the two groups was that the counselors who had been through the training program displayed *more* inaccurate reflections with real clients than did the counselors who had not participated in the program. The training-program counselors in this study seemed to emphasize the form of reflection over the substance of accurately understanding their clients.

The findings by Gallagher and Hargie (1989) can serve as a warning. In practicing the use of reflection, you do not want to lose sight of the fact that your goal is to *accurately* summarize the client's thoughts and feelings. Since understanding those thoughts and feelings is a prerequisite for good reflection, you should first concentrate on appreciating what the client is communicating. You must listen. Only *after* making the effort to understand, do you progress to the next task: putting your comprehension into words you say to the person.

Good reflections usually incorporate only part of what clients communicate. Consequently, you are providing direction when you reflect. By focusing on some material and leaving out other content, you increase the likelihood that the client will engage in additional discussion of what you include, and you decrease the probability of the person further exploring what you exclude.

The tone of your reflection may also influence the nature of the client's response. For example, if an individual says, "I'm so sick of it. No matter what I try, he never listens to me," the tone of your response can be positive and focused on the future, "You really would like to get through to him," or negative and focused on the past, "So far, nothing you've tried has seemed to work." A positive, future-oriented tone may encourage the client to focus on desirable conditions, whereas a negative tone may encourage further description of unpleasant circumstances. Although there certainly are times when reflections with a negative tone are entirely appropriate, you should remember your ultimate purpose is to encourage productive change. And, in order to do that, you must include reflections that are positive and are oriented toward the future. Results of empirical research suggest that when workers frequently use such comments, clients feel more powerful and confident with regard to solving their problems (Bohart et al., 1993).

Problem solving often involves persons in addition to the identified client. When such individuals are available and willing to participate in sessions, and clients agree to their involvement, including those persons in all or part of the session can be both revealing and productive. The basic strategy of reflecting thoughts and feelings applies to those nonclient participants as well.

Emotional Levels of Reflection

Just as forms of interrogation (such as open and closed questions) can be defined according to the range of information being specified, a reflection may be referred to by its feeling level. In terms of emotional content, we can consider three broad categories of reflection.

Factual reflections describe conditions without any reference to emotions. By avoiding feelings, you promote rapid movement through topics.

Surface feeling reflections recognize obvious emotions being expressed. By matching or slightly exceeding the intensity communicated by the client, you encourage the individual to consider issues being discussed.

Underlying feeling reflections suggest emotions that have not been explicitly stated or expressed by the client. When the person accepts the validity of the comment, such statements can powerfully draw attention to deeper issues. On the other hand, if the client is not ready to see the truth of the remark or if the observation is inaccurate, you may create a miscommunication that will take some effort to repair.

Here is an example of a client statement, followed by three different levels of reflection.

Client: After examining the tumor they removed, my doctors say the cells look borderline, and the cancer experts are recommending against chemotherapy. Although I had prepared myself to accept it, I'm relieved that I won't have to go through the chemotherapy regimen. I still get frightened at times, but it's not like I felt before the surgery, when I thought I might soon be dead. I will be glad when I'm strong enough to return to work and to move back to my own place. The bills are piling up and living with my parents is tough on all of us, but it's also wonderful just to be alive.

Worker: **_Factual Reflection_**
The medical report was good, and your main task now is to recover from the surgery.
Surface Feeling Reflection
Occasionally you feel scared, and there are frustrations associated with your rehabilitation. But you're very thankful for the positive medical findings.
Underlying Feeling Reflection
Facing death has been revitalizing and has enabled you to take a fresh look at what really is important in your life.

Empirical research (e.g., Sharpley et al., 2000) has demonstrated that both factual reflections and feeling reflections are associated with higher ratings of rapport. In line with such research, we believe that factual reflections can be useful, and that it is difficult to go wrong with an accurate surface feeling reflection. But our opinion is that underlying feeling reflections are educated guesses, and, for the most part, you should avoid them.

When reflecting emotions, novices sometimes feel limited by their vocabulary. If that happens to be the case with you, we offer the following set of words. Although we hope the list is helpful, there are some dangers associated with it. First, remember you want to be accurate in your reflections; so don't use the words indiscriminately. Second, never have the list in front of you during a role play or when working with real clients; looking down at such a document is distracting to clients and will greatly diminish, if not destroy, your ability to establish positive relationships. Third, do not say words you feel ill at ease using; your vocabulary should remain natural and comfortable.

calm

contented	relaxed	steady
mellow	serene	
peaceful	smooth	

confident

accomplished	courageous	powerful	satisfied	worthy
assured	fearless	proud	strong	
brave	invincible	secure	sure	

excited

cheerful	ecstatic	energized	hopeful
curious	elated	enthusiastic	joyful
delighted	encouraged	exhilarated	overjoyed
eager	energetic	glad	thrilled

angry

aggravated	enraged	incensed	mad	sore
annoyed	exasperated	infuriated	offended	
bitter	fed up	irate	outraged	
cross	frustrated	irked	perturbed	
disgusted	furious	irritated	resentful	

hurt

abused	cheated	embarrassed	pained	troubled
ashamed	crushed	exploited	regretful	violated
belittled	devastated	humiliated	rejected	
betrayed	disgraced	insecure	sorry	

lonely

abandoned	excluded	left out	withdrawn
alienated	ignored	lonesome	
disconnected	isolated	rejected	

perplexed

baffled	hesitant	stuck
bewildered	mystified	torn
doubtful	puzzled	

pressured

burdened	dominated
desperate	impatient
distressed	intimidated

sad/tired

bored	discouraged	exhausted	let down	unhappy
dejected	dismayed	gloomy	pessimistic	
despondent	down	glum	somber	
disappointed	drained	grieving	sorrowful	

scared/anxious

afraid	fearful	jumpy	restless	terrified
agitated	frantic	jittery	stressed	threatened
alarmed	frightened	overwhelmed	shaken	uneasy
apprehensive	horrified	nervous	shaky	vulnerable
dreading	insecure	panicky	tense	worried

surprised

alarmed	shocked
appalled	stunned
dismayed	

Look at where your mark is for option J. What is your opinion of reflection now as compared to before? Review your observer notes and look for examples of reflection. Notice how many contain feelings.

SEQUENCES AND COMBINATIONS OF RESPONSES

Now that you have encountered the basics of interrogation and reflection, it is possible to think about sequences and combinations of those responses. We will focus on three patterns: the funnel sequence, the inverted funnel sequence, and the reflection-interrogation combination.

Funnel sequences begin with a broad probe or question, continue with reflection and possibly some open interrogation, then end with closed interrogation to fill any gaps in information you must gather. Such sequences are appropriate when the client is comfortable talking with you and understands the nature of the information you are seeking.

Here is an example of a funnel sequence that begins with a general inquiry, then transitions to a more specific focus. (Imagine that all of the remarks are being made to the same person and that there is a client response between each one.)

- How was the first day on your new job?
- You realize there is a lot to learn, but you are excited about the challenge.
- What sort of training will you be having?
- You're looking forward to the orientation sessions.
- Once you are trained, what shift will you be working?

Inverted funnel sequences begin with easily answered closed questions, then move to broader responses such as reflection and open interrogation. This technique is the best approach we know for encouraging a client to talk when the individual is reluctant to speak with you.

Here is an example of an inverted funnel sequence. (It is taken from an interaction with a 16-year-old who was hospitalized following a drug overdose suicide attempt. In response to an initial open question of, "How are things going?" the patient said nothing and turned away from the worker. But communication soon began to flow as a result of the following inverted funnel sequence.)

Worker: Did Dr. Matthews see you this morning?
Client: Mmhmm.
Worker: Have they brought you breakfast?
Client: Yeah. (Turning toward the worker with a disgusted look)
Worker: You didn't like the food.
Client: It was awful. Everything was cold, and the fried eggs were all runny. It was almost as bad as that stuff they had me drink last night to make me throw up. I just want out of here.
Worker: You'd really like to go home.
Client: But they're making me stay, even though I've told them I want to go home. This place is terrible. It's boring and there's nothing to do.
Worker: What do you think would need to happen in order for Dr. Matthews to discharge you?

Initially, this client seemed to have no intention of talking with the worker. But two easy-to-answer closed questions evoked minimal responses. Next, two reflections elicited animated descriptions of thoughts and feelings, and then an open question led the interaction toward a discussion of positive change.

A ***reflection-interrogation combination*** takes place as a compound response to the client's most recent remarks. First, you reflect the essence of what the person just communicated, and then you ask a question or state a probe. By having your question or probe follow a reflection, you are able to gather necessary information while still conveying understanding and attention.

Here are several examples of reflection-interrogation combinations. (They are taken from interactions with five different clients.)

- You were surprised by his account. How did you respond to him?
- A fresh start seems to you like it might be worth the risk. Tell me what a new beginning would allow you to do.
- It's hard to stay within your food budget because you use a "country-cooking" style of meal preparation. Give me an example of a "country-cooked" meal.
- Attempting to discipline your children has been an ordeal. What are some of the strategies you've tried?
- Her leaving has you feeling discouraged and adrift. You've been imagining what it would be like if you would just disappear. Are you thinking of killing yourself?

MULTIPLE-CHOICE QUESTIONS

The remainder of the chapter consists of opportunities for you to use material that has been presented. We start with a set of multiple-choice questions. Items 1-7 are with one client, and items 8-20 are with another client. Here are your instructions for this exercise.

- For each of the following client statements, choose the response or responses you believe would be appropriate. (Several items have more than one correct answer.)
- Indicate your selection in writing.

- Read the discussions of *all four* options.
- If you are correct, go to the next item.
- If you are incorrect, think about the explanations and, if necessary, review relevant portions of the chapter; then, once you better understand the issues, proceed to the next question.

1. My mother called last night—I'm about four hours away from home—and she told me how sad she is and how she doesn't have anyone. This is the second time she's called this week. We're very close. We've always been close—through everything. I feel badly about being away from her and just dealing with my life here, when she is back home all alone. She needs me, and I feel very guilty and depressed.
   A. You don't think she really wants you to move back home, do you?
   B. Living a half-day away means that most of your communication is on the telephone or by mail.
   C. Have there been other weeks in which she has called you twice?
   D. It hurts to think of her being so sad.

Discussion of options.

   A. You don't think she really wants you to move back home, do you?
   - Your leading question suggests that you are biased and that you are expecting a certain answer.
   B. Living a half-day away means that most of your communication is on the telephone or by mail.
   - With so much emotion expressed by the client, this factual reflection misses the heart of the person's statement.
   C. Have there been other weeks in which she has called you twice?
   - You may get a simple "Yes" or "No" to your closed question. In addition, your response unnecessarily directs the interaction and changes the focus from the present to the past.
   D. It hurts to think of her being so sad.
   - By providing this surface feeling reflection, you are demonstrating interest and attention, while leaving the client free to decide where the interaction goes next.

2. I feel very ashamed. I know she's having a lot of problems, and I could easily solve them by moving home. But I can't do that because of my responsibilities here.
   A. Why do you think *you* could fix everything?
   B. You regret not doing more for your mother.
   C. I'm sure your mom does not hold you responsible for her problems.
   D. It sounds to me like being here is very demanding, and you are looking for a reason to return home.

Discussion of options.

A. Why do you think *you* could fix everything?
   - Asking a "Why" question is likely to put the client on the defensive. The response you get probably will be a justification, which may not be very productive.
B. You regret not doing more for your mother.
   - Your surface feeling reflection conveys understanding and is likely to encourage the client to continue bringing up new thoughts and feelings.
C. I'm sure your mom does not hold you responsible for her problems.
   - You do not know the client's mother. Consequently, you have no basis for offering such reassurance. This response may distance you from the client, since the person probably does not share your opinion.
D. It sounds to me like being here is very demanding, and you are looking for a reason to return home.
   - Such analysis changes the focus from the individual's opinions to yours. And you may get an angry response if you are incorrect or if the person is not ready to see the validity of your observation.

3. Talking to her has increased the pressure on me. With my work and with her second call of the week, I'm very frustrated. I'm depressed because she's depressed.
   A. The two conversations with her really have you down, and you are thinking that something needs to change.
   B. You feel helpless.

C. I'm sorry you have so much stressing you.

D. It seems you have quite a few responsibilities that you are trying to fulfill. What are some of the stresses associated with your work?

Discussion of options.

A. The two conversations with her really have you down, and you are thinking that something needs to change.
  - This reflection describes the situation and then recognizes the client's feelings and thoughts. By stating that the person desires change, you rephrase the client's frustration with a positive tone that may help the individual move forward, rather than talk another time about being ashamed and depressed. Although you want to recognize the client's emotions, doing nothing but reflecting depressive feelings may result in a downward spiral that leaves both *you* and the client feeling despondent.
B. You feel helpless.
  - Your feeling reflection probably is accurate, but it also is a very strong statement that may suggest there is nothing the client can do. The comment could be improved by emphasizing that the person is feeling helpless *now*. For example, the worker might say, "Right now you're very discouraged."
C. I'm sorry you have so much stressing you.
  - In a worker-client relationship, this expression of sympathy probably is not helpful.
D. It seems you have quite a few responsibilities that you are trying to fulfill. What are some of the stresses associated with your work?
  - The client is focusing on mother-related feelings and issues, but this combination of a factual reflection and an open question may change the topic away from what is foremost on the person's mind.

4. If I don't actually move back home, maybe at least I should try to be there more often. I've been home very little this year, and we really have not had much time to spend together. I am her only child, so I know she needs me.

A. One possible way of helping your mom is to make more frequent trips to see her. What might those entail?
B. What do you do when you are together? How could you improve the time you do spend with each other?
C. What would you do if you were there?
D. Have you told her how you feel?

Discussion of options.

A. One possible way of helping your mom is to make more frequent trips to see her. What might those entail?
  • This reflection-interrogation combination allows you to convey interest and understanding, while also requesting relevant information.
B. What do you do when you are together? How could you improve the time you do spend with each other?
  • Asking a multiple question may confuse the client. A better strategy is to ask one question, then wait for a response.
C. What would you do if you were there?
  • The client's statement ends with a comment of being needed, and your open question encourages further discussion of that issue by requesting concrete examples of actions the person would take.
D. Have you told her how you feel?
  • A brief reply may be the response to this closed question. Your phrasing also suggests that you have decided what the client should do.

5. I guess I just think I should spend some time with her. There are a few jobs around the place that need attention, so we might work on those together. But I imagine the most important thing is for her to have another person there to talk with.
  A. I think you should arrange a visit to see your mom.
  B. What are some tasks the two of you might tackle?
  C. Feeling that you can solve your mother's problems gives you a sense of power.
  D. You would feel better if there were face-to-face interactions taking place.

Discussion of options.

A. I think you should arrange a visit to see your mom.
  • Your statement cuts off the client's discussion of thoughts and feelings. Rather than focusing on what the individual has to say, you give advice, which implies that you believe the person is not capable of making productive plans.
B. What are some tasks the two of you might tackle?
  • The form of this open question is good, but the information you are after is of secondary importance at the moment. Consequently, you may sidetrack the interaction to a minor issue.
C. Feeling that you can solve your mother's problems gives you a sense of power.
  • You are taking a shot in the dark with this underlying feeling reflection. The result may be an unimportant discussion regarding the accuracy of your observation.
D. You would feel better if there were face-to-face interactions taking place.
  • The client's opinion regarding the key activity that ought to happen is the focus of this reflection. But your comment also sets the stage for expanding available options, since you do not say that the client must be the one to provide the interactions.

6. She definitely needs someone to be with her and talk with her. I'm sorry I can't be there all the time, but I have my own obligations here. There is no way that I can be home enough to take care of all her needs. I guess she really has to become less dependent on me.
  A. You feel guilty about not being with her.
  B. It seems you are thinking she might need other sources of support.
  C. You're saying that going to see her would be a mistake, since it would reinforce her dependency.
  D. What comes to mind when you think of her becoming more independent?

Discussion of options.

A. You feel guilty about not being with her.
  - In previous multiple-choice responses 1D and 2B above, you reflected the hurt and regret the person is feeling. Although the client comment in item 6 also contains a statement of regret, there probably is no need to cycle back into a discussion of that emotion.
B. It seems you are thinking she might need other sources of support.
  - This factual reflection of the client's comment puts the emphasis on a positively stated objective that has the potential to become a focus of discussion.
C. You're saying that going to see her would be a mistake, since it would reinforce her dependency.
  - You miss the mark with this reflection. The client has not said or implied that it would be wrong to visit her.
D. What comes to mind when you think of her becoming more independent?
  - Your open question requests the client to reveal additional thoughts on the issue of independence, which seems as though it could become a productive topic.

7. I would feel a lot better if she had some friends she could count on and confide in. She gets along with people at work, but part of her problem is the stress there. So opening up to her coworkers isn't the answer. She should be with friends outside of work who she can talk to and visit.
A. You think she needs time with nonwork friends.
B. How could she develop such relationships?
C. I'm sure that some new friends would make a big difference.
D. Do you know anyone she might spend time with?

Discussion of options.

A. You think she needs time with nonwork friends.
  - You recognize the client's thoughts regarding the possible role of nonwork friends, thereby encouraging further discussion focusing on that perceived need.

B. How could she develop such relationships?
  • Your open question puts the emphasis on how appropriate friendships might be built by the client's mother. But *the mother* is not your client. Instead of discussing plans that a nonclient could make, it generally is better to concentrate on actions that might be taken by the person who has come to see you.
C. I'm sure that some new friends would make a big difference.
  • You have no direct evidence to support your reassurance.
D. Do you know anyone she might spend time with?
  • At this point, there is no need for a closed question. By asking one, you may limit the individual's reply.

The remaining multiple-choice items involve a one-to-one interaction with a 15-year-old in foster care who is seeing you for the first time. In the waiting area is Mrs. Williams, the foster mother, who has brought the young person to your office from school.

8. (You begin the body of the interview by saying, "How are things going?" and the teenager responds by staring at the floor.)
  A. Things aren't that bad, are they?
  B. Why are you staring at the floor?
  C. Did you go to school today?
  D. Would you tell me what's on your mind?

Discussion of options.

  A. Things aren't that bad, are they?
    • The content of this leading question suggests you will find it difficult to accept the validity of any intense discomfort described by the client. Consequently, it becomes less likely that the young person will share such feelings with you.
  B. Why are you staring at the floor?
    • Your "Why" question may be perceived as threatening and provocative. The most probable response is continued silence.
  C. Did you go to school today?
    • Providing a "Yes" or an affirmative head nod is easy for the client to do because all that is required is an acknowledgment of information the student believes you already have.

Consequently, the young person is not surrendering much by answering the question. But even a head shake is more of a response than staring at the floor. And for now, a small indication of cooperation is all you are after.

D. Would you tell me what's on your mind?
- By offering this closed question, you have set yourself up to receive a negative head shake. Barring that, more silence probably is what you will get.

9. (In response to the question, "Did you go to school today?" the client gives an affirmative head nod.)
   A. You'll feel better if you tell me what's on your mind.
   B. You're probably feeling isolated since you are a new student there.
   C. You're having a lot of problems at school, aren't you?
   D. Did Mrs. Williams pick you up at school?

Discussion of options.

A. You'll feel better if you tell me what's on your mind.
- You demonstrate your lack of appreciation for the client's perspective when you offer such reassurance. Although you may believe the statement to be true, the young person is likely to view its guarantee as being worthless.

B. You're probably feeling isolated since you are a new student there.
- By providing this analysis, you put the focus on your opinions, thereby decreasing the probability of the client sharing thoughts and feelings. It also turns out, as you will see later in the interview, that you are wrong.

C. You're having a lot of problems at school, aren't you?
- You have no information on which to base your leading question. And by asking it, you give the client an opportunity to supply a negative response.

D. Did Mrs. Williams pick you up at school?
- The positive qualities of response 8C also exist in 9D. This closed question increases your chances of getting a cooperative reply.

10. (In response to your asking, "Did Mrs. Williams pick you up at school?" the client provides an affirmative head nod.)
  A. I get the feeling you are very angry.
  B. She really goes the extra mile for you, doesn't she?
  C. I guess you would have preferred that our appointment be during school rather than after.
  D. Did you talk on the way over?

Discussion of options.

  A. I get the feeling you are very angry.
    • You have insufficient evidence to make this underlying feeling reflection. Although your comment turns out to be correct, making it now probably will not result in a productive response from the client.
  B. She really goes the extra mile for you, doesn't she?
    • You are focusing on someone other than the client in this leading question. And, given the nature of the responses you've received to this point, you do not have enough information to justify making such a judgment. As you will later learn, your observation is not in tune with how the young person is feeling.
  C. I guess you would have preferred that our appointment be during school rather than after.
    • There is no basis for your observation. Consequently, you probably are distancing yourself from the individual.
  D. Did you talk on the way over?
    • The positive qualities of responses 8C and 9D also characterize this closed question. Another limited expression of cooperation is the most likely result.

11. (The client's response to the question, "Did you talk on the way over?" is "Yes.")
  A. If you can talk with her, why can't you talk with me?
  B. What did you talk about?
  C. Well, I think you should also be talking to me.
  D. Would you tell me what you discussed?

Discussion of options.

A. If you can talk with her, why can't you talk with me?
  • You probably will increase the client's defensiveness by asking a "Why" question.
B. What did you talk about?
  • Having asked three closed questions in a row, you encounter the client's first verbal reply. Now is a good time to try asking an open question, since the individual may answer with another verbal response.
C. Well, I think you should also be talking to me.
  • It is unlikely that the client will respond positively to this advice.
D. Would you tell me what you discussed?
  • Although your idea is a good one, phrasing it in a "Would you" question gives the client an easy opportunity to reply in a negative manner.

12. (In response to, "What did you talk about?" the client says, "The same old stuff.")
A. I'm sorry it wasn't something pleasant.
B. What was this topic that you've discussed before?
C. Was it just as bad this time? Did you really dislike it?
D. It seems to me that you should develop a better attitude toward Mrs. Williams.

Discussion of options.

A. I'm sorry it wasn't something pleasant.
  • Your sympathy is out of place here and probably will seem odd to the client.
B. What was this topic that you've discussed before?
  • This open question pulls for more information. Since you got some actual words in response to your last open question, you are likely to get a few more in reply to this one. In addition, your remark recalls what the client said previously about "the same old stuff," thereby demonstrating that you have been paying attention.
C. Was it just as bad this time? Did you really dislike it?

- You may confuse the client by asking these multiple closed questions. If you do get an affirmative or a negative answer, you can't be certain which question the young person is addressing.
  D. It seems to me that you should develop a better attitude toward Mrs. Williams.
  - It is almost certain that the client's reaction to this advice will be a defensive one.

13. (After you ask, "What was this topic that you've discussed before?" the client says, "Rules.")
    A. Entering a new living situation always involves learning to do a few things in new ways.
    B. I guess that wasn't very pleasant, was it?
    C. So, you were talking about things to do and not to do.
    D. In the past, what sorts of problems have you had with rules?

Discussion of options.

A. Entering a new living situation always involves learning to do a few things in new ways.
   - Your analysis comes in the form of a general observation about life that probably applies to this client. But in offering it you appear to be taking sides with the foster parents, thereby increasing the chances of alienating yourself from the young person.
B. I guess that wasn't very pleasant, was it?
   - You are jumping to a conclusion with this leading question. By putting words in the client's mouth, you decrease the chances of open communication.
C. So, you were talking about things to do and not to do.
   - You acknowledge the teenager's answer with this factual reflection. By using it, you give your client the responsibility for determining where the interaction goes from here.
D. In the past, what sorts of problems have you had with rules?
   - Your open question shifts the focus from the present to the past, which probably is not something you want to do at this point.

14. (Following the reflection of, "So, you were talking about things to do and not to do" the client says, "Like always.")
    A. There are frequent discussions of the expectations Mr. and Mrs. Williams have for you.
    B. Could you tell me what the reason might be for this repetition?
    C. It sounds like they have to repeat a lot of things for you.
    D. Mrs. Williams probably keeps talking about the rules because she is not satisfied with how you are following them.

Discussion of options.

   A. There are frequent discussions of the expectations Mr. and Mrs. Williams have for you.
      • This factual reflection has the same productive characteristics as response 13C. You are again giving the client a chance to determine where the interaction proceeds next.
   B. Could you tell me what the reason might be for this repetition?
      • By phrasing your request as a "Could you" question, you give the client an opportunity to say "No."
   C. It sounds like they have to repeat a lot of things for you.
      • Your comment may be true. But the client is not likely to respond in a productive way, since the statement appears to take the side of the foster parents.
   D. Mrs. Williams probably keeps talking about the rules because she is not satisfied with how you are following them.
      • No doubt you are accurate in this analysis. By providing it, however, you put the focus on your opinion, which seems to favor the foster parents.

15. (In response to your reflection of, "There are frequent discussions of the expectations Mr. and Mrs. Williams have for you" the client says, "Yeah, and I'm sick of it.")
    A. You're fed up with being told what to do.
    B. Do you think your foster parents are tired of it?
    C. Why do you think it comes up so often?
    D. You should tell Mrs. Williams how you feel.

Discussion of options.

   A. You're fed up with being told what to do.

- This is an accurate surface feeling reflection. It acknowledges the client's initial verbal description of a clear-cut emotion. By recognizing the young person's frustration, you are encouraging further exploration of issues associated with that exasperation.

B. Do you think your foster parents are tired of it?
- You put the focus on the foster parents with your question, rather than on the client. And since it is closed, you also give the client an opportunity to reply with nothing more than a brief response.

C. Why do you think it comes up so often?
- This "Why" question is likely to put your client on the defensive.

D. You should tell Mrs. Williams how you feel.
- Your advice probably will not result in a productive response from the client.

16. They just give me too many rules about everything in the house and outside.
    A. Are any of the rules necessary?
    B. Greater freedom is something you would like to have.
    C. It would be nice to be making more of your own decisions.
    D. The feelings of confinement you are having are typical for a person who moves from a less restrictive to a more restrictive environment.

Discussion of options.

A. Are any of the rules necessary?
- Your closed question invites two potential problems. The first is the possibility of a brief response, and the second is the likelihood of a negative reply. With this client, a negative reply would mean the individual wants a home with no rules, and that is not a realistic option.

B. Greater freedom is something you would like to have.
- By phrasing this factual reflection in a way that puts a positive twist on the client's remarks, you invite additional discussion of the freedom issue.

C. It would be nice to be making more of your own decisions.

- The wording of your factual reflection opens the door to a discussion of areas in which the individual would like to have increased autonomy.

D. The feelings of confinement you are having are typical for a person who moves from a less restrictive to a more restrictive environment.
  - This analysis probably is accurate. But, despite the validity of your observation, it has little relevance to exploring the client's thoughts and feelings. Consequently, you are not encouraging movement in a productive direction.

17. Yeah, I need more freedom. But they treat me like a baby. They tell me when and where I can go places, like they don't know that I should be able to make some decisions on my own. I can take care of myself, so why do they think I want a nice cozy home with somebody always telling me what to do?
    A. I'm sure they believe they're doing what's best for you.
    B. You're rebelling against what you really want most and have rarely had, a stable and predictable home environment.
    C. You really would like to be telling them what to do.
    D. You're angry about the restrictions on you. Give me an example of a rule you believe is unfair.

Discussion of options.

A. I'm sure they believe they're doing what's best for you.
  - You are shifting the focus to the foster parents, and you appear to be siding with them. Consequently, your comment may lead to an argument or to a shutdown of communication.

B. You're rebelling against what you really want most and have rarely had, a stable and predictable home environment.
  - This analysis may or may not be true. Even if it is true, the client is likely to respond defensively, rather than admit to the validity of the statement.

C. You really would like to be telling them what to do.
  - You probably are right, but where does this comment lead? You are not likely to negotiate a solution that involves the client supervising the foster parents.

D. You're angry about the restrictions on you. Give me an example of a rule you believe is unfair.
   • The correct responses in items 8-16 have combined to form an inverted funnel sequence designed to get the client talking. In this instance the technique has worked. Now, for the first time, the client's response has been several sentences in a row. By using a combination response (1) to reflect a central feeling expressed by the young person and (2) to request a specific example relating to that emotion, you are encouraging a more detailed discussion of what is troubling the individual.

18. Mrs. Williams says I have to be in by 9:00 on school nights. That's too early. I don't have time to do anything. She's just trying to stop me from being with my new friends.
    A. Tell me what you believe your foster parents *do* want.
    B. You'd like to be with them more.
    C. Having enough time with your friends is important to you.
    D. You're hopeless about conditions ever changing with your foster parents.

Discussion of options.

A. Tell me what you think your foster parents *do* want.
   • By responding with this probe, you change the focus to the foster parents. It is better to continue concentrating on the person with whom you are talking.
B. You'd like to be with them more.
   • You encourage the interaction to move in a positive direction with your factual reflection. By recognizing the individual's desires, you are laying the groundwork for consideration of what the young person would be willing to do in order to have more social time.
C. Having enough time with your friends is important to you.
   • Your factual reflection describes the client's complaint in terms of a positive objective. Consequently, this comment may help to set the stage for an eventual discussion of how the young person could work toward bringing about the desired arrangements.

D. You're hopeless about conditions ever changing with your foster parents.
  • This degree of discouragement was not expressed by the client. Instead of reflecting what the young person actually said, you are reading too much into the individual's statement. Your choice of the word "hopeless" may also give an unnecessarily negative direction to the interview. Rather than moving toward a consideration of adaptive possibilities, the client may pick up on your cue and discuss why nothing will work.

19. Yeah. Although we haven't known each other very long, I've made some really close friends. But Mrs. Williams keeps saying they are a bad influence on me, and she won't let them come over. Without ever meeting them, how does she know they are so terrible?
  A. What would you think about asking Mrs. Williams to come in so that the three of us could discuss issues relating to your friends?
  B. She has you really angry.
  C. Mrs. Williams believes your friends are a bad influence, and she won't let them come over.
  D. You think Mrs. Williams is too unbending when it comes to your friends, but you seem pretty unbending yourself when it comes to Mrs. Williams.

Discussion of options.

  A. What would you think about asking Mrs. Williams to come in so that the three of us could discuss issues relating to your friends?
  • In this situation, you have available the individual about whom the client is complaining. Bringing Mrs. Williams into the discussion might allow for a fuller exploration of relevant issues.
  B. She has you really angry.
  • You have previously acknowledged that the client is angry. At this point, there is no need to reflect that feeling again.
  C. Mrs. Williams believes your friends are a bad influence, and she won't let them come over.

Five Ways of Responding

• There are two problems with this comment. It uses the client's words rather than your own, and it changes the focus from the young person to Mrs. Williams.

D. You think Mrs. Williams is too unbending when it comes to your friends, but you seem pretty unbending yourself when it comes to Mrs. Williams.

   • At this stage of the interview, your confrontational statement is not likely to be productive. Since the client probably will respond defensively, you are risking an argument.

20. I don't care if she comes in. All I want is an even break. I'm happy when I'm with my friends. Why can't the Williams just let me be happy? They're always trying to bring me down. I need to be myself. But how can I be myself if they are always telling me what to do?

A. It's frustrating to have your desires blocked at every turn.

B. Adolescence is a time of transition from childhood dependency to the independence of adulthood. Feeling confined is a typical experience during this period of maturation.

C. It sounds like ways of getting more independence might be a topic for us to discuss with Mrs. Williams.

D. I think if you and Mrs. Williams really listen to each other, everything will work out.

Discussion of options.

A. It's frustrating to have your desires blocked at every turn.

   • This feeling reflection identifies a negative emotion and focuses on the client's perception that the Williams reject all proposals. Don't forget that you may be moving toward a three-way discussion involving Mrs. Williams. Concentrating on unpleasant feelings toward her probably will not encourage productive interaction when she enters the room.

B. Adolescence is a time of transition from childhood dependency to the independence of adulthood. Feeling confined is a typical experience during this period of maturation.

   • Your general observations about life are accurate but not very helpful. There is little chance that these opinions will move the interaction in the direction of adaptive change.

C. It sounds like ways of getting more independence might be a topic for us to discuss with Mrs. Williams.
   - Your comment phrases the client's complaint in a positive manner that draws attention to the idea of negotiating a productive plan.
D. I think if you and Mrs. Williams really listen to each other, everything will work out.
   - You are reaching too far with your reassurance, and the client probably knows your comment is unrealistic. Consequently, the young person may start thinking about what *won't* be accomplished with Mrs. Williams.

SHORT-ANSWER QUESTIONS

Write your answer for each of the following questions.

1. Give a situation in which you believe it would be inappropriate to offer advice.
2. Describe an instance in which you think it would be appropriate to offer advice.
3. Give a situation in which you believe it would be inappropriate to provide analysis.
4. Describe an instance in which you think it would be appropriate to provide analysis.
5. Give a situation in which you believe it would be inappropriate to express sympathy.
6. Describe an instance in which you think it would be appropriate to express sympathy.
7. Give a situation in which you believe it would be inappropriate to communicate reassurance.
8. Describe an instance in which you think it would be appropriate to communicate reassurance.
9. Give an example of an open question.
10. Provide an example of a closed question.
11. Give an example of a leading question and describe difficulties it might create.
12. Cite an example of multiple questions and describe problems they could cause.

13. Give an example of a "Why" question and describe a negative reaction that might result.

14. Provide a surface feeling reflection for the following statement. "My campus job wasn't paying the bills, so I took on a second job at a restaurant. Although it seemed like a good idea at the time, my academics have taken a nose dive. I had a decent grade point average coming into this term, but I don't know if I can make enough money to stay in school and still be a good student. And if I don't have time for the class work, why should I even be here?"

15. Give an example of a funnel sequence.

16. Provide an example of an inverted funnel sequence.

17. Give a reflection-interrogation combination in response to the following statement. "My boyfriend says our relationship is exactly what he wants, but he also says he needs his 'space.' I think him being independent is fine, but when I don't hear from him for days at a time I begin to fear that maybe there *is* a problem between us."

POSSIBLE ANSWERS FOR SHORT-ANSWER QUESTIONS

Use the following answer-checking procedures.

• For each item, compare your answer to the one we provide.
• If you believe your answer is correct, you are done with that item.
• With any question for which you believe your answer is incorrect, consider our answer and, if needed, review relevant portions of the chapter. Keep your original answer that you now think is incorrect, but add to it a response that you believe would be correct.

1. Generally, supportive workers do not give advice before drawing on the client's ability to generate options. For example, it would be too directive to tell a person to get out of a bad marriage rather than to have the individual name and consider available possibilities.

2. It is appropriate to give advice in order to preserve life. For instance, a productive comment to a suicidal person might be, "I

don't want you to be dead. Instead of killing yourself, I would like you to give us a chance to address the difficulties you are facing."

3. In most instances, supportive workers do not provide analysis if the client is capable of developing a meaningful understanding of how things got to be the way they are. For example, an individual is seeing you in order to discuss family problems, but the person changes the subject whenever the focus turns to the problematic relationships. You could analyze the changes in topic and say, "You are resisting our attempts to address the reason for you being here." But it probably would be more effective to have the *client* do the analysis by making a comment such as, "You are here to talk about difficulties with your family. Several times we have been ready to examine that issue, but on each of those occasions you have brought up other topics for us to discuss. What do you think might be the reason for those changes in topic?"

4. Analysis can be appropriate in order to provide a rationale for a recommendation you make. For instance, you might say, "Often there is a biochemical component to low energy, gloomy thoughts, and despondent feelings such as you are experiencing. I think it would be a good idea to have an evaluation regarding your appropriateness for antidepressant medication."

5. It generally is inappropriate to express sympathy in a relationship if you are not in the habit of self-disclosing personal information about yourself to the other individual. With such a person, the following statement would not be helpful, "I'm sorry you have had so many tragedies in your life."

6. It would be appropriate to express sympathy when you are with an individual to whom you regularly self-disclose personal information. In such a relationship, the following comment might be appreciated, "I'm sorry you've been in so much pain."

7. It is inappropriate to communicate reassurance in which the guarantee is worthless. For example, you cannot support a statement such as, "I'm sure that everything will turn out OK."

8. It can be appropriate to communicate reassurance in which the guarantee is backed by facts. For instance, you might be able to say, "The necessary repairs have been made in your apartment, and you have been certified as being eligible for a return of your security deposit. The check will be mailed tomorrow."

9. An example of an open question would be, "How do you feel about being accepted?"

10. An example of a closed question would be, "Are you receiving rental assistance?"

11. An example of a leading question would be, "You've had financial difficulties before, haven't you?" Regardless of the individual's actual financial history, a person who wants to please you may give a positive response, and a person who wants to displease you is likely to give a negative response.

12. Examples of multiple questions include, "Are you willing to accept the help, or do you want to try to make it on your own?" and "What will the program mean to you, and how do you feel about receiving assistance?" If you get a "Yes" or "No" to the first set of questions, you won't know what it means, and either set of questions may be confusing to the client.

13. An example of a "Why" question would be, "Why did you wait so long before coming to us?" Such a question is threatening and may result in a response that is fabricated or distorted.

14. A possible surface feeling reflection would be, "Having gotten your finances in order, it's now really frustrating to see your grades drop."

15. An example of a funnel sequence would be: "How have things gone since our last meeting?" "Knowing the check came through is very satisfying." "You're still anxious about not having enough money to pay your bills. Have you applied for assistance?"

16. An example of an inverted funnel sequence would be: "Did you start the program?" "Is it worth the effort?" "What will you be doing next week?" "You're feeling more hopeful about the future."

17. An example of an appropriate reflection-interrogation combination would be, "Despite your boyfriend's assurance, when days go by without contact you begin to worry about the stability of your relationship. What do you do when you have such doubts?"

FILL-IN-THE-RESPONSE QUESTIONS

This is the chapter's final exercise. It provides you with a series of statements from a single client. For each item, write a worker response that you believe would be appropriate.

1. I've got a problem where I live. I have a new neighbor who is especially inconsiderate. At all hours of the night, this guy plays very loud music that keeps me awake. Often I don't get enough sleep, and then I'm tired the next day.

2. In the morning I need to get moving early. But after a night of his noise, my alarm goes off and I feel like I've hardly been asleep at all. Most mornings this week I just couldn't get myself going because I had been kept awake by the music coming from his place. As the day drags on, I feel tired, and I want to sleep. It's really getting to me. I know I'm not functioning as well as I should be.

3. I can't take it much longer. I've thought about going over there at 2:00 A.M., pounding on his door, and screaming, "Turn down that racket!" But to me that doesn't seem like the right approach. I'm not sure I would get anywhere, and I might just end up making the situation worse.

4. I'm not the kind of person who actually could yell at him. I guess what I really should do is go over when I'm calm, sometime during the day, and sit down and have a talk with him. I ought to just lay out the situation and tell him that I need some peace and quiet.

5. I've thought about asking him not to play his music after 11:00. But I'm not sure if he is the type of person who would take into account how his actions are affecting others. He might not care what someone else wants or thinks. Who knows how he'd respond. I've also wondered if I'm the only one around here who feels this way. I think his noise must be bothering other people too.

6. Maybe it's time to do something. So far, I've just been keeping things to myself and boiling inside. Although I've thought about a few ideas, the fact is that I really haven't done anything yet. But that needs to change. I can't continue to put up with his racket.

POSSIBLE ANSWERS FOR
FILL-IN-THE-RESPONSE QUESTIONS

For each response opportunity, there are many possible correct answers. We list two, and we suggest you use them in the following manner.

- Look at our two answers and think about them.
- Consider relevant material covered in the chapter.
- Read the client statement again, then immediately read your answer and the two options listed here.
- Write another response that you believe might be an improvement on your first effort.
- Repeat this procedure for each of the remaining items.

1. • The nighttime noise has you exhausted.
   • You're really frustrated with his behavior.
2. • It's exasperating to have your life so disrupted.
   • Not having enough energy to face your responsibilities is disheartening.
3. • You've been so mad that you've felt like confronting him in the middle of the night.
   • At times, when you've been so furious, you've imagined going over and yelling at him.
4. • One option would be meeting with him during the day and saying what's on your mind.
   • What might you say to him in such a meeting?
5. • Confronting him by yourself would entail some risks, but you're also thinking there could be others who are fed up with his behavior.
   • Speaking with him yourself is one idea you've had, and you've also considered the possibility that others might be disturbed by what he is doing.
6. • You're ready to decide on an effort you could make.
   • We've talked about a couple of strategies: having a discussion with him, and finding out how others are feeling about the noise. At this point, what possible action would you like to discuss further?

SUMMARY

Most efforts intended to be supportive can be categorized according to five basic ways of responding. Telling the individual what to do is the purpose of advice, but this response runs the risks of rejection, failure, or dependency. When analyzing, you provide your explanation of how circumstances developed, rather than focusing on the other person's thoughts. Being sympathetic means saying how you feel about the client's difficulties and can be interpreted as pity or insincerity, while false reassurance means offering a worthless guarantee that communicates a lack of appreciation for the severity of the situation. Interrogation can come in several forms. Open varieties give the client considerable latitude in responding, but closed types can be answered with one word or with a small bit of information. Questions to avoid include leading questions, multiple questions, and "Why" questions. Reflecting is using your own words to summarize essential ideas and emotions communicated by the other person. At times you may want to employ phrasing that matches a client's negative tone, but it also is necessary for some of your reflections to encourage discussion of productive change. Depending upon the feeling content of your statement, reflections can be classified as factual, surface feeling, or underlying feeling. When working with an individual who is reluctant to talk, a good strategy is to combine interrogation and reflection into an inverted funnel sequence. And, if you want to gather certain information while still conveying interest and understanding, a reflection-interrogation combination is an effective technique.

Chapter 3

CREATING POSITIVE RELATIONSHIPS

Hundreds of empirical studies have demonstrated the importance of the relationship between worker and client (e.g., Beutler, et al., 2004; Lambert & Ogles, 2004; Whiston & Sexton, 1993). The quality of the worker-client relationship is so clearly linked to client improvement that developing a strong therapeutic bond has been described as a foundation for helping services, and training in the development of relationship skills is advocated as "crucial" (Lambert & Barley, 2002, p. 27).

Why is the quality of the relationship between client and worker so important? One reason is to gain the cooperation of clients. Effective collaboration is not something that happens automatically. There is always the potential for clients to sabotage efforts by being unconsciously defensive or purposefully uncooperative. Consequently, decreasing the possibility of defensiveness and increasing the probability of willing cooperation are fundamental needs for human service workers.

Imagine the roles are reversed and you are the client. What sort of worker characteristics might encourage you to honestly explore issues and adaptively deal with them?

After formulating your own answer to the preceding question, consider the following.

It is likely that you would want your worker to be understanding. In addition to demonstrating comprehension of your feelings and beliefs, you probably would like the person to respect your attitudes and to care about your well-being. But efforts at showing interest in you and appreciation for your concerns only would have meaning if you perceived that the individual was being honest with you.

Workers convey understanding, respect, caring, and honesty when they exhibit facilitative levels of three interpersonal skills: empathy, warmth, and genuineness. Carl Rogers (1957) originally identified those three skills, and they continue to be seen as being crucial to the development of positive relationships between workers and clients (e.g., Bohart, Elliott, Greenberg, & Watson, 2002; Pichot, 2001).

Viewing empathy, warmth, and genuineness as *skills* has several implications. First, there are behaviors that contribute to these skills, and there are behaviors that detract from them. Second, it is possible for others to give you feedback regarding your performance of relevant behaviors. And third, if you are receptive to such feedback you will increase your use of productive behaviors and decrease your use of those that are counterproductive.

What are behaviors that might contribute to or detract from empathy, warmth, and genuineness? Let's consider some possibilities.

EMPATHY

Empathy is understanding another person *and* communicating your understanding to the individual. Clients generally experience greater improvement when there is a high level of empathic understanding from the worker, as demonstrated by reviews of empirical studies (e.g., Bohart, et al., 2002; Orlinsky, Ronnestad, & Willutzki, 2004). Additional research (Greenberg, Elliott, Watson, & Bohart, 2001) has shown that the association between worker empathy and client improvement is strongest when worker empathy is rated by clients, as opposed to being rated by either workers or observers. So it is important for clients to perceive that the worker understands.

The research is clear. Understanding is not enough. You must also *communicate* your understanding to clients.

How might a worker do that?

Imagine you have just told us about a recent experience of yours. In response, one of us says "I see" and another one of us says "I understand." Since, in fact, it would be possible for us to say "I see" or "I understand" even if we weren't really listening or didn't have any idea what was just in your mind, it is our position that "I see" and "I understand" do not constitute demonstrations of understanding.

Another possibility is for the worker to repeat several of the client's exact words. Since a parrot can do the same thing, such a response fails to show that the worker actually comprehends the meaning of what the client is communicating.

If it's not empathic to parrot or to simply say you understand, then how *do* workers express empathy? One of the best ways to demonstrate understanding is to reflect what the client has communicated. As you recall, reflection is using fresh words to summarize essential thoughts and feelings expressed by another person. When you accurately reflect in a caring way you are being empathic.

It has been asserted that effective reflections go beyond simple paraphrasing of the client's statements (e.g., Greenberg, et al., 2001). The goal is to be able to express in your own words the understanding you have of the client's experience, which may include thoughts and feelings the client has not directly verbalized. As we mentioned in Chapter 2, however, it is important not to go too far beyond what the client has communicated. There should be evidence for the thoughts and feelings you are reflecting, such as the client's demeanor or tone of voice. (We will discuss nonverbal communication in Chapter 7.) In the absence of such evidence you are simply guessing that the client might be feeling a particular way. If you guess and miss, you demonstrate a lack of empathy.

How will you know whether your reflections are conveying empathy? Often you will get indications from clients when they are feeling understood. For example, after a particularly accurate reflection a client may respond with, "Yes. Exactly."

Another way to determine how well you are expressing empathy is to get feedback from knowledgeable observers. Available research suggests that observer ratings of worker empathy are more strongly associated with client improvement than are workers' self-ratings (Greenberg, et al., 2001). Practicing or working without feedback is not nearly as conducive to learning as having knowledgeable observers critique what you do. So we encourage you to obtain feedback from such observers. Seek their comments on the accuracy and apparent impact of your reflections in role plays or in recorded interactions with clients (produced with their permission).

Being truly empathic also involves understanding when the client will benefit from reflection and when reflection may not be what the client needs. Based upon their review of relevant research, Bohart et al. (2002) hypothesized that some clients, at particular points, may find expressions of empathy to be too intrusive. Consequently, an important part of building relationships may be understanding when to do something other than reflect feelings, such as using the inverted funnel sequence discussed in Chapter 2 or helping the client to consider alternatives, as discussed in Chapter 4.

WARMTH

Demonstrating warmth toward clients is another relationship skill that research studies have shown to be associated with productive change, particularly when clients clearly perceive the worker to be warm (e.g., Farber & Lane, 2002). Warmth, or unconditional positive regard (as Rogers termed it), has a number of meanings. One aspect of warmth is recognizing the client's fundamental worth as a human being, separate from any evaluation of the person's behavior. Such nonjudgmental respect does not mean that you agree with the client. Instead, it is your acknowledgement of the individual's right to have his or her own values, beliefs, and attitudes.

Being warm does not prevent you from encouraging clients to consider the consequences of their behavior, although warmth does suggest that you refrain from offering judgmental comments conveying your own opinions of issues being discussed. Rather than making judgments for the client, you leave ultimate decision-making responsibility with that person.

When you are warm you communicate caring. Primarily through your demeanor, the client can tell that you truly are interested in his or her well-being.

In essence, being warm requires that your interaction style signals the following message: "I care about you. I hope things work out for you. But I'm not going to tell you what to do."

Of course, this attitude of acceptance needs to be coupled with common sense. For example, a magazine writer once asked Carl Rogers how he would respond if, during a session, a suicidal client were about to leap to his death out of Dr. Rogers' office window. Rogers told the writer that he would not let the person jump (Hall, 1967).

Clearly, saying "Don't jump" is a judgmental comment. In addition, though, it is one that communicates caring and demonstrates common sense. Our position, as was Rogers', is that judgmental comments can be entirely appropriate if their purpose is to preserve life.

Sometimes you may find yourself ready to make judgmental statements that do not arise from a need to preserve life. Instead, they have their origin in your dislike for the client. If you find yourself not liking the person, you should consider the source of your feelings and how to handle them.

One appropriate response can be to admit to yourself that you don't like the person, and then to be certain that you go "by the book" in your interactions with the individual. If this is your approach, you must remain vigilant for any negative reactions on your part, so that the service you provide continues to be appropriate and professional.

If you come to believe that your own personal reactions are likely to interfere with your ability to do your job, then you can seek to establish alternative service arrangements for the client. Making such arrangements may involve a number of possibilities, including transferring the client to a colleague or referring the person to another organization.

It always is acceptable to discuss negative reactions with your supervisor or with a professional colleague. On the other hand, an inappropriate method of handling such feelings is to deny their existence and to try sweeping them under the rug.

Just as you may have negative feelings toward certain clients, there may be clients who have negative feelings toward you. In such situations, demonstrating warmth involves being willing to listen to those negative emotions. Expression of unpleasant feelings toward human service workers is not uncommon. When it happens to you, try to keep from making matters worse. Research suggests that ignoring those feelings or responding in a defensive or hostile manner may interfere with the development of a relationship and prevent productive change (Safran, Muran, Samstag, & Stevens, 2002). Alternatively, reflecting the negative feelings and, when appropriate, accepting responsibility for your role in those feelings can demonstrate that you care about the person and are interested in working collaboratively with the individual.

GENUINENESS

The third interpersonal skill, genuineness, is meaning what you say. There are only a few research findings supporting a direct association between genuineness and productive change, but it has been suggested that genuineness may contribute to change by strengthening the worker-client bond and facilitating client perception of empathy and warmth from the worker (Klein, Kolden, Michels, & Chisholm-Stockard, 2002). As with empathy and warmth, being genuine requires that you do some things and avoid others.

When you are genuine you are truthful in what you say to the person. But genuineness does not compel you to say everything you are thinking. As long as you are honest in what you do say, you are being genuine.

Genuineness also suggests that you are being yourself with clients and that you are not hiding behind a professional facade. For instance, you do not develop a special set of phrases to be used with clients. Rather than talking in a stereotyped manner, your speech and phrasing are the same as you would use in polite conversation.

Opportunities for being genuine also occur when you do not hear or do not understand what a client says. On such occasions you should say that you did not hear, and you should ask the client to repeat the comment. Or you should say that you did not understand, and you should request clarification. Never feign understanding or pretend that you hear.

One more frequently encountered area that requires genuineness is in the realm of committing yourself or an organization to a course of action. You must be careful not to make promises you can't keep. When you do make a commitment, be sure you have the authority to enforce it. This means following through with what you said would be done. And it also means never making promises on behalf of other organizations when those entities retain the authority to determine eligibility and to select the services that will be offered.

Empathy, warmth, and genuineness are three key skills, but research on the helping relationship also has addressed a broader concept, termed the therapeutic alliance. In addition to what we already have discussed with regard to the development of a worker-client bond, the idea of alliance emphasizes consensus and collaboration when determining goals and activities for pursuing those goals, and it includes feelings of partnership and energetic hope as both the worker and the client do their part to bring about progress (Horvath & Bedi, 2002). Researchers have found that the existence of such a cooperative alliance is consistently related to client improvement (e.g., Martin, Garske, & Davis, 2000). Additional ways of enhancing consensus and collaboration include problem solving (discussed in Chapter 4) and establishing goals, objectives, and plans (addressed in Chapter 6).

MULTIPLE-CHOICE QUESTIONS

Items 1-7 involve one client; questions 8-14 concern a second individual; and items 15-20 focus on a third person. Your instructions are the same as in the previous chapter.

- For each of the following client statements, choose the response or responses you believe would be appropriate. (Several items have more than one correct answer.)
- Indicate your selection in writing.
- Read the discussions of all four options.
- If you are correct, go to the next item.
- If you are incorrect, think about the explanations and, if necessary, review relevant portions of the chapter; then, once you better understand the issues, proceed to the next question.

1. I'm really worried. My husband's union went out on strike a month ago, and he's out with them. Meanwhile, there's no money coming in. We haven't paid any bills in three weeks. I just don't see how we're going to pull through this.
   A. What are the bills that need to be paid?
   B. Because your husband is not presently working, there is no income available to meet your needs.
   C. The financial strain has you really anxious.
   D. Has he gone out on strike before?

Discussion of options.

   A. What are the bills that need to be paid?
- So early in the interaction this information is irrelevant. Instead of asking such a question, you should be focusing on exploring the client's thoughts and feelings.

   B. Because your husband is not presently working, there is no income available to meet your needs.
- Your response accurately captures the person's thoughts, but it ignores her feelings. Reflecting the emotional aspect of your client's message helps to develop a positive working relationship.

   C. The financial strain has you really anxious.
- This surface feeling reflection demonstrates your empathic understanding of the client.

   D. Has he gone out on strike before?
- Asking this closed question may lead to a simple "Yes" or "No." In addition, you unnecessarily shift the focus from the present to the past.

2. My husband is so proud. He won't even consider asking for any financial help. He just says, "Don't worry. They will hire us back." In the meantime, we have to live. We have to support ourselves. But he flips out every time I even suggest that I could get a job.
   A. You are in an extremely tough situation, and I feel badly for you.
   B. It sounds as though your husband comes from a family where only the man works outside of the home, but that type of situation rarely exists today.
   C. Why haven't you been more assertive with your husband?
   D. Without another source of income, you fear what the future may hold.

Discussion of options.

   A. You are in an extremely tough situation, and I feel badly for you.
- Although you may feel sympathy for the client, expressing pity is not likely to be helpful to the person.

B. It sounds as though your husband comes from a family where only the man works outside of the home, but that type of situation rarely exists today.
- By analyzing how the husband got to be the way he is, you are moving the focus away from what the client has to say. Such a shift is inappropriate at this point in your relationship.

C. Why haven't you been more assertive with your husband?
- One of your objectives is to enlist the client's cooperation by decreasing her defensiveness. You move in the opposite direction, however, by asking a "Why" question that requires her to defend her actions.

D. Without another source of income, you fear what the future may hold.
- This surface feeling reflection empathically summarizes what your client has expressed and allows her to decide where the interaction should go next.

3. Even before he went out on strike, we were living paycheck to paycheck. He made just enough to cover the rent, utilities, and groceries. But we were never able to save anything. Now there hasn't been a paycheck in several weeks. The rent is due, and, with it getting colder outside, we need to get fuel oil. But every time we talk about bills or money, we seem to get into a fight. I'm just so angry at him.
A. Your frustrations are boiling over.
B. Maybe you should leave him?
C. What will happen if you don't pay your rent?
D. Are your fights a new occurrence or have you always had these types of arguments?

Discussion of options.

A. Your frustrations are boiling over.
- This surface feeling reflection conveys empathy.
B. Maybe you should leave him?
- Making such a suggestion is not an appropriate response for a supportive worker.
C. What will happen if you don't pay your rent?

- Your response shifts the focus away from the strong emotions expressed by the client.

  D. Are your fights a new occurrence or have you always had these types of arguments?
  - This confusing multiple question may sidetrack you to the past.

4. I've mainly been trying to keep my thoughts to myself because when I do bring up my concerns, it ends up in a huge argument. And I don't want to fight. But he's got to realize how bad the situation is. He's letting his pride rule his head. He's too proud to let me work. He just doesn't seem to see the seriousness of our predicament.

   A. Have you ever been able to discuss the strike without getting into an argument?

   B. Something has to change, and you're desperate to communicate your point of view in a way he will appreciate.

   C. I'm sure everything eventually will turn out OK.

   D. In order to avoid arguing with your husband, you go along with the old-fashioned notion that the wife should stay at home.

Discussion of options.

   A. Have you ever been able to discuss the strike without getting into an argument?
   - This closed question could potentially lead to a "Yes" or "No" response.

   B. Something has to change, and you're desperate to communicate your point of view in a way he will appreciate.
   - Your surface feeling reflection empathically recognizes the client's thoughts and feelings.

   C. I'm sure everything eventually will turn out OK.
   - By offering reassurance, you minimize the person's concerns and suggest there really isn't anything to be worried about.

   D. In order to avoid arguing with your husband, you go along with the old-fashioned notion that the wife should stay at home.
   - Making a judgmental comment, as you do here, fails to foster the warmth necessary for an effective relationship.

5. I don't think he's really considered what may happen. He's so sure that everything will be fine. And I hope he's right, I truly do. But we have to have another plan to fall back on, just in case the strike isn't successful. I don't mean to be a pessimist, but I don't want to bury my head in the sand either.
   A. You're making an effort to look on the bright side of things, but you also feel responsible for planning ahead, in case your husband does not return to his job.
   B. You don't actually think you're a pessimist, do you?
   C. Although you'd like to have a positive outlook, your stronger desire is to be able to protect your family's welfare.
   D. How have you and your husband settled differing opinions in the past?

Discussion of options.

   A. You're making an effort to look on the bright side of things, but you also feel responsible for planning ahead, in case your husband does not return to his job.
      • You communicate understanding by reflecting what your client has expressed.
   B. You don't actually think you're a pessimist, do you?
      • This leading question seeks agreement rather than a genuine response.
   C. Although you'd like to have a positive outlook, your stronger desire is to be able to protect your family's welfare.
      • Your surface feeling reflection is accurate and empathic.
   D. How have you and your husband settled differing opinions in the past?
      • This open question makes an unnecessary transition from the present to the past.

6. Well, I wish he would agree for me to work part-time, but he won't. I guess if things got really bad, my parents could help us out until we were back on our feet. But I would rather not have to ask them for money.
   A. Your husband's stubbornness may cause the eventual downfall of your family.
   B. How do your parents feel about lending you money?
   C. Will your husband agree to your parents helping you out or will he refuse their help too?

D. Requesting financial assistance from your parents is an available option, but it's one you're feeling uneasy about.

Discussion of options.

A. Your husband's stubbornness may cause the eventual downfall of your family.
  • Your comment is too judgmental for a supportive interaction.
B. How do your parents feel about lending you money?
  • You may need to know such information later if you discuss this option in detail. But, so early in the interaction, you should be focusing your comments on the client.
C. Will your husband agree to your parents helping you out or will he refuse their help too?
  • This multiple question may be confusing, and it shifts attention away from your client.
D. Requesting financial assistance from your parents is an available option, but it's one you're feeling uneasy about.
  • The empathic understanding you convey in this remark probably will help to cultivate an effective working relationship.

7. I just don't know where to go from here, and that's why I'm talking to you. I figured you could give me advice on dealing with my husband and could tell me how we might be able to get out of our financial bind. What do you think I should do?
A. You were hoping I would be able to provide you with some answers.
B. Since your husband's expectations for the future seem unrealistic, it appears that you need to be the one taking the necessary steps for insuring your family's well-being.
C. I care what happens to you, and I hope things work out. But, rather than telling you what to do, I'm going to do my best to assist you in making your own decisions regarding your course of action.
D. It would be comforting to believe that there is someone who has all the answers. But in reality, the best you and I can do is to collaborate on the decisions you're facing. So, let's think about some of the choices you have.

Discussion of options.

A. You were hoping I would be able to provide you with some answers.
  • Simply reflecting the person's misunderstanding of your purpose might be an adequate response on some occasions, but for this particular instance, we believe there are better options available.
B. Since your husband's expectations for the future seem unrealistic, it appears that you need to be the one taking the necessary steps for insuring your family's well-being.
  • Telling the individual what to do suggests that you know better than the client how she should act. Such a presumption does not show respect for the person's own problem-solving abilities.
C. I care what happens to you, and I hope things work out. But, rather than telling you what to do, I'm going to do my best to assist you in making your own decisions regarding your course of action.
  • Defining your role is an appropriate response.
D. It would be comforting to believe that there is someone who has all the answers. But in reality, the best you and I can do is to collaborate on the decisions you're facing. So, let's think about some of the choices you have.
  • Your empathic response recognizes the client's desire for guidance, addresses the nature of your relationship, and moves the interaction in a productive direction.

Questions 8-14 involve a different client.

8. My wife is in the hospital with a bad case of pneumonia, and I don't know what to tell our four-year-old son, Jeremy. It's been six days since the kid has seen his mother, and he's starting to ask a lot of questions about what's going on. I haven't told him much at this point because I don't know how he'll handle it. I don't want to scare him.
  A. Your wife has been quite ill, and Jeremy is wondering about her.

B. You feel unsure of what you should say to Jeremy. You don't want your explanation to frighten him.

C. I see what you're saying, and I can understand why you're concerned.

D. Because you've recognized the need to appropriately address Jeremy's confusion, you're nervous about what to say to him. I know of a program that specializes in working with families who have a member in the hospital, and I'm sure they would be willing to speak with you about Jeremy.

Discussion of options.

A. Your wife has been quite ill, and Jeremy is wondering about her.
- Although this factual reflection is correct, it focuses on the person's wife and son. Keeping your remarks centered on the client is more likely to facilitate the communication of empathy and warmth.

B. You feel unsure of what you should say to Jeremy. You don't want your explanation to frighten him.
- By offering this accurate surface feeling reflection, you are fostering an effective working relationship between you and the client.

C. I see what you're saying, and I can understand why you're concerned.
- Saying that you "see" and "understand" does not demonstrate empathy.

D. Because you've recognized the need to appropriately address Jeremy's confusion, you're nervous about what to say to him. I know of a program that specializes in working with families who have a member in the hospital, and I'm sure they would be willing to speak with you about Jeremy.
- Making promises on behalf of others is risky. A more responsible approach is limiting yourself to commitments that you (or your organization) are capable of fulfilling.

9. I've just never had to deal with anything like this before. My wife is so sick, and I'm trying to be there for her. But my son needs me too. I want to make this whole ordeal as easy on him as I can, but I'm not quite sure how to do that.

A. Trying to provide support for your wife and son has you facing tasks that are new for you and that are very demanding.
B. You've never had to go through anything like this, with your wife so sick and with Jeremy needing you to make things easy on him.
C. What are you going to do about Jeremy?
D. It probably would have been better to have been honest with Jeremy from the start. Now you're trying to make amends by looking for the best way to discuss the subject with him.

Discussion of options.

A. Trying to provide support for your wife and son has you facing tasks that are new for you and that are very demanding.
   • By using fresh words to accurately reflect your client's predicament, you convey empathy and warmth.
B. You've never had to go through anything like this, with your wife so sick and with Jeremy needing you to make things easy on him.
   • Parroting the person's message fails to demonstrate empathy.
C. What are you going to do about Jeremy?
   • The client just explained to you that he is unsure of how to handle Jeremy. By disregarding that message, your comment communicates inattention and a lack of empathy.
D. It probably would have been better to have been honest with Jeremy from the start. Now you're trying to make amends by looking for the best way to discuss the subject with him.
   • Criticizing your client may lead to defensiveness on his part.

10. I wish there was someone to help me with all of this. I feel so helpless. . . . I can't make my wife better. I can't calm Jeremy's fears. I've been doing what I thought was right, but I don't think it's been enough.
   A. The efforts you've been making on your own seem insufficient, and you long to do more.
   B. Since your best efforts haven't met the needs of your family, you feel inadequate and completely overwhelmed.
   C. Although you've been working hard to care for those you love, it's been discouraging to find that your efforts haven't worked better.

D. Doing your best is all anyone can ask of you.

Discussion of options.

A. The efforts you've been making on your own seem insufficient, and you long to do more.
   • Your empathic response is likely to foster rapport.
B. Since your best efforts haven't met the needs of your family, you feel inadequate and completely overwhelmed.
   • You've summarized the person's thoughts and feelings, but your response leaves little room for hope.
C. Although you've been working hard to care for those you love, it's been discouraging to find that your efforts haven't worked better.
   • This understanding remark is an effective surface feeling reflection that may contribute to a productive relationship with your client.
D. Doing your best is all anyone can ask of you.
   • Making such a pat response does not show appreciation for the feelings of inadequacy the person has shared with you.

11. I want to spend more time with both of them. It's really a letdown when I have to work late. On those days, I only get one hour to visit my wife at the hospital and barely an hour to play with Jeremy before getting him ready for bed. That's just not enough time for my family. They need extra attention right now, and I need them too.
   A. If being together is that important to you, then family-time needs to be the top priority in your life, at least while your wife is ill.
   B. What are some of the reasons for working overtime?
   C. There just aren't enough hours in the day to spend the quality time with your family that you desire.
   D. You value your time with your family, and it's disappointing when you feel you've been shortchanged.

Discussion of options.

A. If being together is that important to you, then family-time needs to be the top priority in your life, at least while your wife is ill.

- An inappropriate way of attempting to assist your client with his concern is telling him what to do. Rather than giving advice, help him work toward productive change by respecting and encouraging his ability to find his own solutions.
B. What are some of the reasons for working overtime?
  - The person's answer to your question will yield information that is irrelevant to the present focus of the interaction.
C. There just aren't enough hours in the day to spend the quality time with your family that you desire.
  - This response is devoid of the feeling conveyed in your client's last remarks. Ignoring the person's emotional expression may detract from an atmosphere of empathy and warmth.
D. You value your time with your family, and it's disappointing when you feel you've been shortchanged.
  - The feelings shared by the client are accurately captured in your empathic response.

12. (Imagine a low-flying airplane prevented you from hearing the comments your client made in item 11. The person has stopped speaking and is now waiting for you to reply.)
  A. I didn't hear what you were saying. Please tell me again what you just said.
  B. Go on.
  C. I see what you mean.
  D. (You remain silent.)

Discussion of options.

A. I didn't hear what you were saying. Please tell me again what you just said.
  - Because of your honest response, the client is likely to perceive you as a genuine individual, and he probably will appreciate your efforts not to miss anything he has said.
B. Go on.
  - Although the client may continue, you will have damaged your credibility with the person if he guesses that you actually did not hear his last remarks.
C. I see what you mean.

- This outright lie will result in significant negative consequences if the person does not believe you.
D. (You remain silent.)
  - Your silence may become very awkward.

13. I feel better going to bed knowing that during the day I've spent plenty of time with my family. When I've had to cut back on being with them, I think we all feel down when the day is over. I guess what I'd really like is to find a way to be with them more, especially while my wife is hospitalized.
    A. You feel satisfied at the day's end if a lot of your time was spent with your wife and son.
    B. Being with Jeremy and your wife is fulfilling for you, and you want to figure out how to have additional time with them.
    C. Your aim is to increase the amount of time with your family, especially while your wife is ill.
    D. When you don't spend time with them, your wife and son also miss the contact.

Discussion of options.

   A. You feel satisfied at the day's end if a lot of your time was spent with your wife and son.
     - You have made an adequate surface feeling reflection, but you have missed a significant piece of information. The client's goal, mentioned at the end of his comments, is an important point to reflect.
   B. Being with Jeremy and your wife is fulfilling for you, and you want to figure out how to have additional time with them.
     - Not only have you accurately reflected the person's feelings, but you have captured the heart of his message as well. This effective response communicates understanding.
   C. Your aim is to increase the amount of time with your family, especially while your wife is ill.
     - Although your reflection is accurate, you omit any mention of how the client feels. Letting the person know you understand his emotions, as well as his situation, will help to build a positive relationship.
   D. When you don't spend time with them, your wife and son also miss the contact.

- You are better off making a response that focuses on the client.

14. Spending more time with Jeremy might also help me to tell him about his mom. Maybe it's not that I don't know what to say to him, but that I haven't found a good occasion to say it. I guess when I know we're only going to have a little time together, I don't want to spend it getting him worried over his mother. I'd rather just enjoy his company.
   A. On many days you've only had an hour to play with Jeremy.
   B. The excuses you have for not communicating with Jeremy are that you would rather play with him and that the news regarding your wife would be anxiety provoking for him.
   C. You don't feel having an honest conversation with your son is a good way to use your time with him.
   D. Not only would greater contact with your son be satisfying for you, but it might also provide a better opportunity for you to explain the situation to him.

Discussion of options.

   A. On many days you've only had an hour to play with Jeremy.
      - Reflecting only one small segment of the person's remarks is not an efficient response. Instead, you should focus on the essence of the client's message
   B. The excuses you have for not communicating with Jeremy are that you would rather play with him and that the news regarding your wife would be anxiety provoking for him.
      - Saying that the client is making excuses for his behavior may prod him into creating rationalizations for his actions. By encouraging him to take a defensive stance, you are not facilitating a relationship that sets the stage for productive change.
   C. You don't feel having an honest conversation with your son is a good way to use your time with him.
      - Your judgmental response seems cold and critical.
   D. Not only would greater contact with your son be satisfying for you, but it might also provide a better opportunity for you to explain the situation to him.

- Using a positive tone to reflect the person's thoughts and feelings is likely to help the client continue addressing issues.

The remaining multiple-choice items are with a different client.

15. For the past several years I've been working for the same program. I have gotten several promotions, so that I'm now an assistant manager at my facility. The organization has a manager position that will be opening up in another town, and I've been offered that job. It would mean more money and more responsibility, but it would also mean that I would have to move. And I'm not sure I want to do that.
    A. Thinking about moving has you distraught.
    B. A tough decision is confronting you.
    C. You're confused about whether or not to take their offer.
    D. Right now, you're not sure what you want to do.

Discussion of options.

A. Thinking about moving has you distraught.
   - Your attempt at empathy identifies a feeling the client has not expressed.
B. A tough decision is confronting you.
   - This accurate reflection conveys understanding. Labeling the decision as "tough" has demonstrated your appreciation for the client's dilemma, and because there was no specific feeling expressed by the client, your response is an appropriate reflection of the circumstance the person faces.
C. You're confused about whether or not to take their offer.
   - The client has not expressed disordered or mixed-up thinking that would indicate confusion.
D. Right now, you're not sure what you want to do.
   - Although your reflection is accurate, it fails to contain enough fresh words.

16. In terms of my career, the new job would be an exciting opportunity with quite a few challenges. The program I would be heading has been going quite well, and they are looking to expand it. Actually, I'm very flattered that they would ask me to be the per-

son to take charge. On the other hand, during the past couple of years I've put a lot of time and effort into getting my place shaped up, and I would really hate to leave it after all of that work.

A. What are you going to do?
B. You're thinking about sitting back and enjoying your place, rather than moving forward and accepting the opportunity you've been offered.
C. You regret that pursuing this career opportunity would require new living arrangements.
D. How much time do you have to decide?

Discussion of options.

A. What are you going to do?
  • You are jumping too quickly to deciding what to do.
B. You're thinking about sitting back and enjoying your place, rather than moving forward and accepting the opportunity you've been offered.
  • This comment is overly opinionated. It conveys the impression that you believe the client should take the new job.
C. You regret that pursuing this career opportunity would require new living arrangements.
  • By making this surface feeling reflection, you effectively communicate empathy.
D. How much time do you have to decide?
  • Your question asks for information that is not necessary for you to have right now.

17. What if I left my place for the new position, and it didn't work out? I would have made a pretty big sacrifice with little or nothing in return. Then there is the other side. If I don't take advantage of this promotion now, who knows when I might get another chance to be the boss? I just wish I could be more certain that being manager for this program would actually work out.

A. Accepting the new job would be easier if you were more confident about how long it might last.
B. Since you've been successful with the organization to this point, it seems to me that you probably would be successful in the new position.

    C. Maybe you could commute to the new job so you wouldn't lose your place if being manager fell through.

    D. You're distressed about the possibility of moving.

Discussion of options.

    A. Accepting the new job would be easier if you were more confident about how long it might last.
- This nonjudgmental reflection enhances your chances for developing a positive relationship.

    B. Since you've been successful with the organization to this point, it seems to me that you probably would be successful in the new position.
- By making such a biased remark, you are attempting to direct the client toward accepting the promotion.

    C. Maybe you could commute to the new job so you wouldn't lose your place if being manager fell through.
- Your suggestion is not needed at this point.

    D. You're distressed about the possibility of moving.
- Although you are trying to be empathic, there is no evidence to support your perception that the client is distressed.

18. If I knew the job was going to last at least a year, I think it would be worth the risk. In fact, I don't believe I really would be taking much of a chance if they gave me that long to prove myself. The operation is small enough that I'm pretty sure I could make any necessary adjustments if I had a year to implement them.

    A. If there were assurances of having a year to work, you probably would be willing to make the move.

    B. You'd be willing to accept the offer if you knew it would be good for at least twelve months.

    C. Given sufficient time, you're certain you would be successful.

    D. It seems to me that being worried about leaving your place was just a smoke screen. Your real concern is whether you'll be given enough time in the new position to prove yourself.

Discussion of options.

    A. If there were assurances of having a year to work, you probably would be willing to make the move.

- You have accurately reflected the client's position.

B. You'd be willing to accept the offer if you knew it would be good for at least twelve months.
- This reflection demonstrates your understanding of the client's thoughts.

C. Given sufficient time, you're certain you would be successful.
- Since the client is not certain of being successful, you have misunderstood the individual.

D. It seems to me that being worried about leaving your place was just a smoke screen. Your real concern is whether you'll be given enough time in the new position to prove yourself.
- Your comment is unnecessarily confrontational.

19. What I need to do is press for a commitment that I will have at least a year to prove myself. If they would agree to a year, I think I would take the risk and make the move. And if they aren't willing to give me a year, then I'll probably just stay where I am.

A. We have a managerial opening in our organization. I'll bet they would give you a year, and you wouldn't even have to move.

B. Being denied the guarantee of a year would lead you to reject the offer. What might be some other consequences of asking for such an assurance and being turned down?

C. Don't you think you'd seem a little pushy if you made such a request?

D. Now that you've decided how to respond to the promotion offer, is there anything else you'd like to discuss today?

Discussion of options.

A. We have a managerial opening in our organization. I'll bet they would give you a year, and you wouldn't even have to move.
- You probably are not being genuine when you make this comment, since you are unlikely to have the power to back it up.

B. Being denied the guarantee of a year would lead you to reject the offer. What might be some other consequences of asking for such an assurance and being turned down?

• The client has begun considering options and you have gone along by offering a reflection, then nonjudgmentally asking the individual to consider additional consequences associated with the course of action under discussion.

C. Don't you think you'd seem a little pushy if you made such a request?

• Asking such a leading question implies a judgmental attitude on your part.

D. Now that you've decided how to respond to the promotion offer, is there anything else you'd like to discuss today?

• Such a response is premature. You still have some work to do with the current topic.

20. I don't think there would be any negative repercussions resulting from me asking for a year to show what I can do. It seems to me that I could explain the reasoning behind my request so they would understand my need for such an interval. And if they decide not to give it to me, I still think they would see my viewpoint as being a reasonable one.

A. Since you don't perceive any drawbacks to this option, I would encourage you to request the twelve months.

B. You don't think there would be any negative repercussions resulting from asking for a year to show what you can do.

C. You're comfortable with the idea of asking for twelve months.

D. How would you ask for the time, and who would you talk to about it?

Discussion of options.

A. Since you don't perceive any drawbacks to this option, I would encourage you to request the twelve months.

• There is no need for you to take a position regarding this strategy.

B. You don't think there would be any negative repercussions resulting from asking for a year to show what you can do.

• Remember to use fresh words.

C. You're comfortable with the idea of asking for twelve months.

• Your comment accurately reflects what the client has communicated.

D. How would you ask for the time, and who would you talk to about it?
   - We recommend that you avoid asking multiple questions. Also, both of these questions ask for detailed information that is not necessary at this point.

SHORT-ANSWER QUESTIONS

Write your answer for each of the following questions.

1. According to this chapter, what characteristics are clients likely to want in their workers?
2. What three interpersonal skills, identified by Carl Rogers, help workers to develop positive relationships with clients?
3. Define empathy.
4. What "way of responding," discussed in Chapter 2, tends to convey empathy?
5. Give an example of an instance in which you were empathic to another person, and describe how that individual responded to your empathy.
6. When interacting with a client, how might a "warm" worker behave?
7. A client is angry because a friend of a neighbor keeps parking her car in front of his mailbox, thereby preventing delivery of mail for that day. The client says, "The next time I find her car blocking my mailbox I'm going to slash her tires." What is your response?
8. A married client tells you that there is a gun in her house, and that she has thought about using it on herself. Even after getting a commitment from her that she will not kill herself during the coming week, you are worried about the availability of the gun. In light of the chapter's comments on warmth, discuss the appropriateness of making the following statement? "For the time being, I believe it would be in your best interest for there not to be any guns in the house. So I would like you to talk to your husband about the presence of guns in your home, and ask him to remove the gun you know about, as well as any other guns that might be there. How would you feel about having such a conversation with him?"

9. With regard to instances in which you believe your personal dislike for a client is likely to adversely affect your ability to do your job, what are appropriate responses discussed in the chapter?
10. Define genuineness.
11. The chapter discusses typical endeavors engaged in by genuine workers. Name those actions.
12. Think of worker behaviors that can hamper genuineness. Give an example of such an instance, and describe its effect on the interaction.

POSSIBLE ANSWERS FOR SHORT-ANSWER QUESTIONS

The answer-checking procedures remain the same as before.

- For each item, compare your answer to the one we provide.
- If you believe your answer is correct, you are done with that item.
- With any question for which you believe your answer is incorrect, consider our answer and, if needed, review relevant portions of the chapter. Keep your original answer that you now think is incorrect, but add to it a response that you believe would be correct.

1. We suggest that clients usually want workers to demonstrate the following: understanding of what they are thinking and how they are feeling; respect and caring for them; and honesty.
2. Carl Rogers identified empathy, warmth, and genuineness as essential skills for workers who want to develop positive relationships with their clients.
3. Empathy is understanding another individual and communicating your understanding to the person.
4. Reflection is a good way to convey empathy.
5. One of us had a client who described his usual daily routine of going to work, not having enough tasks there to keep him busy, having no escape from listening to a radio station that he hated, and sharing a small office with a coworker who seemed to talk incessantly about the same topics. In response to the worker comment, "You dread going to work," the client responded, "Yes. Exactly," then continued sharing his work-related frustrations.

6. When with a client, a warm worker would do the following: demonstrate respect for the person, whatever the individual's behavior; refrain from being judgmental when helping the client to consider consequences of actions; and maintain a demeanor characterized by interest and caring.

7. A possible response is, "What might happen if you slashed the tires on her car?"

8. Since your objective is to preserve the client's life, we believe the response in question 8 is appropriate.

9. After trying to "go by the book," if you find yourself unable to do your job effectively because you dislike the client, the following appropriate actions are discussed in the chapter: transferring the client to a coworker, referring the person to another organization, and discussing your reactions with a supervisor or with a professional colleague.

10. Genuineness is meaning what you say.

11. Genuine workers do the following: they are natural; they admit when they do not hear or do not understand clients; and they make promises only when they can keep them.

12. In the film *Man Trouble*, a worker repeatedly uses the phrase, "I hear you," then later demonstrates that he really hasn't heard much at all when he calls a client by a name she has said she hates. One participant rolls his eyes at the gaff, and the maligned client gives the worker a look of disbelief.

FILL-IN-THE-RESPONSE QUESTIONS

Listed below are a series of client statements. For each one, write a worker response that you believe would be appropriate.

1. At work I just got my first performance evaluation, and I was very disappointed. My supervisor rated me as unsatisfactory on punctuality. And, since I'm still a probationary employee, that rating could cost me my job.

2. In the entire evaluation period, I was only late for work one time, and that was an emergency. My mother called that morning to talk about some trouble my brother was in. And I ended up talking to him as well, so I didn't get off the phone until the time I

usually leave for work. I called to let my supervisor know what had happened and that I wouldn't be on time. And when I got to work, there was no talk about me being late, so I thought there was no problem. But I guess now I've found out that family emergencies don't count as legitimate reasons for being delayed.

3. I don't know if it's realistic for me to continue working there. Things are bound to come up so that I'll probably be late other times. After all, I do have a life outside of work. But my supervisor doesn't seem to recognize that. I think it's unfair to penalize me for being human. And I think the way it was done was really underhanded.

4. I know I'm not perfect. Like everybody else, I make mistakes. But when I do something wrong and don't know it, I deserve to be told right then. A couple of months later I don't want to be blindsided with a negative write-up of my behavior. I take pride in my work, and I try to do a good job. And I'm definitely *not* accustomed to receiving documents that term my efforts unsatisfactory.

5. Getting written up for unsatisfactory performance certainly isn't something I want to go through again. But I'm not quite sure what to expect if I stay with this job. I don't know if my punctuality really was unsatisfactory or if maybe giving new employees an unsatisfactory rating on something is a standard practice that allows the organization to get rid of a probationary person they don't want to keep.

6. I guess it's possible I'm reacting too strongly. Maybe I need to find out more about how performance ratings are used in the organization. I do like working there, and I would prefer to stay if I could believe that my boss will be fairly evaluating my efforts.

POSSIBLE ANSWERS FOR
FILL-IN-THE-RESPONSE QUESTIONS

For each response opportunity, there are many possible correct answers. We list two, and, as in previous chapters, we suggest you use them in the following manner.

- Look at our two answers and think about them.
- Consider relevant material covered in the chapter.

- Read the client statement again, then immediately read your answer and the two options listed here.
- Write another response that you believe might be an improvement on your first effort.
- Repeat this procedure for each of the remaining items.

1. • Getting the poor rating was discouraging.
   • It was disheartening to receive the negative evaluation.
2. • Since you thought the issue of arriving late that day had been resolved, you were surprised when it resulted in the unsatisfactory evaluation.
   • Providing support to your family that day unexpectedly damaged your performance rating.
3. • You feel betrayed by your supervisor's actions.
   • You're angry at your supervisor.
4. • Being described as unsatisfactory embarrasses you.
   • You feel hurt by the report.
5. • You're uncertain about the true meaning of the evaluation.
   • The actual significance of the rating is something you're wondering about.
6. • Feeling you can trust your supervisor is important.
   • Confidence in your supervisor is something you'd like to have.

SUMMARY

Productive change is more likely when you have positive relationships with clients. You promote such relationships when you are skilled in conveying empathy, warmth, and genuineness.

Empathy is understanding the other person and communicating your understanding to the individual. And empathy is what you usually communicate when you reflect.

Warmth involves being respectful, caring, and nonjudgmental. But being warm should not prevent you from helping clients to consider the consequences of their actions, and it should not stop you from taking steps necessary to preserve life.

Genuineness requires that you come across as being honest and natural. Clients must perceive you as being trustworthy in order for any of your other relationship-building efforts to be worthwhile.

Chapter 4

PROBLEM SOLVING

Clients often bring up problems they consider important and troublesome. One possible response is to tell them how to deal with the difficulties. As we discussed in Chapter 2, though, advice has a number of drawbacks: it may be rejected; the person may fail to successfully implement the suggestions; and telling the person what to do may foster an authoritarian atmosphere that encourages dependency.

An alternative to giving advice is to engage clients in problem solving. By helping them generate their own ideas for coping with challenges, you foster two conditions that empirical research has linked to productive change: a collaborative working relationship (Tryon & Winograd, 2002) and autonomous decision making (e.g., Senecal, Nouwen, & White, 2000; Vansteenkiste, Simons, Sheldon, Lens, & Deci, 2004). Other researchers have found that people experience improvement in emotional well-being when they focus on coping with problems (Nezu, Nezu, Felgoise, McClure, & Houts, 2003; Orlinsky et al., 2004; Spence, Sheffield, & Donovan, 2003) and succeed in implementing internally-motivated plans (e.g., Koestner, Lekes, Powers, & Chicoine, 2002; Sheldon & Houser-Marko, 2001). Collaborative problem solving can also result in what Bandura (1997) calls a mastery experience. Clients who believe they have successfully coped with an issue in a supportive nonauthoritarian context have increased confidence and motivation to deal with additional problems. Furthermore, clients who engage in problem solving learn a skill they can apply during future coping efforts.

We are using the term "problem solving" because it is a phrase that most people understand, and it is a topic for which a body of evidence exists. The point has been made, though, that clients may view the term "problem" as an unpleasant way of conceptualizing what is happening (e.g., Pichot, 2001). As you read the material that follows, note that when talking with clients there is no need to use the terms "problem" or "problem solving." For example, we would never ask clients, "What is your problem?" Instead we prefer more neutral questions such as, "How are things going?" or "What is on your mind today?"

Although there are many approaches to problem solving (e.g., Nezu, 2004; Richard, 2003), one possibility is to think of the process as involving three phases: (1) exploring thoughts and feelings, (2) considering alternatives, and (3) developing plans. By engaging clients in those steps, you help them gain insight and prepare personally meaningful plans for change that they can use to cope with challenges. Let's now take a closer look at how to facilitate such outcomes.

EXPLORING THOUGHTS AND FEELINGS

The exploration phase involves you and the client developing a shared understanding of both challenging circumstances and emotions associated with those situations. Opening up and freely releasing one's thoughts and feelings sometimes is referred to as *ventilation*. So, if you hear staff members talk about a client having "vented," it simply means the person engaged in the free-flowing expression of emotion-laden material.

During the client's initial revelations, patiently listen to the person. Focus on what the individual is communicating, and assume ignorance.

As a novice worker, it is easy to approach each client in a fresh manner. As you gain experience, however, you will begin to see recurring patterns in certain kinds of interactions. Using your accumulated observations to generate hypotheses is good, but jumping to conclusions is ill-advised. Rather than racing ahead and assuming you know what the client is going to say next, you need to stay with the person and understand what *this* individual is actually communicating.

When discussing areas of concern, it is helpful to spend some time focusing on specific examples. You can address those concrete instances in a number of ways. You might do any of the following: reflect episodes the client spontaneously describes; ask for an account of the most recent occurrence; request a description of a typical instance; or tell the client to pretend to be watching a video recording of the episode and to provide a detailed account of what the recording shows.

In addition to exploring events that have occurred, there also is a need to focus on distressing emotions. Such feelings must be fully felt before they can be left behind. Occasionally, once is not enough and it may be necessary to have repeated discussions involving the same unpleasant emotions. When such repetition takes place, there usually is a gradual diminishing of distress as the client becomes more and more desensitized to the issues.

Some individuals try to handle ongoing distress by sweeping it under the rug. Attempting to hide unpleasant feelings becomes maladaptive when it leads to further difficulties, as the concealed issues begin interfering with the person's life. For example, a review by Diane Berry and James Pennebaker (1993) indicated that health difficulties are more frequent among persons who do not reveal negative experiences than among individuals who confide in human service professionals.

Results of empirical research indicate that being able to encourage the expression of intense negative emotions is a characteristic of skilled workers (Kivilighan, 1989). During your own interactions with actual clients, you probably will encounter individuals who communicate unpleasant feelings in many ways, including crying. Consequently, you need to think about how you will respond when a person cries.

Here is an approach to crying that we take. In the interviewing room there is a box of tissue accessible to the worker, but out of the client's reach. If the individual begins to cry, the worker places the tissue box near the person and holds it until the client takes a tissue (then leaves the box near the individual). Moving and holding the box communicates that it is acceptable to cry. The worker then reinforces this nonverbal message with patient silence and accurate reflection.

If a client brings up multiple areas to be addressed, there eventually must be a narrowing of the focus. When this is the case, you can review the issues that have been raised, and then ask a question such as, "We can more closely examine any of these areas, where do you think we should start?"

Among the issues on which you choose to focus, there ought to be at least one that shows promise of being amenable to change. Rapid progress should be possible in that area.

For example, when starting an intervention with the family of a behavior disordered child, getting ready for school in the morning is a common issue for an initial therapeutic focus. Although preparing for school rarely is the reason for which the family sought assistance, it usually is an area that is plagued with real difficulties. Reasons for selecting this focus include the following: you can count on it to occur five times during most weeks; the process is associated with a number of easily measured tasks; you know each episode will be resolved one way or another within a brief period of time; and it is an issue with which therapists generally are able to help families make rapid progress. Once experiencing improvement in this area, the family members become convinced as to the value of therapy, and they become more motivated to work at implementing the insights they are achieving.

Enhancing motivation is an important reason for selecting an issue in which quick progress is achievable. By seeing concrete evidence of improved coping, clients often experience increases in self-efficacy. They become more confident in their ability to address problems, and they become more committed to working with you in a productive alliance.

Another facet of selecting issues on which to work is, in counseling terminology, *ownership* of the problem. Clients must perceive that they are, to some degree, responsible for the development of what they now want changed. If clients deny any role in the creation of the problem, it often is the case that they are unable or unwilling to bring about any meaningful adjustments in that area.

For example, let's say a husband enters counseling because of marital difficulties with his wife. She refuses to see the therapist, so the sessions are only with him. He consistently accuses his wife of causing their problems, and he maintains that she must be the one to change. He believes all of his reactions to her are appropriate, and he is unwilling to modify anything about himself. With the wife not participating in therapy, and with the husband refusing to own any aspect of the problem, there will be no progress toward improving the marriage.

Frequently there are external conditions that clients would very much like to change but that they cannot influence. Nevertheless, being unable to modify the circumstances does not preclude progress in a different realm. Clients still can adjust the ways in which they respond to undesirable situations. Adaptive possibilities flourish when clients recognize that they can alter their own thoughts, feelings, and responses, no matter what others in their environment might do. (To avoid becoming part of the problem, you must be careful not to inadvertently close doors by implying that particular distressing circumstances *make* a client respond in certain ways. For example, it would be inappropriate for you to say to the person, "Your roommate makes you angry.")

Occasionally clients bring up problems that other people have encouraged them to address. If clients focus on those issues simply to please others or to relieve guilt, they often do not benefit from problem solving. The process is more likely to be successful if clients tackle issues that are personally meaningful to them. According to a series of research findings, people work harder and make greater progress when they focus on internally-motivated plans rather than on goals they think others want them to achieve (Sheldon & Elliot, 1998, 1999; Sheldon & Houser-Marko, 2001; Koestner et al., 2002). Research has also shown the increased emotional well-being that people experience after following through with their plans is even greater when they perceive that what they did was consistent with their own values and preferences (Sheldon & Elliot, 1999; Sheldon & Kasser, 1998). Consequently, clients are more likely to benefit from problem solving if the worker, by exploring thoughts and feelings, can help them to identify issues that are personally important to them.

So during the exploration phase, a skilled worker tries to discover issues that clients are personally motivated to address and for which they accurately perceive some responsibility. Those are areas in which change can be facilitated.

The exploration phase can continue as long as new information keeps emerging. But if you find the interaction is covering old ground that already has been adequately explored, it is probably time to move to the next phase of problem solving. By the end of the exploration stage, you and the client should have developed a clear understanding of the problematic circumstances and related feelings. And if it seems appropriate, you can summarize the issues that have been discussed. When recapping, you may find it helpful to include a statement such as, "You would like to (fill in the desires)." This type of comment prepares clients for the next phase of problem solving (considering alternatives). It also gives them an opportunity to correct you if you have misunderstood their needs or their desire for change.

CONSIDERING ALTERNATIVES

Often there is a natural progression from the exploration phase to considering alternatives. If that is not the case, such as when problems are large and multifaceted, you may need to assist the person in selecting areas on which to focus. Helping clients to divide concerns into manageable segments may be one of the most important forms of assistance you offer. Once a focus has been identified, the client and worker can begin thinking about alternatives.

The objective of the alternatives phase is to consider in detail two or three promising options. Ultimately, this discussion involves clients identifying the likely positive and negative consequences associated with each viable possibility.

Before narrowing the focus to the best available possibilities, however, you may need to help clients generate a range of options. Two ways of getting ideas on the table are brainstorming and exploring a series of three questions.

Brainstorming calls for clients to name multiple possibilities in rapid succession without critically evaluating any of them. Adolescents often like this technique because it allows them to make outrageous statements that generate no more of a response from you than, "OK, what else could you do?"

Either with or without brainstorming, another approach is to explore the following questions.

- What have you tried?
- What have you thought about trying?
- Right now, as we are talking, what other possibilities come to mind?

By using reflection and judicious interrogation, you start with the first area (What have you tried?). Upon completing that survey, you move to the second topic (What have you thought about trying?). And, if necessary, you can progress to the third question (Right now, as we are talking, what other possibilities come to mind?).

When beginning to address alternatives, it's helpful to be specific. For example, if a client has expressed a desire to get more exercise, you might want to ask, "What have you previously done in order to increase the amount of exercise you get?" Or, you could use a reflection-interrogation combination such as, "You would like to increase the amount of exercise you get. What have you tried in order to do that?"

Occasionally workers rush into considering alternatives before fully exploring the issues to be addressed. You will realize that you've rushed to the consideration of alternatives if you begin to ask, "What have you tried. . . ." and you have difficulty filling in the rest of the question. If you find you are unable to ask an explicit question or to formulate a specific reflection-interrogation combination, you should return to the exploration of thoughts and feelings until the focus for the alternatives phase is clear to both you and the client.

During the discussion of what has been tried, you acknowledge failed efforts, but the emphasis should be on what has worked, or on what might work with modifications. Although recent efforts tend to take center stage, it may also be productive for clients to describe ways they coped with similar episodes in the past. In addition to identifying relevant coping efforts that might be used again, reflecting clients' past successes may encourage them to believe they have the ability to deal with the current problem.

When you have explored all three areas and there still is a need to generate more options, another technique is to have clients describe how they have seen others handle such situations. Sometimes these discussions can produce worthwhile material, especially if the focus is on persons whom clients like or admire. Thinking about how others have successfully coped with similar problems may also raise clients' confidence in their own ability to cope with the challenges.

Having encouraged the client to generate options, there still may be other possibilities you believe should be discussed. If that is the case, you can suggest the ideas that have come to mind. When making such suggestions, supportive workers employ a style that is low-key and nonjudgmental. For example, you might say, "Last month I was working with an individual in a similar situation. That person coped with the issue by. . . . I'm wondering what you might think about trying something like that."

There will be times when you know that an option being discussed has difficulties associated with it. On such occasions it is appropriate for you to share your information and for clients to consider those disadvantages.

Remember, though, *clients* are the ones who must accept or reject options, not you. Whether you agree or disagree with a course of action is of secondary importance (except in life-threatening situations). Instead, the decisions being made should reflect the fundamental values and beliefs of your clients. As demonstrated by previously cited research, clients experience more success and greater increases in well-being when they work on plans that are personally meaningful.

One way of helping a client think through an option is to have the person role play an application of that possibility. In acting out the scenario, you can participate as a role player. But since you probably don't know the absent participants, it often is better for them to be represented by empty chairs. When a response is needed from an individual represented by a chair, one option is for the client to move to the chair and provide the appropriate comments for that person. Since role playing tends to bring in different perspectives and to make intentions concrete, processing such interactions after the role play often identifies issues needing discussion.

Whether options are generated through role playing, information you provide, or general consideration of likely consequences, it may be appropriate to identify potential problems associated with implementing a possibility under consideration. When an alternative appears to be worth keeping, it may be productive to encourage the development of contingency responses. Such fall-back positions are most necessary when the primary option is risky, but still deserving of a try.

Of course, all options involve some risk, and the client cannot develop a specific response for every possible eventuality. Rather than attempting to anticipate an infinite number of occurrences, it is more realistic to focus on the most likely ones. And sometimes the best strategy is simply to help the person recognize that difficulties may arise and that adaptation may be necessary.

When you do assist in the development of back-up positions, that activity can occur during the alternatives stage or during the third phase of problem solving, creating a plan. That is the phase you move to after considering the most promising possibilities. Hopefully, one or more of those options can become the basis for formulating a course of action.

DEVELOPING A PLAN

In a problem-solving interaction, your efforts culminate in the development of a plan. Regardless of its makeup, the plan is a good one if it has four characteristics.

- *Negotiated.* Rather than dictating courses of action, you ought to collaborate with clients so that plans develop out of a joint effort. It is more likely that the tasks will be consistent with the individual's personality, values, and attitudes if the plan is the result of collaboration, rather than being a mandate from the worker. The world's leading expert on the client is–the client. Although the worker may be a crucial source of support, clients should be the ones to decide what options will work best for them. They should not leave the interaction feeling that they have been pressured toward a certain direction; instead they need to come away believing they have chosen a course of action. As demonstrated by reviews of empirical literature (e.g., Deci & Ryan, 1987; Lewis & Osborn, 2004) and by clinical observations (e.g., Pichot, 2001), compared to coercion, perceived self-control has a variety of advantages, including less anxiety, more optimism, higher self-esteem, and–most importantly–greater persistence in attempting to implement the plan.
- *Focused in the present.* Work on the plan should begin today or tomorrow, although components in the more distant future can also be included.
- *Specific.* Concrete tasks are clearly described. There ought to be no doubt about what needs to be done or when an objective has been achieved. The plan should specify the responsibilities of each participant, including the client, the worker, the worker's organization, and other sources of support. The plan should also include implementation strategies. Reviews of research findings indicate

that people are more successful at accomplishing their plans if they have established specific methods for implementing them, such as describing when and where they will carry out the tasks and how they will handle obstacles (Gollwitzer, 1999; Koestner et al., 2002).

- ***Realistic.*** It is likely, not just possible, that the client will engage in the tasks. If planned tasks are to be of any use, participants must be capable of following through with them.

Having developed a plan, the *client* should verbally review its components. If omissions or misunderstandings become apparent, discuss those areas until there is a shared view of what is anticipated.

The following dialog demonstrates how problem solving could be addressed in an interaction.

Worker: What's on your mind today?

Client: Well, I have an upcoming problem, and I'm not exactly sure how to handle it.

Worker: Mmhmm.

Client: For three years I was a dispatcher for a law enforcement agency, and then I returned to school last semester. I didn't work last term, and I really need to get a job. So, I recently accepted a position as a crisis intervention worker. This is going to be a new experience for me. As a dispatcher I helped get interveners to the scene, but I wasn't there myself. Being a crisis worker will involve a new set of responsibilities for me. I'm not sure if I'm trained well enough to do crisis intervention, and I wonder if I will be able to handle it.

Worker: Mmhmm.

Client: I start next week, and I feel that other than my helping skills class, I have no real training in human-service intervention. Although I have my dispatcher background and my class preparation, both of which helped me get the position, I don't know if I will be able to do this new job.

Worker: So you've worked as a dispatcher, but your duties did not involve face-to-face contact with people in need of help. You've taken a course in helping skills. And that, combined with your experience as a dispatcher, landed you the crisis worker position.

Client: Mmhmm.

Worker: But it's scary to think about going into this new area.

Client: Yeah *really*, because it's going to be so different. In the past I've mainly helped to arrange some sort of physical intervention, and now I will be expected to deal with emotional problems. It's different from being a dispatcher where we could say, "OK, we understand the problem. Here's what we're going to do." The crisis job will be something new. Also, they haven't been real specific on what sort of orientation I'll have.

Worker: Mmhmm.

Client: With my dispatcher job, I had a senior person who was with me as a guide for six weeks. But the crisis job is more or less just going to be learn-on-your-own. I'll have a couple days with another crisis worker, but then I'll be alone. So when I'm on duty, I'll be the only crisis worker there. Whatever happens to come up, I'll have to deal with.

Worker: Mmhmm.

Client: I don't know. . . . I guess I'm worried about what they might want me to do. Am I going to get into situations that I can't handle? Like, are they going to ask me to go out into the field and break-up domestic violence situations? In addition to outreach—which means going to the client's location—the program does both telephone and walk-in intervention. So, if I have some highly intoxicated person who walks into my office, how am I going to handle that?

Worker: (Pause.) Well, you have a number of concerns with regard to this new position. One area is the difference between being a dispatcher and doing crisis intervention. As a dispatcher you were very directive and action oriented, and you're thinking that might not be appropriate for a crisis worker. Then in terms of training, at the law enforcement agency you had a supervisor who was with you for several weeks to help you become acclimated to your new position, but that lengthy orientation period is not available at the crisis intervention program. And you're uncertain about your ability to fulfill the expectations of the job. You're also apprehensive about the pressure associated with being alone much of the time. Since the modes of service involve outreach as well as walk-in and telephone contacts, you are worried about how you're going to be able to cope with those new experiences.

Client: Yeah . . . very worried because I really don't know what to expect. I start next week. But I also have another concern. I'm a student, and I'm attending school full-time. Budgeting my time is going to be a problem.

Worker: Mmhmm.

Client: This job that I'm taking involves working all three shifts. So, I'm trying to plan when I'm going to be working. But I also have to study. I don't want my grades to slip. Then there are the usual activities of daily living.

Worker: Mmhmm.

Client: So, I will really have to juggle my time.

Worker: In addition to the uncertainties associated with making the transition from being a dispatcher to being a crisis intervention worker, you're also anticipating time pressure with regard to all of the duties that you have to perform.

Client: Yeah, I tend to be a perfectionist. When I set out to do something, I want to do it the best I can. I don't like to let things slide. I prefer to stay on top of what's going on. And I'm hoping I'll be able to do that.

Worker: (Pause.) But you believe there may be a possibility that you won't live up to your high expectations of yourself?

Client: Well, sure. I mean, there *is* only so much that one person can do in a twenty-four hour day. I'm concerned that I might let myself down, let my employer down, and let down my professors at school. And I'm trying to get into graduate school, so grades are very important. I don't want to let them slide just because I'm working. But I need to work too. I mean, the bills have to be paid. So, yeah it's a struggle.

Worker: Part of the pressure that you're experiencing is related to the demanding expectations you have for yourself, particularly with regard to maintaining your academic performance.

Client: Right, mmhmm.

Worker: Let's review what we've covered. You're making the shift from being a dispatcher to being a crisis worker. You will be starting a new position in which the orientation period will be less structured than in the law enforcement job you had. You have questions about the nature of the work you're going to be doing, and you have worries about the time pressure that you're putting on yourself.

Client: Right, yeah. Yeah, that's it.

Worker: Other issues that you'd like to bring up?

Client: No, those are my main concerns right now.

Worker: All right. (Pause.) We've identified a number of areas on which we might focus. One is the transition from dispatching to crisis work. Another area would be the specifics of the new position in terms of the training that you will have and the expectations that you'll face on the job. A third area to consider would be time pressure, especially as it relates to the need to maintain your academic performance. So of those three areas—making the shift from dispatching to crisis work, the nature of the new job, and the time pressure—which of those might you like to discuss further?

Client: The time. The time pressures.

Worker: OK. You are a college student.

Client: Mmhmm.

Worker: You are now attending classes.

Client: Mmhmm.

Worker: And you will be starting a new job.

Client: Right.

Worker: What kinds of decisions are you faced with in terms of managing your time?

Client: Well, I'm trying to prioritize. I want to do my best in everything, but when I have a limited number of hours for school, it is going to come down to how much time am I going to spend studying? The work schedule is something I don't really have too much control over. Basically, they'll tell me when I'm working, and I'll have to be there.

Worker: Mmhmm.

Client: So that's out of my hands. But for the other hours of the day, I'm just going to have to try to make a time budget. You know, like a financial budget. I could decide that certain hours will be spent on studying and that other hours will be spent on homework.

Worker: (Pause.) So your schedule at the crisis intervention center will pretty much be set by them. . . .

Client: Yeah. I mean, I think once I'm there for awhile I may have some say in my schedule.

Worker: Mmhmm.

Client: But for right now, the schedule is more or less determined by them.

Worker: OK.

Client: So I will just have to work when they tell me to.

Worker: Mmhmm. And your class schedule is set.

Client: Yeah, right.

Worker: Other aspects of your time that have already been established by someone else?

Client: Saturday is the day I try to do the laundry and the housework.

Worker: Mmhmm.

Client: That's about it.

Worker: So we have a couple of areas that are fixed. One would be your work schedule; the other is your class schedule.

Client: Mmhmm.

Worker: And we have a couple of more areas—studying and housework—that might allow some flexibility.

Client: Mmhmm.

Worker: You said you were thinking of making a schedule that would allow you to keep track of what you need to be doing each day.

Client: A schedule would be a reminder to me that, hey, this is what I need to be doing now.

Worker: Mmhmm.

Client: That might be helpful.

Worker: (Pause.) You've thought about trying to develop a schedule to remind you of tasks you need to be doing.

Client: Mmhmm. I've also thought about trying to get some private time and focus on what needs to be done.

Worker: Mmhmm.

Client: And say, "OK, this is the time for me to do my school work" or whatever it is I need to do.

Worker: Mmhmm.

Client: But that tends to create tension with my roommates.

Worker: Mmhmm.

Client: If I post a schedule, though, they can see it too. They can say, "This is your private time that you need for studying; we'll leave you alone then."

Worker: Mmhmm.

Client: So a posted schedule might work not only for me but also might allow us to get along better.

Worker: You think that if you display the schedule, your roommates might read it and help you meet it.

Client: I think they would at least understand why I'm tucked away in my room; they wouldn't think I'm doing it to avoid them.

Worker: In the past, what other strategies have you used that again might be helpful for you in terms of managing your time?

Client: Hmm. . . . I don't know if I've really tried anything other than just going at it as the time goes along. I mean, just trying to fit things in as I can.

Worker: Plugging away. (Pause.) What else have you thought about trying?

Client: Really, nothing else. I've never actually had a plan.

Worker: OK.

Client: That's part of my problem.

Worker: But you are working on a plan now.

Client: Mmhmm.

Worker: The idea you have come up with is to develop a schedule and to put it up so that both you and your roommates would see it. . . .

Client: Mmhmm.

Worker: . . . so that hopefully things might go a little bit more smoothly when you need to have some time to yourself.

Client: Mmhmm.

Worker: Other ideas that come to you now in terms of how you might be able to manage your time?

Client: Well, at my crisis job I will be given the freedom to read if it's a slow night. If we don't have calls or if we don't have walk-ins, I will be allowed to do other work.

Worker: Mmhmm.

Client: It means I could do homework there *if* it was a quiet night. Now, of course, I won't know that until it happens. But I can always take my homework with me, just in case it would be quiet so I could do it.

Worker: You anticipate that there may be times at your job when you would be able to focus on your studies.

Client: It could happen, yeah.

Worker: So you're going to be prepared by taking your school materials with you in case some free time should develop.

Client: Yeah. Mmhmm.

Worker: All right. Other ideas that come to mind in terms of managing your time?

Client: No, not really.

Worker: So, we've talked about two ideas: having a schedule, and taking your homework with you so that if you did have free time at work you could spend some effort on your academic assignments.

Client: Mmhmm.

Worker: Other ideas that come to mind?

Client: I think that's all.

Worker: You're saying you would be comfortable with a schedule and with being prepared to do homework at work, if the opportunity arises.

Client: Right. Yeah.

Worker: So you have decided on two tasks: you will post a schedule and you will take your homework to work with you. (Pause.) Sometimes it's helpful to work out a few details ahead of time and to think about problems that might come up. For example, when will you have time to develop and post the schedule?

Client: I actually have some free time tonight, and I have a computer program that I could use to develop a shell for the schedule. So I could make up the first schedule tonight and then use the shell to make a new schedule each week.

Worker: When will you do the weekly schedules?

Client: Well, I know that I won't have to work Sunday evenings. So every Sunday night I could make a schedule for the week.

Worker: So you'll develop a form tonight that you can use to make a weekly schedule every Sunday night.

Client: Right.

Worker: What things might interfere with using the schedule?

Client: Well, when I tried to make a schedule a few years ago I would forget to look at it.

Worker: So the schedule won't be helpful if you don't see it.

Client: Right.

Worker: What could you do to increase the chances that you'll look at the schedule?

Client: I could post it on my bedroom door. That way I'll see it every time I go to my bedroom and my roommates will also be able to see it.

Worker: Posting the schedule on your door will serve a couple of purposes.

Client: Yes. And I could ask my roommates to help me stick with the schedule. That way they'll be reminded about it, and they'll also help me stay with it.

Worker: Well, you've worked out a number of details for how and when you'll develop the schedule, and you've come up with a way to remind yourself about the schedule that will also get your roommates involved with helping you.

Client: Mmhmm.

Worker: Are there any other details regarding the schedule that we should address?

Client: No. I think that's it. I really believe the schedule is going to help this time.

Worker: You've worked out some details for implementing a schedule, and you're feeling more confident that you will use it productively.

Client: Mmhmm.

Worker: The other idea was taking your homework to work with you in case you have some free time. What details should we address regarding that plan?

Client: I don't think I'll have any problems with that. I'll just have to remind myself to pack a bag with some homework before I leave for work.

Worker: (Pause.) So, we have addressed the issue of time management.

Client: Mmhmm.

Worker: There were two other areas you brought up. One was making the transition from being a dispatcher to being a crisis worker. . . .

Client: Mmhmm.

Worker: And the other was the expectations associated with your new position in terms of the training you're going to be having and the nature of the work you'll be doing.

Client: Mmhmm.

Worker: Are there topics that you'd like to discuss with either of those issues?

Client: Well, I don't think so right now. I'm going to be starting this job next week. So maybe once I actually get into it and see what the orientation is going to be like and see what their expectations are going to be, I'll know more about what the issues are. But I think my main worry was the time restraints.

Worker: OK.

Client: Maybe I could see you next week after I've already had a couple days on the job.

Worker: That would be fine. When would be a convenient time for you next week?

Client: How about if we meet at the same time next Friday?

Worker: So, that'll be Friday at 10:00.

Client: Mmhmm.

Worker: And at that time you will have gotten your feet wet.

Client: Yeah, a little anyway.

Worker: And by then a few of the work-related issues might be more concrete so that we could discuss them more fully.

Client: Yeah, sounds good.

Worker: For now, you have decided to use some strategies for time management. We talked about two specific plans. I'd like you just to review those for me.

Client: Well, the first thing I need to do is make a schedule tonight and post it on my bedroom door so that not only myself but my roommates can see that throughout the day these are the hours I'm going to be doing whatever, work, classes, or studying. And I'll ask my roommates to help me stick with the schedule. Also, when I go to work, take my homework with me. If there's a quiet evening, I can use some of that extra time to fit in homework.

Worker: OK. And how are you feeling about that plan?

Client: Good. Really good.

Worker:	So, you have two tasks: make a schedule and have home-work available at work.
Client:	Mmhmm.
Worker:	And we're going to meet again this coming Friday at 10:00 in the morning. We can see how you are doing with your plan and also check-in with the situation at your new job.
Client:	OK. Sounds great.
Worker:	I look forward to seeing how things work out.
Client:	Yeah, me too. Thanks a lot.

In this interaction the worker talked quite a bit, eventually speaking only slightly less than the client. It would also have been acceptable for the worker to have talked less. The converse, however, probably is not true. Significantly more talk from the worker may have constituted too much input.

Throughout the interaction the worker relied on nonverbal expressions of interest ("Mmhmms"). The first verbal response by the staff member was a reflection (interrupted with an "Mmhmm" from the client) that recognized the nature of the situation and how the person was feeling. Next, the worker summarized the issues confronting the individual and the emotions associated with those pressures. The staff member then offered a reflection that recognized the existence of job-related uncertainties, as well as the issue of time pressure.

The client's lofty goals were the focus of the next two verbal responses. The worker asked a closed question intended to verify that the client feared being unable to live up to self-determined expectations, and then reflected the essence of those expectations.

At this point in the interaction, the staff member decided to focus the discussion more narrowly. To this end the worker did the following: summarized the issues and emotions that had been discussed, asked if there were other topics the client wanted to bring up, specifically identified the three areas the person had described earlier, and asked which of those the individual wanted to discuss further.

When the client chose time pressure as a topic in need of additional attention, the worker summarized the circumstances with regard to that issue, and next asked an open question intended to draw out specific choices the person needed to make. The staff member encouraged the discussion of time factors by using nonverbal expressions of interest, a brief verbal response ("OK"), four factual reflections, and an open question.

During the exploration of time factors, the client mentioned the option of developing a schedule, and the worker then moved the problem-solving process into the alternatives phase by using a factual reflection to reintroduce the topic of a schedule. The staff member supported the client's positive comments about a schedule by offering frequent "Mmhmms" and two factual reflections.

The worker continued with the consideration of alternatives by asking an open question about other strategies that had been helpful in the past. After reflecting the client's response, the staff member asked an open question regarding what the person had thought about trying. The worker acknowledged the client's responses with an "OK." When the individual said that not having a plan was part of the problem, the staff member pointed out that they were in the midst of working on one, and then summarized the client's idea of developing and posting a schedule. Next, the worker used an open question to draw out other options the client might have thought about trying, and then recognized the person's responses through an "Mmhmm" and two factual reflections.

In order to check for any further ideas the client was thinking about, the staff member asked an open question regarding other ideas that might have come to the individual. When the client did not offer any more possibilities, the worker summarized the two options that had been discussed and encouraged the client to think about specific issues related to carrying out those ideas. To help the client develop implementation strategies for using a schedule, the worker asked four open questions and reflected the client's responses to those questions. The worker asked a closed question to check for any other details that needed to be addressed and reflected the client's increasing confidence in the plan. The worker then reminded the client about the idea of taking homework to work and asked an open question regarding its implementation. The staff member then reviewed the options and issues that had been covered, and asked a closed question to discover whether there were other topics the client wanted to explore. When the person responded that there might be an area that could best be discussed at a later date, the worker agreed, and then turned the focus to setting a time for a subsequent meeting and establishing an agenda for that session. (If there had been other areas to consider in the present meeting, the worker could have returned to the exploration phase of problem solving with regard to those topics.)

At this point, the plan actually had been developed, so the staff member requested the client to review its two components. After the person's summary, the worker asked an open question to see how the client was feeling about the plan. Since the person indicated commitment to the two endeavors, the staff member brought the interaction to a close by naming the two tasks, verifying the subsequent meeting, reviewing the agenda for that meeting, and expressing interest in learning how events developed.

This problem-solving interaction fulfilled its objective. The client came away with a plan that was negotiated, focused in the present, specific, and realistic.

Subsequent contacts with this individual would offer opportunities to monitor progress regarding implementation of the plan. Efforts intended to reinforce, refine, and expand coping efforts would be crucial, because in the final analysis, *it is what clients do between interactions with you that matters most.* We must not lose sight of that fact. The ultimate objective of human services is to provide opportunities for clients to better cope with the demands they face. Facilitating client progress is the goal, and helping skills are only a means to that end.

MULTIPLE-CHOICE QUESTIONS

Items 1-7 involve one client; questions 8-15 concern a second individual; and items 16-24 focus on a third person. Your instructions are the same as in the previous chapters.

- For each of the following client statements, choose the response or responses you believe would be appropriate. (Several items have more than one correct answer.)
- Indicate your selection in writing.
- Read the discussions of all four options.
- If you are correct, go to the next item.
- If you are incorrect, think about the explanations and, if necessary, review relevant portions of the chapter; then, once you better understand the issues, proceed to the next question.

1. I have had it with my roommate. She is the biggest slob. She leaves her clothes everywhere and never, I mean *never*, picks-up

after herself. I don't have the extra time to clean up her messes just because she feels like being lazy. I have enough to worry about!

A. Your roommate sounds like an inconsiderate person.

B. What have you tried in the past to get her to change?

C. The sloppy habits of your roommate are frustrating.

D. Being a busy person, you're unable to keep the place clean by yourself.

Discussion of options.

A. Your roommate sounds like an inconsiderate person.
  - This comment puts the focus on the roommate rather than on the client.

B. What have you tried in the past to get her to change?
  - It is inappropriate to call for a discussion of options so early in the interaction. You should first explore the client's thoughts and feelings.

C. The sloppy habits of your roommate are frustrating.
  - Your response gets the exploration phase off to a good start by accurately reflecting the client's feelings about her roommate's inconsiderate behavior.

D. Being a busy person, you're unable to keep the place clean by yourself.
  - You ignore the client's strong feelings by focusing only on facts in your reflection. It misses the heart of what the client has said.

2. I'm sick of having to do everything. I wash the dishes and do the cleaning. And her clothes will stay on the floor for days unless I pick them up. It's too much. She doesn't help at all! But she is my friend, and I care about her. I don't want to lose her friendship over this.

A. Although you're very irritated with her, you're not ready to give up on the relationship.

B. You still want to be her friend, but because of her insensitive behavior, you question whether she wants to be your friend.

C. You like her, but you hate her messiness.

D. How have your roommate's habits affected the relationship between you?

Discussion of options.

    A. Although you're very irritated with her, you're not ready to give up on the relationship.
- By reflecting the client's feelings and thoughts, you are continuing to explore the problem.

    B. You still want to be her friend, but because of her insensitive behavior, you question whether she wants to be your friend.
- The client has not expressed this sentiment. Perhaps such material eventually will come out, but for now, you are assuming too much.

    C. You like her, but you hate her messiness.
- You encourage further exploration by making this accurate surface feeling reflection.

    D. How have your roommate's habits affected the relationship between you?
- With this response you move away from the client's distressing feelings. For the time being, it is better to stay with those emotions in order to encourage a full airing of concerns, which gives the client a chance to vent her feelings.

3. The difference in our approaches to keeping up the place is really putting a strain on us. I'm worried that, if these circumstances continue, our friendship will be permanently damaged.
    A. Have the two of you been friends long?
    B. How do you feel about telling your roommate what's bothering you?
    C. You worry that if these circumstances continue they will permanently damage your friendship.
    D. You fear your relationship may be at risk.

Discussion of options.

    A. Have the two of you been friends long?
- This closed question asks for unnecessary information and moves away from the person's distressed feelings.

    B. How do you feel about telling your roommate what's bothering you?
- You are indirectly suggesting that the client should commu-

nicate her feelings to the roommate. By offering this advice you discourage the person from generating options herself.

C. You worry that if these circumstances continue they will permanently damage your friendship.
   • Your reflection is accurate, but it does not use fresh words. Simply repeating the client's phrasing suggests minimal involvement on your part.

D. You fear your relationship may be at risk.
   • This reflection demonstrates that you understand both the problem and the client's emotions.

4. I feel like my roommate and I have to work this out now because I can't handle it anymore. I want to resolve the matter so that her sloppiness changes but our friendship doesn't. I'm just not sure what to do to make that happen.

A. You have nowhere to turn.
B. So, a task for us would be to figure out how to get things moving in a positive direction.
C. What are some areas in which you and your roommate get along?
D. Tell me how you think you are going to resolve these issues with your roommate.

Discussion of options.

A. You have nowhere to turn.
   • You are incorrectly implying that the client has no options.

B. So, a task for us would be to figure out how to get things moving in a positive direction.
   • Although you recognize the client's current uncertainty, your statement also focuses the discussion on productive coping.

C. What are some areas in which you and your roommate get along?
   • Difficulties between the client and her roommate are the current focus of the interaction. It is better to stay with that topic, rather than shift the attention to a new area of discussion.

D. Tell me how you think you are going to resolve these issues with your roommate.

- You ask the client to solve the problem without the benefit of considering various alternatives. Brainstorming and the three "What" questions discussed in the chapter are more realistic ways of generating options. In addition, since "these issues" is vague phrasing, the client may not know how to respond.

5. I do value the friendship we share, but her clutter makes me so mad. Something has to change. It can't go on like this. I just don't know what to do or say next.
   A. You'd like to get things moving forward.
   B. Don't you think your roommate knows how her habits are affecting you?
   C. But you do believe that action is necessary. What have you tried in the past to resolve the messiness issue with your roommate?
   D. I'm sure we can work this out without you losing your roommate as a friend. Your fundamental relationship is so strong; I'm certain it can weather this storm.

Discussion of options.

   A. You'd like to get things moving forward.
      - Although accurate, you just made a very similar reflection. Repeating the same idea is unlikely to elicit new thoughts or feelings from the client.
   B. Don't you think your roommate knows how her habits are affecting you?
      - This is a leading question.
   C. But you do believe that action is necessary. What have you tried in the past to resolve the messiness issue with your roommate?
      - The client is now repeating herself and is not adding any new information. Consequently, it is time to move from the exploration stage to the alternatives phase of problem solving. That change in focus is likely to occur because of your combination response. You have reflected her desire for change, and the focus for the alternatives phase is clear because of the explicit wording in your question.

D. I'm sure we can work this out without you losing your room-mate as a friend. Your fundamental relationship is so strong; I'm certain it can weather this storm.
   • Because you cannot guarantee this positive outcome, you have offered false reassurance.

6. Well, I've tried dropping hints to my roommate, some subtle, some not so subtle. But she's just not getting the picture. I don't know if she's ignoring my hints or if she just hasn't picked up on them.
   A. Do you believe clues are ever going to work or do you think you need another strategy?
   B. How did you expect your roommate to react to your hints?
   C. One strategy you've tried is to confront her in an indirect way.
   D. Although you have tried to point out her bad habits, your roommate doesn't care how you feel.

Discussion of options.

   A. Do you believe clues are ever going to work or do you think you need another strategy?
      • Remember that multiple questions can confuse communica-tion with the client.
   B. How did you expect your roommate to react to your hints?
      • Your question calls for further discussion on an option that the client has just described as being unsatisfactory. Concentrating on past failures is not likely to help the indi-vidual develop adaptive options.
   C. One strategy you've tried is to confront her in an indirect way.
      • This is an accurate reflection that does not dwell on the neg-ative.
   D. Although you have tried to point out her bad habits, your roommate doesn't care how you feel.
      • You are making an assumption about the client's roommate.

7. The innuendoes didn't work at all. I guess I should have tried a different approach.
   A. What else have you thought about doing?
   B. Do you think anything is really going to work?

C. Don't be disappointed about the decision you made.
D. You attempted indirect suggestions. What else have you considered?

Discussion of options.

A. What else have you thought about doing?
  - You are moving the discussion away from past failures by encouraging the client to explore other possibilities she has considered.
B. Do you think anything is really going to work?
  - Your disheartening closed question does not facilitate problem solving.
C. Don't be disappointed about the decision you made.
  - Telling the client how not to feel is an ill-advised response. It implies the individual's present frustration is unimportant.
D. You attempted indirect suggestions. What else have you considered?
  - This combination response facilitates continued examination of options.

Another client is interviewed in items 8-15.

8. My supervisor just changed a policy at work, and it's making my job impossible. His modification is unnecessary, and it's doing a lot more harm than good.
   A. But you still feel the job is worth keeping.
   B. You're really unhappy about the new procedure.
   C. I had a supervisor like that once. It was a frustrating experience. I can tell you how I handled the situation if you would like.
   D. Your boss isn't doing his job very well.

Discussion of options.

A. But you still feel the job is worth keeping.
  - You are assuming the client already has considered quitting as an option and has discarded that possibility. But there is nothing in the person's remarks to support your conclusion.

B. You're really unhappy about the new procedure.
- By reflecting how the client feels about the change at work, you show you have been listening attentively. This is a positive beginning to the exploration stage.

C. I had a supervisor like that once. It was a frustrating experience. I can tell you how I handled the situation if you would like.
- The client has not come to discuss difficulties you've had. At this point in the interaction, there is no need for such self-disclosure from you.

D. Your boss isn't doing his job very well.
- By commenting on the supervisor, you have moved the spotlight away from the client and onto the boss. Rather than shifting attention to persons who are not present, it is better to focus on the individual in front of you.

9. I don't know where he comes up with these schemes. The new rule doesn't even make sense. It's ridiculous.
A. The new directive seems unnecessary to you.
B. Tell me how the change is affecting you.
C. What would you do if you were the supervisor?
D. This new policy came out of nowhere, and it is creating havoc in your workplace.

Discussion of options.

A. The new directive seems unnecessary to you.
- The person is likely to continue exploring issues in response to your reflection.

B. Tell me how the change is affecting you.
- By inviting such discussion, you are targeting the interaction on an area that needs to be examined.

C. What would you do if you were the supervisor?
- Requesting this speculation moves the interaction too quickly into the alternatives phase.

D. This new policy came out of nowhere, and it is creating havoc in your workplace.
- This is an inaccurate reflection and assumes much more than the person has said.

10. I'm the evening manager at a grocery store. The new policy states that employees can work only in the department they're hired for. So if a cashier calls in sick at the last minute, I can't grab someone else in the store to fill in. This really puts me in a bind. Work backs up, and I end up staying two or three hours past the end of my shift.

A. It sounds like there already have been some times when you became frustrated with the results of the new instructions.

B. You want the supervisor to turn control of the employees over to you.

C. Is there anything you can do about this aggravating job restriction?

D. Accomplishing your managerial tasks has become difficult. Give me an example of an instance when the new rule interfered with your job.

Discussion of options.

A. It sounds like there already have been some times when you became frustrated with the results of the new instructions.
   • Your reflection recognizes the person's feelings and suggests you would like to hear about a recent problematic episode.

B. You want the supervisor to turn control of the employees over to you.
   • Although this observation may be true, it is not an accurate reflection of what the client just said.

C. Is there anything you can do about this aggravating job restriction?
   • Asking clients to think of options before fully examining their circumstances and emotions is an unproductive approach to problem solving.

D. Accomplishing your managerial tasks has become difficult. Give me an example of an instance when the new rule interfered with your job.
   • At this point the client has not fully described the circumstances at work. The nature of that situation will become clearer because of your combination response that requests a description of a specific incident.

11. About two weeks ago, a cashier hurt her back one hour before clock-in time. No one I called could come in to take her shift on such short notice. Before the new policy, I could just grab a spare shelf stocker, someone from the deli, or maybe a bagger. Within a few minutes I'd have them on the register line. But not on that night! My supervisor had his eye on me to make sure I would enforce the new rule. That left me stuck cashiering when customer lines got too long. I was able to get the cash books done, but when it was time to go home, I still had to tally the stamp, lotto, and gift certificate receipts, plus make the night deposit. I got home three hours late. And the next evening I had a reprimand in my box for working too much overtime. I can't win!

   A. The new guidelines don't seem realistic when it comes to the actual demands of your job. Consequently, you find yourself feeling trapped and exasperated with regard to your boss' expectations.

   B. So you're pretty much stuck because of this new policy. It sounds like whatever you do, there are going to be problems with the action you take.

   C. It seems like this whole problem could have been avoided if your supervisor had talked with you before changing the policy.

   D. What did you do in response to the reprimand?

Discussion of options.

   A. The new guidelines don't seem realistic when it comes to the actual demands of your job. Consequently, you find yourself feeling trapped and exasperated with regard to your boss' expectations.
  - This reflection effectively summarizes the person's situation and feelings.

   B. So you're pretty much stuck because of this new policy. It sounds like whatever you do, there are going to be problems with the action you take.
  - You assert that a good solution does not exist. Such an attitude on your part is not likely to facilitate problem solving.

   C. It seems like this whole problem could have been avoided if your supervisor had talked with you before changing the policy.

- Your credibility will be damaged if you are incorrect. And because this analysis is not needed to solve the immediate problem, you take an unnecessary risk by expressing such an opinion.

D. What did you do in response to the reprimand?
- There would be no difficulty with this open question if you had first made a reflection to demonstrate your understanding of the thoughts and emotions the client just shared.

12. That pretty much sums it up. And I don't know what to do about it. I haven't tried anything because I can't think of what to do. I've been racking my brain for days, and I still can't come up with any ideas. That's why I came to you. I figured you would have some answers.

A. Then you haven't spoken to your supervisor directly. It seems to me that's the first thing you should do. A one-to-one conversation could help to clarify the issues.

B. I'm sorry. I don't know how to help you.

C. Well, I can't tell you what to do.

D. Sometimes it is helpful to look at what other people have tried in similar situations. How is the day-shift manager dealing with the new policy?

Discussion of options.

A. Then you haven't spoken to your supervisor directly. It seems to me that's the first thing you should do. A one-to-one conversation could help to clarify the issues.
- A supportive worker's role is not to give advice. Instead of saying what the individual should try, it is better to engage the person in a problem-solving process that helps the *client* create a solution.

B. I'm sorry. I don't know how to help you.
- Brainstorming and other techniques can help to generate options during the alternatives phase. Consequently, this response is inappropriate.

C. Well, I can't tell you what to do.
- Although you may be right, making such a comment will not promote the problem-solving process.

D. Sometimes it is helpful to look at what other people have tried in similar situations. How is the day-shift manager dealing with the new policy?
  • The client's statement provides answers to all three "What" questions of the alternatives phase. But because of your response, a new resource for developing alternatives is now available. The person can use your comment as a spring-board for generating new ideas.

13. I've really only observed the day manager once when she was in the midst of a similar crisis. She had the supervisor himself filling in! It was a riot to see the boss running the register, bagging groceries, and doing other odd jobs. I don't know how she got him to do it.
A. She probably asked him, don't you think?
B. Seeing him in those roles was amusing. What other thoughts do you have about the supervisor substituting for absent employees?
C. Let's take a look at some other possibilities that might be available. What else has the day manager tried?
D. That sounds like a unique arrangement. I also wonder how she did it.

Discussion of options.

A. She probably asked him, don't you think?
  • Asking a leading question is unlikely to generate a productive reply from the client.
B. Seeing him in those roles was amusing. What other thoughts do you have about the supervisor substituting for absent employees?
  • After reflecting the person's comment, you ask the client to share more thoughts about the boss lending a hand. Your request is likely to result in further consideration of this alternative.
C. Let's take a look at some other possibilities that might be available. What else has the day manager tried?
  • Your question directs attention away from using the supervisor as a last-minute replacement. Getting the boss involved

is a viable option and should not be shunted aside by changing the interaction's focus.

D. That sounds like a unique arrangement. I also wonder how she did it.

- In a vague way, you have asked the client to consider the other manager's solution. There is a better response listed in this group.

14. I liked it. I was surprised at first, but he seemed to fit right in with the other employees. It looked like a few workers were giggling at the boss' efforts, but overall I think he was doing an OK job. Maybe I ought to try the same thing with him.

A. You're thinking of seeking some help from him yourself. How might you go about doing that?

B. So this is the option you've settled on. Let's figure out how you would go about doing it.

C. Obtaining the supervisor's assistance when you are short-handed seems like it might be an idea worth considering.

D. The boss' participation shocked you.

Discussion of options.

A. You're thinking of seeking some help from him yourself. How might you go about doing that?

- Your combination response recognizes the client's thoughts and requests further information on the topic.

B. So this is the option you've settled on. Let's figure out how you would go about doing it.

- There may be other alternatives to be evaluated before deciding on which ones to use. And making that final selection is the client's responsibility.

C. Obtaining the supervisor's assistance when you are short-handed seems like it might be an idea worth considering.

- You have accurately reflected the client's sentiment, thereby encouraging the person to continue evaluating this option.

D. The boss' participation shocked you.

- Reflecting only a minor aspect of the client's remarks does not demonstrate attentive listening. In order to communicate your understanding of the person's message, you should summarize the essence of the message. Because the material you reflect also directs the focus of the interaction, try not to become side-tracked by secondary issues.

15. I'm still not sure what *I* would actually do. I think using the boss is a great move. And it certainly seemed to work for her. But I wonder how she convinced him to help out.
    A. I imagine all she did was tell him she needed his help.
    B. You can't figure out what she did to get the boss involved.
    C. Getting your boss to work alongside the staff appears to you like it would be an option worth examining.
    D. How could you find out what she did?

Discussion of options.

A. I imagine all she did was tell him she needed his help.
   • Allow the client to consider possible strategies rather than cutting off such efforts by expressing your opinion.
B. You can't figure out what she did to get the boss involved.
   • This reflection is accurate, but it does not encourage the person to develop ideas about how to achieve similar results.
C. Getting your boss to work alongside the staff appears to you like it would be an option worth examining.
   • You reflected similar material in question 14. Making virtually the same statement twice in a row may not be very useful, since the second comment probably will fail to generate new ideas or expressions from the client.
D. How could you find out what she did?
   • You are giving the individual an opportunity to explore a path that may lead to recruiting the supervisor's help. Perhaps as the person investigates this option, some workable alternatives will emerge.

The remaining multiple-choice items involve a client in his second interaction with the worker. During the first session, this person had expressed frustration and anger toward his landlord, who recently had doubled the rent. In addition to airing his dislike of the landlord, the client had been apprehensive and uncertain about his future living arrangements. The plan he developed was to look for available apartments by checking the classified ads in the daily newspaper.

16. Nothing has really changed since last week. I still have to pay twice the rent if I want to stay where I'm living. I have two weeks left before I have to decide whether to accept the new lease agreement or to decline the contract and move out. I checked the newspaper again for other apartments, but everything I found was either too expensive or too far away from my job.

A. You're still facing the dilemma of whether or not to stay in your apartment. With regard to the possibility of moving elsewhere, you've looked at the newspaper classifieds, which so far have not been productive. What other efforts have you made?

B. You'll be forced to make a choice one way or the other very soon. The earlier you make up your mind, the more time you will have to prepare for the implementation of your decision.

C. You mean in all of those ads there wasn't a single apartment that you could have considered?

D. I'm sorry you aren't having any luck. It's tough to find an apartment these days.

Discussion of options.

A. You're still facing the dilemma of whether or not to stay in your apartment. With regard to the possibility of moving elsewhere, you've looked at the newspaper classifieds, which so far have not been productive. What other efforts have you made?

- Your combination of a summary and a "What" question have quickly focused the interaction on the alternatives phase of problem solving. Since the exploration phase for this topic was completed during the last session, and the same issue is the focus of the current session, the timing of the response is appropriate.

B. You'll be forced to make a choice one way or the other very soon. The earlier you make up your mind, the more time you will have to prepare for the implementation of your decision.

- Advising your client on how he should respond to his predicament is not the best way to help. Instead, guide him through the problem-solving procedure so he can learn to apply the same process in future decision-making situations.

C. You mean in all of those ads there wasn't a single apartment that you could have considered?
  • This question takes a confrontational approach and is likely to elicit a defensive response.
D. I'm sorry you aren't having any luck. It's tough to find an apartment these days.
  • A sympathetic comment is not what the person needs to facilitate his problem-solving efforts.

17. I spoke to the landlord yesterday to try and work out a deal. What a waste of time! He slammed the door on me before I even got a chance to make my proposal. How can anyone be so unreasonable?
A. You were unable to get him to listen to your ideas.
B. Sounds like he's not a very friendly person. His response was rude and certainly was an overreaction.
C. The attempt you made at a compromise was unsuccessful, and, if possible, you're even more exasperated with him.
D. I don't know. You would think he would be more cooperative. After all, you've been a good tenant so far. It seems like he should want to maintain your relationship.

Discussion of options.

A. You were unable to get him to listen to your ideas.
  • You ignore the client's feelings.
B. Sounds like he's not a very friendly person. His response was rude and certainly was an overreaction.
  • This judgmental observation will not contribute to the problem-solving process. In addition, your comment focuses attention on the landlord rather than on your client.
C. The attempt you made at a compromise was unsuccessful, and, if possible, you're even more exasperated with him.
  • You have accurately reflected the person's remarks.
D. I don't know. You would think he would be more cooperative. After all, you've been a good tenant so far. It seems like he should want to maintain your relationship.
  • It is unlikely there will be benefits from your well-meaning, but ineffective, comment. When selecting responses for this

client, remember that problem solving is the goal of the interaction.

18. I'm furious at him! He's really put me in a bind. I don't see how to work this thing out. There's no way I can stay in the apartment because I can't afford it. And even though I know I have to move, finding a new place seems impossible. I don't know where I could go.
    A. What are you going to do?
    B. Although you hate the way it has come about, moving somewhere else seems to be what you've concluded you must do. You've been looking in the newspaper for available apartments. What else have you thought about trying with regard to locating new living accommodations?
    C. Your landlord's actions have left you no way out. It seems that whatever you choose to do, you lose. If you stay, you'll probably be evicted for not paying your rent. And at the present time, there's really nowhere else you can go.
    D. I'm sure there are lots of things you could do. How about renting a room in someone's home, finding a roommate to split the costs, or moving in with a friend?

Discussion of options.

A. What are you going to do?
  • If the client had the answer to this question, he wouldn't need to see you.
B. Although you hate the way it has come about, moving somewhere else seems to be what you've concluded you must do. You've been looking in the newspaper for available apartments. What else have you thought about trying with regard to locating new living accommodations?
  • Your reflective comment recognizes the client's anger, but it also focuses attention on his decision to move. By using the second "What" question, you direct the interaction back into considering alternatives.
C. Your landlord's actions have left you no way out. It seems that whatever you choose to do, you lose. If you stay, you'll probably be evicted for not paying your rent. And at the present time, there's really nowhere else you can go.

- A positive tone and an emphasis on viable options are important for successful problem solving. Neither one of those factors is present in this counterproductive remark.

D. I'm sure there are lots of things you could do. How about renting a room in someone's home, finding a roommate to split the costs, or moving in with a friend?
- It is much better to encourage the person to generate his own options rather than suggesting ideas yourself. Your advice will not help the client to develop his own problem-solving skills, and it may foster a sense of dependency on you.

19. I've been meaning to get some additional newspapers and local publications that list available apartments, but I haven't gotten around to it yet. I've also thought about driving through neighborhoods and looking for "for rent" signs. That would take a lot of time though.

A. Although you've had good intentions, so far you have made no progress on your apartment search. Now you're under even more pressure than you were before.

B. Checking apartment listings and searching for structures displaying rental signs are two strategies you've considered. What do you think about those possibilities?

C. You believe looking for posted rental signs isn't worth your while. It would take a lot of effort that isn't very likely to pay off.

D. Getting more information on nearby apartment rentals is one option; another idea, although more time consuming, would be to look for posted rental signs.

Discussion of options.

A. Although you've had good intentions, so far you have made no progress on your apartment search. Now you're under even more pressure than you were before.
- You have no recognition of the two alternatives the client just suggested. And you are not likely to help him come up with a solution by pointing out his failure to solve the problem.

B. Checking apartment listings and searching for structures displaying rental signs are two strategies you've considered. What do you think about those possibilities?

• You are likely to get further discussion of options in response to your reflection-interrogation combination.

C. You believe looking for posted rental signs isn't worth your while. It would take a lot of effort that isn't very likely to pay off.

• Your response discounts the option of looking for posted rental signs and fails to recognize the possibility of finding additional information from printed apartment listings. If your intent is to foster effective problem solving, you should keep all viable alternatives open until the client evaluates and selects which ones to use in formulating a plan.

D. Getting more information on nearby apartment rentals is one option; another idea, although more time consuming, would be to look for posted rental signs.

• Summarizing the choices discussed so far, as you have done here, will help the client to consider those options and perhaps will spark some new ideas.

20. Driving around and looking for signs doesn't seem very efficient, but I probably *should* get more publications on available apartment rentals. I have several friends who ended up finding apartments that way. In fact, that's how I found my current place.

A. You believe collecting apartment listing publications would be a good way to get some leads on a new place to live. What other ideas can you think of right now that might be helpful?

B. Keeping in mind last week's accomplishments, what has changed that leads you to believe you'll follow through with your plans this time?

C. Gathering rental information is something you've done before. It seems like you've decided that's where you need to be putting your efforts.

D. Even with a lot of information, it's going to be very difficult to find an affordable apartment in just two weeks.

Discussion of options.

A. You believe collecting apartment listing publications would be a good way to get some leads on a new place to live. What other ideas can you think of right now that might be helpful?

- By using a combination response that ends with the last "What" question, you have encouraged further consideration of alternatives.

B. Keeping in mind last week's accomplishments, what has changed that leads you to believe you'll follow through with your plans this time?

- This question is likely to provoke a defensive attitude from the client. Instead of criticizing the person's previous effort, help him formulate a plan in which follow-through is likely to occur.

C. Gathering rental information is something you've done before. It seems like you've decided that's where you need to be putting your efforts.

- Generating alternatives probably will stop as a result of your comment which suggests settling on this one option.

D. Even with a lot of information, it's going to be very difficult to find an affordable apartment in just two weeks.

- The negative attitude apparent in your statement probably will diminish the client's motivation for dealing with the problem.

21. If worse comes to worse, I could always move in with my sister until I find a place of my own. I'm pretty sure she would let me, although I haven't really talked to her about it.

A. Wouldn't you feel like you were imposing if you had to stay with your sister?

B. Speaking to her would probably be a good idea and one that you should act on right away.

C. What else could you do?

D. Living with your sister may be an option if you are unable to find an apartment.

Discussion of options.

A. Wouldn't you feel like you were imposing if you had to stay with your sister?

- This leading question may discourage the person from considering a feasible alternative.

B. Speaking to her would probably be a good idea and one that you should act on right away.

- It is better to let the client come to this conclusion himself, rather than directing his decision with your opinions.

C. What else could you do?

- Although you're eager to obtain more alternatives, neglecting to comment on the sister option before asking your "What" question may suggest to the client that you are disregarding this alternative. Your question would be more productive if you had first reflected the idea he just shared.

D. Living with your sister may be an option if you are unable to find an apartment.

- You have rephrased the person's statement and specified it as an option. This comment will foster your efforts toward generating alternatives, evaluating them, and developing a plan.

22. I guess I should ask her about it soon—just in case. With only two weeks left, I could very well end up living in my car if I don't find a place to go. And being homeless is certainly not something I want.

A. Time is running out, and I'm glad you recognize that fact. It's important for you to act quickly in making new living arrangements.

B. You know that living in your car isn't really a possibility. Let's try and think of other solutions.

C. We've discussed three options so far: obtaining rental information, driving through local residential areas, and moving in with your sister. What else comes to mind?

D. You feel that even though it's probably too late, it couldn't hurt to ask for your sister's help.

Discussion of options.

A. Time is running out, and I'm glad you recognize that fact. It's important for you to act quickly in making new living arrangements.

- This statement implies an attitude of superiority on your part.

B. You know that living in your car is not really a possibility. Let's try and think of other solutions.

- Unless you can see into the future, you can't say for sure

what will happen with your client. Consequently, expressing your opinion of the car option is not very helpful.

C. We've discussed three options so far: obtaining rental information, driving through local residential areas, and moving in
with your sister. What else comes to mind?
   • Listing the ideas already mentioned not only helps to orga-
     nize the information discussed, but also shows the client
     that progress is occurring during the interaction. Your open
     question pulls for more options.

D. You feel that even though it's probably too late, it couldn't hurt
to ask for your sister's help.
   • The individual never said it was too late to check with his sis-
     ter, and in reality it may not be.

23. Getting rental listings, driving around, and checking with my sister are about all of the possibilities I can think of. But as I said,
driving around doesn't seem like a smart idea. The other two
things sound good though. I have some time, later today and
tomorrow morning, when I could work on them.

A. Within the next twenty-four hours you could locate more
apartment information and you could speak to your sister.
How does that plan sound to you?

B. How much time will you have?

C. So it seems like you've made a decision. You won't drive
through neighborhoods looking for signs, but you will follow
through on the other things we've discussed.

D. Do you think you could follow through with this plan?

Discussion of options.

A. Within the next twenty-four hours you could locate more
apartment information and you could speak to your sister.
How does that plan sound to you?
   • By defining the plan, you help the client develop a clear pic-
     ture of actions he can take. In addition, you ask for the per-
     son's opinion of the proposal. This request will elicit infor-
     mation as to whether the plan is realistic. If the client is not
     completely comfortable with the plan, you can assist him in
     making necessary changes or clarifications.

B. How much time will you have?

- The information you receive in response to this question may or may not be relevant to the person's plan. Even if the question is relevant, such details should be worked out after the plan itself has been established in the minds of both the client and the worker.

C. So it seems like you've made a decision. You won't drive through neighborhoods looking for signs, but you will follow through on the other things we've discussed.
- This attempt at establishing a plan is vague and could lead to a misunderstanding between you and the client. When discussing a prospective strategy, it is important to be clear and concrete about the options selected for action.

D. Do you think you could follow through with this plan?
- It is better to specifically define what you are discussing before referring to any set of options as a "plan."

24. The plan is fine except that I'm a little nervous about talking to my sister. We get along OK, but we haven't lived in the same house since we were kids. In fact, I've never even spent the night at her place. When you think about it, me staying with her is a really big favor to ask.
    A. It is a lot to ask. Do you think she would let you do it?
    B. You're having misgivings about asking your sister. Let's try a role play. Pretend your sister is seated in that chair, and tell her what's on your mind.
    C. Maybe we should figure out a new plan and forget about relying on your sister. Let's focus on finding apartment listings. What are some of the specific sources you could check?
    D. The idea of asking your sister for help has you a bit uneasy. What might you say to her?

Discussion of options.

A. It is a lot to ask. Do you think she would let you do it?
- By emphasizing the magnitude of his request, you may increase the client's feelings of uncertainty regarding this alternative. Expressing your negative opinion of the option may eliminate the person's sister as a resource, thereby making problem solving more difficult. In addition, your closed question implies that you have not been listening

attentively since the client gave you his answer in a previous remark.

B. You're having misgivings about asking your sister. Let's try a role play. Pretend your sister is seated in that chair, and tell her what's on your mind.
- You have zeroed in on what the person has identified as the weakest part of the plan. Having the client act out a possible encounter with his sister should help him think through issues associated with approaching her.

C. Maybe we should figure out a new plan and forget about relying on your sister. Let's focus on finding apartment listings. What are some of the specific sources you could check?
- With only two weeks left to find a new place to live, the client needs to take action. So, before throwing out a potentially valuable alternative, you should fully explore the desirability of the option.

D. The idea of asking your sister for help has you a bit uneasy. What might you say to her?
- This combination response recognizes the client's anxiety and moves the discussion toward further examination of the option that is troubling him.

SHORT-ANSWER QUESTIONS

Write your answer for each of the following questions.

1. State the defining characteristics of an interaction's exploration phase.
2. What is done during the alternatives phase?
3. Explain what happens in the final stage of problem solving.
4. When there are multiple difficulties, what is one type of problem you should address in the initial plan?
5. Cite three questions that can be helpful in discovering options.
6. Give two additional methods a worker can use to encourage a client to generate problem-solving possibilities.
7. Provide the four elements of a good plan.
8. In addition to discussing an option, what else can you do to help a client consider a specific alternative?

9. When a person blames circumstances and other people for his or her problems, what do you need to encourage in the client?
10. Describe the eventual task of the worker when the client bounces from one topic to another.
11. State how you can be sure a plan is clear to the client.
12. How can you help the client make a more specific plan?
13. Think of a problem that someone you know wrestled with and eventually solved in a satisfactory way. Keep that example in mind as you provide brief responses to question 13 and to all of the remaining short-answer items. What were the pressures facing the person?
14. Prior to deciding on a strategy for handling the difficulty, how did the individual feel?
15. For what part of the problem did the person take responsibility?
16. Before adopting the approach that finally worked, how did the individual try to deal with the problem?
17. Did the person think about an option and decide not to try it? If your answer is "Yes," briefly describe any possibilities that received consideration but no action.
18. Did the individual receive assistance from anyone who engaged the person in a problem-solving interaction? If your answer is "Yes," provide a brief description of that assistance.
19. Think of how the individual resolved the problem. In terms of what the person did, how consistent were those actions with the individual's values and beliefs?
20. What was the time frame in which the problem-resolving actions took place?
21. What tasks were involved in bringing the problem to a resolution?
22. How realistic was the person's plan?
23. What was the final outcome with regard to the problem?

POSSIBLE ANSWERS FOR SHORT-ANSWER QUESTIONS

The answer-checking procedures remain the same as before.

- For each item, compare your answer to the one we provide.
- If you believe your answer is correct, you are done with that item.
- With any question for which you believe your answer is incorrect,

consider our answer and, if needed, review relevant portions of the chapter. Keep your original answer that you now think is incorrect, but add to it a response that you believe would be correct.

1. The exploration phase is spent discovering the client's thoughts and feelings about the situation.
2. Generating and evaluating various options are the tasks of the alternatives portion of the interaction.
3. In the last part of problem solving, efforts are made to develop a plan.
4. Try to address at least one problem that has the potential for rapid progress.
5. You can elicit alternatives by asking the following questions: "What have you tried?" "What have you thought about trying?" and "Right now, as we are talking, what other options come to mind?"
6. Two additional strategies for developing new ideas are brainstorming and considering what others have tried.
7. A plan is likely to succeed if it is negotiated, focused in the present, specific, and realistic.
8. Another means of evaluating an alternative is for the person to role play the possible option.
9. To some degree, the client must own the problem if progress is to be made.
10. The worker needs to narrow the focus of the discussion.
11. Asking the person to describe the plan is a technique that allows you to confirm or clarify the client's understanding of what is to be done.
12. In order to increase the specificity of a plan, you can help the client identify the responsibilities of all participants. You can also encourage the client to think about implementation strategies, such as when and how to carry out the plan and ways to address possible obstacles.
13. The individual in our example was a student who needed an internship placement. He had done a previous internship at the headquarters of a large organization, and for his next placement he contacted a branch office of that organization. He was told it was almost certain that they would give him an internship, but

that a final decision would be made at some unspecified point in the future. After months of waiting, he received a form letter notifying him of his rejection by the branch office. Upon receiving that news, there was little time left before his next placement had to be finalized. If arrangements were not made by the impending deadline, he would miss out on the upcoming internship cycle.

14. The student felt betrayed by the branch office, and he was angry at himself for not having investigated other possible placement opportunities.

15. He admitted that he should not have counted so heavily on the branch office coming through for him. He also realized that if there was going to be an internship in his immediate future, he would have to work quickly.

16. He attempted to check with the internship coordinator for his program, but that individual was unavailable for the week ahead. (This example did not take place at Shippensburg University.) He did speak with some friends, and he got several potential leads from them.

17. Yes. He thought about the leads provided by his friends. But because of the financial costs involved with those opportunities, he did not follow up on any of them. He also considered calling two individuals he knew from his internship at the headquarters office, thinking that they might be able to put in a good word for him at the branch office. But he eventually decided against asking them to use their influence in an attempt to change the decision that had been made.

18. Yes. He discussed the matter with one of his professors. During that interaction he developed a plan for attempting to arrange an internship.

19. The student eventually contacted five organizations that he previously had discounted because he had seen them as being undesirable internship settings. Although he still had questions about their desirability, in the interaction with his professor he realized that he actually had no factual information regarding the quality of the experience he might get at those organizations. Consequently, he became more open-minded about testing the accuracy of his opinions concerning the five organizations. Otherwise, all of the actions he took were consistent with his previous values and beliefs.

20. The time from his rejection by the branch office until the internship deadline was two weeks.

21. Based upon his talk with the professor, the student decided to consult a directory, and he selected five organizations to contact regarding a possible internship. He wrote a memo describing his situation, then sent the memo and a resume to each organization.

22. The student was capable of following through with the plan, and he did. But he had no guess as to what sort of responses he might receive from the five organizations.

23. Representatives from three of the five organizations called him. After a number of telephone interactions, each of the three entities eventually offered him an internship. He accepted the offer from the organization that seemed to have the most structured experience with the greatest variety of ongoing activities. His placement there was fast-paced, wide-ranging, challenging, frustrating, tiring, eye-opening, and in the end, very productive.

FILL-IN-THE-RESPONSE QUESTIONS

Listed below are a series of client statements. For each one, write a worker response that you believe would be appropriate.

1. My parents are splitting up. Because I'm the oldest, I feel it's my responsibility to make sure my brothers and sisters get through this ordeal. I don't want them to get chewed up as this divorce stuff grinds on. It's not fair to them.

2. I know there's not a lot I can do, but I'd like to help out . . . not just with the kids, but with my parents too. I love both of them, but I think they're past loving each other anymore. The divorce is going to be tough on them.

3. It sounds a little crazy, like I'm trying to be a hero or something. But my parents have given me so much. Although I realize I can't fix their marriage, I would like to make the divorce easier. Then everyone can get on with their lives.

4. This whole situation is wearing on us all, and it hurts me to see the people I love become so sad and angry. I wish things were how they used to be, but I know that isn't going to happen. I just want this chaos to be over.

5. I keep hoping this is all a bad dream, but I know it's reality. My parent's marriage is over. It's hard to accept that, after so many years of being together, they can't work things out anymore. But in my heart, I know it's too late.

6. Sometimes I just want to run away, and other times I want to be strong for my family. It's all so confusing and stressful. I feel like parts of my life are just falling to pieces. What I really want to do is work through it myself, so I can have it together for when I need to comfort one of my brothers or sisters, or my mom or my dad.

POSSIBLE ANSWERS FOR
FILL-IN-THE-RESPONSE QUESTIONS

For each response opportunity, there are many possible correct answers. We list two, and, as in the preceding chapter, we suggest you use them in the following manner.

- Look at our two answers and think about them.
- Consider relevant material covered in the chapter.
- Read the client statement again, then immediately read your answer and the two options listed here.
- Write another response that you believe might be an improvement on your first effort.
- Repeat this procedure for each of the remaining items.

1. • You have a sense of obligation regarding the well-being of your sisters and brothers.
   • Trying to protect your brothers and sisters is important to you.
2. • You want to care for your entire family during this time.
   • Recognizing the difficulty of coping with divorce, you want to support your parents as well as your brothers and sisters.
3. • Thinking about all you've received from your mom and dad inspires you to do what you can for them now.
   • You believe that, somehow, your efforts can help to smooth this transition.
4. • It's painful to watch your family become so distraught.

- Things are very different now than they were in the past, and your family's present situation is very draining for everyone.
5. • Although you believe you need to accept your parent's decision to get a divorce, it isn't easy to do.
   - You recognize the importance of dealing with the end of your parent's marriage, but it's still tough to handle.
6. • Confronting the scary issues you're facing would help you feel better prepared to support your family.
   - You believe you need to cope with your own anxieties before you'll really feel ready to help your family members.

SUMMARY

You can view problem solving as having three phases: exploring thoughts and feelings, considering alternatives, and developing a plan. Exploring thoughts and feelings requires that you patiently attempt to understand specific circumstances, as well as the distressing emotions associated with those situations. You should recognize the degree of responsibility that clients take for various difficulties, and you should be alert for at least one problem area that is personally meaningful to the client and shows potential for quick progress. Such productive change can be in environmental conditions or in how clients respond to those conditions.

Considering alternatives ultimately involves the detailed examination of two or three possibilities. But you first may need to encourage clients to generate options through brainstorming or through the exploration of three areas: what they have tried, what they have thought about trying, and possibilities they can think of presently. Other techniques for bringing out ideas include considering the efforts of others in similar situations and offering suggestions yourself. Remember, though, that clients retain the responsibility for final decisions on accepting or rejecting ideas. One approach for helping them make such decisions is to role play an application of the option under consideration.

The goal in developing a plan is the creation of a strategy that is negotiated, focused in the present, specific, and realistic. Clients should review agreed-upon tasks so that you can address any omissions or misunderstandings.

Chapter 5

FINE-TUNING

Now that you have encountered a fair number of concepts, this chapter discusses some common errors made in implementing those ideas. In our experience, when novice workers receive corrective feedback it usually relates to one or more of the areas discussed below. Although several of these problems have already been addressed, we present them again in order for this chapter to contain a comprehensive list of fine-tuning issues.

Concentrating on nonproductive behavior is not pleasant, but identifying such difficulties can help you weed out tendencies that may detract from your efforts. Although we are focusing on mistakes, you can avoid most of these errors by implementing four principles: (1) use the least amount of authority necessary to accomplish your objectives, (2) demonstrate your understanding of the client, (3) talk in ways that seem natural and unrehearsed, and (4) remember your ultimate purpose is to encourage productive change. The opposites of those principles are the pitfalls to avoid: (1) asserting too much authority, (2) speaking in ways that fail to demonstrate understanding, (3) employing phrasing that seems artificial and programmed, and (4) using terms that can hinder movement toward productive change. Most of those mistakes will not apply to you, and you need not worry about them. Instead, focus on the few recurring errors that you do find yourself making, and keep the relevant caveats in mind as you hone your skills.

USING TOO MUCH AUTHORITY

One common difficulty is being too directive. This can occur in a number of ways, including the following: using an opening phrase that implies you are going to solve the client's problem, making opinionated statements, offering general observations about life, giving advice, being too quick to suggest options, concentrating on persons other than the client, inappropriately changing the topic, interrupting, not recognizing alternatives discussed by the client, making judgmental exclamations, and offering to take an action that would be better for the client to initiate. All of those mistakes will be discussed, but we will start with a group of errors that share the theme of inappropriate interrogation, as demonstrated by the following: asking unnecessary closed questions, several questions in a row, "Why" questions, and multiple questions, as well as routinely making reflections into questions.

Asking Unnecessary Closed Questions

One of the most common mistakes by novice workers, and by trained professionals who have forgotten their roots, is asking unnecessary closed questions. Remember that it is best not to ask a closed question unless you would be satisfied with a brief reply.

Asking Three or More Questions in a Row Without Reflecting Any of the Client's Responses

When you get replies to questions you ask, don't keep asking more questions. Instead, reflect the answers you are getting. (An exception to this may occur when you are purposefully using an inverted funnel sequence.)

Asking "Why" Questions

If you want to put your client on the defensive, ask "Why" questions. The responses you get often will contain rationalizations as the client becomes increasingly uncomfortable. If those are not results you want, abandon "Why" questions.

Asking Multiple Questions

Confusing responses, a confused client, or both can result from multiple questions. Such interrogation tends to occur when you try to cover too much at once or when you rephrase a question you've just asked. If you are having trouble with these issues, you can get on track again by following two principles. (1) Maintain a moderate pace. (2) Wait for the client's response before concluding that a question needs to be rephrased.

Routinely Making Reflections Into Questions

Occasionally, you may be so unsure of a reflection that you make it into a question with your tone of voice. Doing that when you are uncertain is acceptable. But when you routinely use your tone of voice to change reflections into questions, you are doing a lot of unnecessary interrogating.

Starting the Interaction by Taking Responsibility for Solving the Client's Problems

Some workers immediately assume responsibility for resolving the client's difficulties by beginning the interaction with a question such as, "How can I help you?" Rather than putting the focus on yourself, it is better to remember that a supportive worker's task is to assist clients in developing their own problem-solving abilities. With this in mind, a more productive way to open might be, "How are things going?" or "Tell me your reason for contacting us."

Making Judgmental Comments

Another common error, displayed by both new and veteran workers, is making judgmental statements. Often these are positive opinions expressed when clients are discussing options or plans. For example, a client says, "I will just tell her what she has been doing, how I feel about it, and what I think should happen" and the worker responds with, "I think that would be a good idea." But whether conveying agreement or disagreement, such responses place some decision-making responsibility on the worker, thereby decreasing the client's independence. Consequently, a more productive acknowledgment of a client's decision may be to offer a statement that merely recognizes the person's opinion of the option, such as, "You're ready to be assertive with her."

Offering General Observations About Life

When sharing truisms you think are applicable, you focus on your own ideas rather than on what clients believe. Consequently, it is almost always better to reflect. For example, a client says the following. "I'm on my own for the first time, and I'm really feeling shaky. When I come home at night there's no one here but me. That's not what I'm used to." You could respond with a general observation about life, such as, "It takes time to get used to a new living situation." Rather than providing your analysis of the circumstances and offering a general observation about life, it would be better to focus on the client by reflecting thoughts and feelings. For example, one possibility might be, "Living alone is new for you, and you're feeling uneasy about it."

Giving Advice

When you are in a supportive helping mode, telling clients what to do is not your role. So for the most part, stay away from advice.

Suggesting Options Too Soon

Remember that you do all you can to pull for client-generated options. Only after making that effort is it appropriate for you to offer additional ideas for consideration.

Focusing on Someone Other Than the Client

Clients often discuss problems that involve other people. But rather than concentrating on the thoughts and feelings of those other individuals, you can bring such persons into the discussion by focusing on your *client's* ideas and emotions as they relate to those persons. For example, "He really got angry" changes the focus to the other person, whereas, "You were surprised by his anger" keeps the focus on the client.

Inappropriately Changing the Topic

For reasons that briefly may make sense to them, workers sometimes change topics rather than encourage clients to continue productive discussions. But appropriate input from clients is what you want. So, when you are getting relevant discussion, you should support those efforts rather than attempting to divert them.

Interrupting

Occasionally, clients engage in monologues and must be interrupted. In less drastic situations, however, interruptions generally are unnecessary. When you find that you have interrupted inappropriately, it may be best simply to stop talking and to let the client continue. When eventually there is an opportunity for you to speak, be sure *not* to start with the same phrasing you used when you interrupted. Otherwise it will appear as though you haven't been listening to the client since you last spoke.

When the need to interrupt a client outweighs the risk of hurting the person's feelings, remember to be honest, tactful, and respectful with your interruption. In the following example, the worker interrupts a client who for the last 35 minutes has been venting nonstop about the intricate legal proceedings of a car accident she had last year. "Excuse me, Mrs. Jones, I can tell it's important to you that I understand the specific details of your accident and its legal entanglements. But before our session is over today, I want to make sure that you leave with some concrete plans for dealing with your frustrations over these exasperating experiences. If moving in that direction is OK with you, I would like you to tell me about some of the things you've been doing that have helped you cope with the great amount of stress you've been under." Those remarks use polite language, address her in a respectful manner, reflect the overall topic and feelings she has discussed, explain why you want to learn about another aspect of what has been happening, and give her a new direction for the discussion. Hopefully those efforts have minimized the trauma of cutting her off and will move the interaction into a more productive mode.

Failing to Recognize Options Generated by the Client

Sometimes the problem is not with what you say but with what you don't say. When a client puts energy into exploring an option, don't ignore those efforts. Instead, recognize the client's contribution.

Making Opinionated Exclamations

If you want to come across as being unskilled, this is a good way to do it. By blurting out a statement such as, "Oh, my God!" you strip away any semblance of professional demeanor. So, if you want to provide supportive help, avoid editorial expletives.

Offering to Take Action That the Client Is Fully Capable of Doing

Being supportive sometimes means acting on behalf of clients. But you do not want to be too hasty with offers of assistance. Before saying you will do something for the client, be sure it really is necessary for *you* to accomplish the task.

SPEAKING IN WAYS THAT FAIL TO DEMONSTRATE UNDERSTANDING

Demonstrating understanding requires focused effort on your part. When this task eludes workers, it tends to do so in one or more of the following ways: relying on vague terms for referring to content; ignoring feelings; using feeling terms that are too broad; saying, "Tell me more" before reflecting what you already know; posing questions the client already has answered; saying "I see" or "I understand;" inappropriately diminishing the intensity of your comments by using qualifiers; unintentionally reducing an event's importance by saying "just;" and repeating the phrase "you know."

Using Terms Such as "Situation," "Stuff," or "This" to Refer to Circumstances You Have Not Specifically Reflected

It is possible to conduct an entire interaction without ever identifying the circumstances being discussed. Instead, they may be referred to in a nebulous way with terms like "problem," "concern," "situation," "stuff," or "this." Such phrasing is acceptable only *after* you have reflected the nature of the conditions being described. Remember, in order to demonstrate understanding you must reflect both feelings and the particular conditions under discussion.

Failing to Reflect Feelings

We have seen some workers avoid reflection of specific content, and we have observed others do entire interactions without reflecting any feelings. If you ignore the emotional component of a client's message, you are not engaging in supportive helping. So, remember to include feeling reflections.

Using Vague Feeling Terms

All clients with distressing emotions are "concerned," "upset," and "bothered." Since such vague terms apply to almost any client, they do not demonstrate that you understand the particular person you are interviewing. In order to do that, you should use more specific terms to identify the emotions you perceive.

Making a Statement Such as "Tell Me More" Without First Reflecting What the Client Already Has Told You

Appearing wooden and stiff often is the net result of using pat phrases like "Tell me more." Such directives certainly do not demonstrate understanding, and they may even suggest uneasiness or lack of attention. In order to show that you comprehend what the client is communicating, you need to reflect rather than try to rely on trite responses.

Asking Questions the Client Already Has Answered

Asking a question the client already has answered lets the person know, in a very demonstrable way, that you have not been listening. Since *attention* is what you should be communicating, supportive helping requires that you listen and that you demonstrate your understanding of the client's message. If you want to ask a question while still demonstrating understanding, one good technique is a combination response in which you offer a reflection and follow it with a question that has come to mind.

Saying "I See," "I Understand," or "I Know How You Feel"

Such responses do not demonstrate that you see, understand, or know. If showing what you've learned is what you hope to do, you are better off reflecting.

Using Qualifiers That Diminish the Intensity of Your Comments When That Is Not Your Intent

If you wish to lessen the intensity of your statement, you can do so by using qualifiers such as "kind of," "a little," and "sort of." But you should omit such phrases if you want your comment to carry its full impact.

Inappropriately Decreasing the Importance of an Event by Saying "Just"

When you make a response such as, "You're just having trouble with your youngest child," one connotation is that the difficulty is really not very significant. Since belittling the client's issues is not something you want to do, a better comment would be, "Trying to get your youngest child to obey has become a taxing experience."

Saying "You Know"

Frequent use of this phrase only serves to blur the focus of what you are trying to communicate. So, if you wish to speak clearly and concisely, avoid peppering your remarks with "you know."

TALKING IN WAYS THAT SEEM ARTIFICIAL
AND PROGRAMMED

Supportive helping involves a variety of techniques. But, as you recall, the eventual goal is to incorporate these methods into a personal style that is both natural and effective. Unfortunately, rather than demonstrating that you are responding as an authentic individual, it is possible to come across as artificial and programmed. This robotic style is often associated with two behaviors: employing repetitive phrasing, and parroting what a client has said.

Using Repetitive Phrases

If you want it to appear as though your intent is to parody supportive helping, then begin all of your reflections with "So," "Well," "It sounds like," "You feel," "You're feeling," or "I hear you saying." That last phrase is *so* hackneyed that Hollywood scripts now use those words when the character speaking to them is intended to be an unflattering caricature of an individual attempting to facilitate therapeutic change. Since you want to be perceived as a *competent* professional, don't begin reflections with, "I hear you saying." On the other hand, it can be appropriate to use "So," "Well," "It sounds like," "You feel," and "You're feeling," as long as you mix them with other openings.

Frequently Restating Exact Words Used by the Client

Rote repeating of phrases is not reflection and adds nothing to the interaction. Avoid frequent parroting of client comments, unless you want to come across as being an automaton.

USING TERMS AND PHRASES THAT CAN HINDER
MOVEMENT TOWARD PRODUCTIVE CHANGE

The ultimate purpose of supportive helping is to encourage productive change. But that objective can become more difficult to attain when workers create road blocks or detours by using certain responses. Problematic comments include statements that suggest clients "must" react in certain ways, as well as words or phrases that are unnecessarily strong.

Saying That Something "Makes" the Client Act or Feel Certain Ways

In supportive helping, there are two fundamental realms for productive change. One is the client's environment, and the other is how the client responds to that environment. As we mentioned in Chapter 4, although some situations cannot be altered, how the client acts in response to those situations often can be modified. But you may imply that changing one's reactions is impossible when you use phrases such as "makes you," "made you," "must be," or "must have." Automatic responses are implied if you offer the following sorts of remarks: "Their rudeness makes you feel unimportant" or "You must feel awful when they speak so harshly to you." It is best to avoid such phrasing if you want to leave open the possibility of clients changing how they react.

Using Strong Words and Phrases Without Considering Their Impact

The term *depressed* can carry a lot of labeling implications. Unless you are ready to discuss the diagnostic definitions and therapeutic options for depression, you may want to rely on less clinical words, such as "sad" or "down."

Often occurring in conjunction with depression are two other powerful terms: *hopelessness* and *helplessness*. Although you might be accurately reflecting a client's feelings, saying, "It's hopeless" or "You're helpless" may suggest nothing can be done, and that rarely is what you want to communicate. On the other hand, you leave open the door for change when you make reflections such as, "It's been discouraging" or "You're tired of trying and not succeeding."

There also are other phrases that tend to cut off discussion of options. For example, after reflecting, "There's nothing you can do" or "You're at a dead end," where do you go from there?

Additional terms that can create unwanted effects are nonclinical emotional labels having negative connotations. These include adjectives such as "jealous," "spiteful," and "vindictive." Rather than using those sorts of words, you may want to employ alternative phrasing.

MULTIPLE-CHOICE QUESTIONS

The first 6 items are with one client; items 7-13 are with a second person; and items 14-20 involve a third individual. Your instructions are the same as in the previous chapters.

- For each of the following client statements, choose the response or responses you believe would be appropriate. (Several items have more than one correct answer.)
- Indicate your selection in writing.
- Read the discussions of all four options.
- If you are correct, go to the next item.
- If you are incorrect, think about the explanations and, if necessary, review relevant portions of the chapter; then, once you better understand the issues, proceed to the next question.

1. The teachers in our school district are on strike, and the school board is refusing to negotiate with them. I think the board and the teachers should be talking to each other. So at the last school board meeting I was able to get on the agenda in order to express my opinions. When it was my turn, I got up to speak. But I froze, and I couldn't say anything. I was so embarrassed that I just left the room. I felt like such a fool.
   A. Good grief!
   B. So, you were sort of overwhelmed.
   C. You were ashamed of your performance.
   D. You felt badly about how you handled the situation.

Discussion of options.

   A. Good grief!
      • Your opinionated exclamation is inappropriate.
   B. So, you were sort of overwhelmed.
      • It does not make sense to precede the word "overwhelmed"

with a qualifier such as "sort of." How can someone be kind of completely overpowered?

C. You were ashamed of your performance.
   • This reflection is on target.
D. You felt badly about how you handled the situation.
   • Before using the term "situation," it is better to define the circumstances.

2. I had lots of things I wanted to say. But when I got up and the spotlight was on me, and all of those people were looking at me, I just lost it. I froze.
   A. As you rose to speak, you were thinking about the message you wanted to deliver, but then you began to focus on your own nervousness?
   B. At first, you were thinking about the opinions you wanted to present, but then you became very self-conscious.
   C. You really overreacted to the pressures that night, and you seem to be overreacting now as you continue to ruminate about what happened.
   D. Being the center of attention was frightening, and your prepared thoughts left you.

Discussion of options.

A. As you rose to speak, you were thinking about the message you wanted to deliver, but then you began to focus on your own nervousness?
   • There is no need to make this reflection into a question.
B. At first, you were thinking about the opinions you wanted to present, but then you became very self-conscious.
   • You have accurately reflected the client's comment.
C. You really overreacted to the pressures that night, and you seem to be overreacting now as you continue to ruminate about what happened.
   • This is a judgmental statement that criticizes the client.
D. Being the center of attention was frightening, and your prepared thoughts left you.
   • Your reflection demonstrates that you understand the client.

3. I was really charged up. I wanted to tell the board that they had a responsibility to our children and that they were letting our kids down by refusing to negotiate. But I'm the one who ended up letting the kids down by not being able to deliver my comments. I thought that what I had to say was important. Instead of making my point, though, all I did was end up looking like a bumbling idiot.

A. When you found yourself unable to deliver your remarks, how did the board react?

B. It sounds like you have children who are missing school. Tell me what you've been doing to help them cope with the strike.

C. Why were you so intimidated?

D. Failing to deliver your message was disappointing.

Discussion of options.

A. When you found yourself unable to deliver your remarks, how did the board react?
- You have shifted the focus away from the client.

B. It sounds like you have children who are missing school. Tell me what you've been doing to help them cope with the strike.
- As with option A, this comment changes the topic away from what the client has been discussing.

C. Why were you so intimidated?
- This "Why" question may threaten your client.

D. Failing to deliver your message was disappointing.
- You provide an accurate surface feeling reflection of what the client has said.

4. I finally took a stand on something. And I really never had done that before. But when I got up there and lost it, I also lost all of my confidence. I still would like to get my point across, but I feel so humiliated.

A. You regret having failed in your initial effort, but you continue to believe that you have something important to communicate.

B. Before going to the meeting, did you spend some time practicing what you were going to say?

C. You wish you had done better, but you still have ideas you want to express to the school board.

D. You are concerned about your performance, but you still have a need to convey your thoughts to the board.

Discussion of options.

A. You regret having failed in your initial effort, but you continue to believe that you have something important to communicate.
  • This is an accurate reflection of your client's thoughts and feelings.
B. Before going to the meeting, did you spend some time practicing what you were going to say?
  • It is not necessary to ask this closed question.
C. You wish you had done better, but you still have ideas you want to express to the school board.
  • This reflection is accurate, but it does not recognize the client's feelings.
D. You are concerned about your performance, but you still have a need to convey your thoughts to the board.
  • The feeling term "concerned" is vague. You can do a better job of identifying specific emotions.

5. I was there for the kids, and I let them down. I know I lost my courage that night, but I really don't want that to stop me. I need to get it together so I can effectively get my point across to the board.
A. As you think back to that evening, how did you feel?
B. So, you would sort of like to try again in some way.
C. You don't want to be stopped by what happened at that meeting. Instead, you want to effectively get your point across to the board.
D. You're determined to persevere.

Discussion of options.

A. As you think back to that evening, how did you feel?
  • You already have the answer to this question.
B. So, you would sort of like to try again in some way.
  • By using the phrase "sort of," you diminish the intensity of your comment, and that probably is not your intent.

    C. You don't want to be stopped by what happened at that meeting. Instead, you want to effectively get your point across to the board.
- Your response repeats exact words and phrases used by the client.

    D. You're determined to persevere.
- This is an accurate reflection of the client's comments.

6. I hope I never make a fool of myself like that again. But I just can't let this issue drop. Either I need to request to speak to the board again, or I need to let them know my thoughts in some other way.

    A. Failing, like you did that night, is not something you want to do.

    B. I see.

    C. One option is speaking again, but there might also be other possibilities.

    D. You don't really plan on trying to speak to them again, do you?

Discussion of options.

    A. Failing, like you did that night, is not something you want to do.
- This comment fails to recognize the options brought up by the client.

    B. I see.
- Making such a response does not demonstrate understanding.

    C. One option is speaking again, but there might also be other possibilities.
- You have provided an accurate reflection that facilitates the problem-solving process.

    D. You don't really plan on trying to speak to them again, do you?
- Your judgmental leading question conveys the idea that you believe she should not attempt to speak again.

The next 7 items are with a different client.

7. My mother broke her hip about three months ago, and since she got out of the hospital, she's been living with me. I've had to take care of her, and she's not the easiest person to take care of. I'm really tired and at the end of my rope.
A. Providing for her needs has become an exhausting experience.
B. So your difficulties just relate to her staying with you.
C. Tell me more.
D. The demands of your mother's convalescence have you really depressed.

Discussion of options.

    A. Providing for her needs has become an exhausting experience.
      • You make an accurate surface feeling reflection.
    B. So your difficulties just relate to her staying with you.
      • Although you may not intend it, using the word "just" may suggest that you believe the client's problems are not very significant.
    C. Tell me more.
      • You are more likely to demonstrate interest and understanding if you reflect your impressions.
    D. The demands of your mother's convalescence have you really depressed.
      • When used by a human service professional, the term "depressed" can be seen as being very strong. Unless you are prepared to deal with the labeling implications of "depressed," avoid this term.

8. Yeah, that's pretty much it. My mother has always been the dominating type. Even before her accident she thought it was her duty to constantly tell me what to do. I could cope with her in short stints, but now she's living in my house. I have my own way of cleaning, my own way of disciplining my children, and here she is, constantly trying to tell me what I should be doing.
A. You've come to dread her critiques of your behavior.
B. The daily routine at your house has become a frustrating experience, as you receive one type of criticism after another.
C. It seems to me that you haven't been assertive enough with your mother.

D. You are upset about your mother's interference in your life.

Discussion of options.

A. You've come to dread her critiques of your behavior.
  • Your reflection is on target.
B. The daily routine at your house has become a frustrating experience, as you receive one type of criticism after another.
  • You provide an accurate surface feeling reflection of the client's comment.
C. It seems to me that you haven't been assertive enough with your mother.
  • This is a judgmental statement that is inappropriate for a supportive worker.
D. You are upset about your mother's interference in your life.
  • Most clients are "upset." Try to be more specific in identifying feelings to reflect.

9. We have been apart for years. But, because of her injury, I have to be her caregiver, plus look after all of my usual responsibilities. Between her and my kids, I have absolutely no life of my own.
A. It's draining to have so many people depending on you.
B. You should have a meeting with your mother and your kids so that you can tell all of them exactly how you are feeling.
C. What do your kids think about the changes brought about by your mother's presence?
D. So, it has been quite some time since you and your mother lived together.

Discussion of options.

A. It's draining to have so many people depending on you.
  • This is an accurate surface feeling reflection.
B. You should have a meeting with your mother and your kids so that you can tell all of them exactly how you are feeling.
  • Your advice implies the client is incapable of generating alternatives.
C. What do your kids think about the changes brought about by your mother's presence?

- At this point in the interaction, it is better to keep the focus on your client, rather than changing it to others involved in the situation.
D. So, it has been quite some time since you and your mother lived together.
  - Your reflection is accurate, but it does not contain a feeling component. You can do better.

10. Although I feel like I can't take it much longer, I don't know what else to do. I have two younger sisters, but they have their own lives. Since I'm the oldest, I've felt that I should be the one to look after my mother. I know she is going to need care for at least a few more months. But I'm tired, and I want my own life back.
  A. As you look ahead to the future, you feel hopeless because of your commitment to provide the assistance that your mother continues to need.
  B. You have taken a lot of responsibility on yourself, but at this point the frustrations of caring for your mother make you want to give up.
  C. My gosh! You mean you have taken this burden on yourself, and you haven't even asked your sisters for help?
  D. So you decided to care for your mother on your own, but, at this point, you really need a change in those arrangements.

Discussion of options.

  A. As you look ahead to the future, you feel hopeless because of your commitment to provide the assistance that your mother continues to need.
    - This might be an accurate reflection, but the term "hopeless" is very strong. Rather than opening doors to available possibilities, it implies that there are few, if any, opportunities for change.
  B. You have taken a lot of responsibility on yourself, but at this point the frustrations of caring for your mother make you want to give up.
    - Although there are probably alternatives regarding care for the client's mother, it is possible that the client will continue to provide the needed support. If the latter is true, the only option for change will be in how the person views the

task of supplying that assistance. But by using the phrase "make you," you have implied that providing care will always result in feelings of discouragement. Thus, you have closed the door on a potential area for progress.

C. My gosh! You mean you have taken this burden on yourself, and you haven't even asked your sisters for help?
- Your opinionated exclamation is followed by a judgmental statement that suggests advice. Consequently, on at least three different counts, this is not an appropriate response for a supportive worker.

D. So you decided to care for your mother on your own, but, at this point, you really need a change in those arrangements.
- By highlighting the client's role in the decision-making process and by recognizing the desire for change, you are giving the person an opportunity to begin thinking about alternatives.

11. I did take charge and decide what should be done. But my one sister and her husband don't have a home situation that is conducive to my mother living with them. They're just starting out, and they only have a one-bedroom apartment. And my other sister has three children, with the oldest being five, so she can't take her. Plus, both of my sisters live several hours away. By staying with me, though, my mother has been able to remain in her home community. That's been important, especially with regard to friends from the church who regularly come by to visit her.

A. One possibility you haven't mentioned is a nursing home. I'm wondering what you might think about using such a facility.

B. Although you've provided most of the care yourself, another important source of support has been the church.

C. Your mother living with you seemed to be the best option. And one positive outcome of your decision has been her ability to see church friends.

D. You still don't think your sisters are going to be much help?

Discussion of options.

A. One possibility you haven't mentioned is a nursing home. I'm wondering what you might think about using such a facility.

• You have inappropriately changed the subject. For now, stay with the topics the client is discussing.

B. Although you've provided most of the care yourself, another important source of support has been the church.

• By recognizing contributions of the church members, you focus the interaction on a resource that may have additional potential for the client.

C. Your mother living with you seemed to be the best option. And one positive outcome of your decision has been her ability to see church friends.

• This reflection is accurate and notes a source of support that may deserve further discussion.

D. You still don't think your sisters are going to be much help?

• Your response does not need to be a question. But even if you make it into a reflection, it would not do much to move the interaction in the direction of productive change.

12. Yeah. She looks forward to their visits. And when they're here, I actually feel like I can take a breather for a few minutes. During their stay she doesn't criticize me, and she has them take care of little needs that might come up, like getting her some water or adjusting her position in the bed.

A. With regard to your sisters, it has been you, not them, who have made the decision that you would be supporting your mother.

B. Your mother really likes to have her church friends visit.

C. So, having the church members over does provide some relief for you.

D. What would you think of having her church friends over more often?

Discussion of options.

A. With regard to your sisters, it has been you, not them, who have made the decision that you would be supporting your mother.

• Your response inappropriately changes the subject, and it fails to recognize the option being discussed by the client.

B. Your mother really likes to have her church friends visit.

- You are focusing on the mother, rather than on your client.
C. So, having the church members over does provide some relief for you.
  - This comment keeps the interaction centered on a continuing source of support.
D. What would you think of having her church friends over more often?
  - At this point in the interaction, there is no need to make such a suggestion.

13. I guess they have been the one bright spot in all of this. Maybe getting them more involved is what I need to do. Their visits have been pretty short. I guess one possibility would be seeing if some of them might be willing to stay a little longer, so I could get a bit more of a break.
    A. I could get in touch with the church and see if they would be willing to organize some regular times to provide relief for you.
    B. One possibility would be seeing if some of them would be willing to stay a little longer, so you could get more of a break.
    C. Involving her church friends seems like a good idea to me. I really believe that is an option you should seriously consider.
    D. You think talking to them about longer visits might be worth a try.

Discussion of options.

  A. I could get in touch with the church and see if they would be willing to organize some regular times to provide relief for you.
    - You are offering to take a step that the client probably is fully capable of doing.
  B. One possibility would be seeing if some of them would be willing to stay a little longer so you could get more of a break.
    - Your response repeats exact words used by the client.
  C. Involving her church friends seems like a good idea to me. I really believe that is an option you should seriously consider.
    - Although positive, your comment is much too judgmental to be used by a supportive worker.

D. You think talking to them about longer visits might be worth a try.
  • This accurate reflection continues the positive momentum with regard to the church member resource.

The remaining multiple-choice items are with a different client.

14. My brother is very intelligent and talented. Although I don't have bad abilities myself, I'm really not in the same ball park as him. So while I'm all but ignored, it seems that he is always getting tons of praise. Just to be around him drives me nuts sometimes. Even though I love him, I can't seem to kick these feelings of jealousy.
  A. Do you want your brother to do worse? Or do *you* want to do better?
  B. You're bothered about the issue of recognition, and you'd like to have more of what you see your brother getting.
  C. Although you have different talents from your brother, you long for your own positive attention.
  D. This situation has you really discouraged.

Discussion of options.

  A. Do you want your brother to do worse? Or do *you* want to do better?
    • Your multiple closed questions might confuse the client, and the answer, especially if it is a simple "Yes" or "No," might confuse you. Also, you have conceptualized the issue in an overly simplistic way.
  B. You're bothered about the issue of recognition, and you'd like to have more of what you see your brother getting.
    • It is better to use a more specific feeling word than "bothered."
  C. Although you have different talents from your brother, you long for your own positive attention.
    • You respond with an appropriate surface feeling reflection.
  D. This situation has you really discouraged.
    • Rather than using a term such as "situation," it is better to reflect the nature of the circumstances, so that both you and

the client have a clear understanding of what you are discussing.

15. I feel like I do my best, but it never seems good enough to get me the kind of attention he gets. I wish it could be me who was the sunshine in the room for once. Our family makes a big commotion about his successes, but mine don't seem to matter to them.
    A. You'd kind of like them to focus on you a little more.
    B. When you do well, you crave for your relatives to take notice.
    C. You feel helpless to change the response of your family members.
    D. Tell me more.

Discussion of options.

A. You'd kind of like them to focus on you a little more.
   • By using the qualifiers "kind of" and "a little," you diminish the intensity of your comment, which in this case you probably do not want to do.
B. When you do well, you crave for your relatives to take notice.
   • You have provided an accurate surface feeling reflection.
C. You feel helpless to change the response of your family members.
   • Although it might be accurate, your use of the strong term "helpless" has the potential to shut off consideration of problem-solving opportunities.
D. Tell me more.
   • You have enough information to make a reflection. Consequently, if you are going to offer a response, you are better off demonstrating your understanding than making a statement that fails to show your comprehension of the client's message.

16. Although I think they see me as a failure, I'm a person with feelings, and it hurts to be viewed as second class. I get so angry at them for not trying to understand me and for not seeming to care about what is happening in my life.
    A. It's exasperating to miss out on the support you know they are capable of giving.

B. Why are their opinions so important to you?

C. So it's just your family's reaction that has you so unhappy.

D. You're angry at them for not trying to understand what is happening in your life.

Discussion of options.

A. It's exasperating to miss out on the support you know they are capable of giving.
- Your surface feeling reflection effectively demonstrates understanding.

B. Why are their opinions so important to you?
- This "Why" question may elicit a defensive reaction from the client.

C. So it's just your family's reaction that has you so unhappy.
- Using the word "just" could give the client the impression that you are downplaying the importance of the topic under discussion.

D. You're angry at them for not trying to understand what is happening in your life.
- Your response employs too many of the words used by the client.

17. I question myself as to why I can't let go of the jealousy. I try to be rational about it, but that doesn't seem to work. I guess I should count this problem as another one of my failures that I haven't been able to overcome.

A. Wow! You're really down on yourself.

B. You feel hopeless regarding your ability to make any changes on this matter.

C. But if you could get your family's approval it would make you happy.

D. So if you were able to dispel these feelings of envy, you would see such a change as a positive achievement.

Discussion of options.

A. Wow! You're really down on yourself.
- Your opinionated exclamation is out of character for a supportive worker.

B. You feel hopeless regarding your ability to make any changes on this matter.
   - Your use of the term "hopeless" may be accurate, but it does nothing to encourage problem solving on the part of the client.
C. But if you could get your family's approval it would make you happy.
   - This is exactly the kind of interaction in which you want to avoid any implication that others' actions can *make* the client react in a certain way.
D. So if you were able to dispel these feelings of envy, you would see such a change as a positive achievement.
   - You have identified a relevant emotion, and you have phrased your response in a way that has the potential to facilitate movement toward goal setting and problem solving. In this case, it is possible that plans may focus on how the client responds to the unequal distribution of praise and attention, since those undesirable circumstances may continue whatever the person does.

18. Yes. I would like to feel more secure in myself. So far, I think I have seen myself as a failure. And that's not a very pleasant way to be living my life.
    A. What could you and your brother do to get along better?
    B. You believe it might be important for you to alter the way you view yourself.
    C. If you're right about that, you know, changing the way you see yourself might be something to consider.
    D. Having confidence in yourself would be an experience you would welcome.

Discussion of options.

A. What could you and your brother do to get along better?
   - Your question is an inappropriate attempt to change the topic.
B. You believe it might be important for you to alter the way you view yourself.
   - Your comment encourages movement toward productive change.

C. If you're right about that, you know, changing the way you see yourself might be something to consider.
  • The phrase "you know" is unnecessary.
D. Having confidence in yourself would be an experience you would welcome.
  • This reflective response is likely to foster continued problem-solving progress.

19. Yeah. I guess I really need to take a look at my own attitudes about myself.
  A. What are some attitudes you would like to change?
  B. What do you think should be different? Which attitude should you address first?
  C. You're sort of ready for a change in some of your attitudes.
  D. In terms of attitude change, you might want to concentrate more on yourself and not worry so much about how others react to your brother.

Discussion of options.

  A. What are some attitudes you would like to change?
    • This open question focuses the interaction on a potential area for new coping efforts. Preceding your inquiry with a reflection was not necessary in this case, since the client's comments were brief, expressed no new feelings, and were entirely related to your question.
  B. What do you think should be different? Which attitude should you address first?
    • Your intent will be clearer if you ask one question at a time, rather than attempting multiple questions.
  C. You're sort of ready for a change in some of your attitudes.
    • By using the phrase "sort of," you decrease the intensity of the need for change when you should be backing that desire.
  D. In terms of attitude change, you might want to concentrate more on yourself and not worry so much about how others react to your brother.
    • It's too soon to make such a suggestion. Instead of being so directive, supportive workers first encourage clients to generate options themselves.

20. I guess I would like to be more self-confident. I would like to be able to do my best at something and then feel good about the effort. If possible, I would like those positive feelings to come from inside, so that however my family might react, I would know in my own mind that I could take pride in what I did.
    A. You think you should be your own judge, rather than depending so much on your family's evaluations?
    B. Do you believe it's really possible for you to make your own decisions and feel comfortable about them regardless of how your family might respond?
    C. You'd like to have your own inner point of reference that would give you a realistic way of determining the value of your accomplishments.
    D. I see.

Discussion of options.

   A. You think you should be your own judge, rather than depending so much on your family's evaluations?
- This response is not bad, but there really is no need for it to be a question. Consequently, we believe there is a better option among the other three possibilities.

   B. Do you believe it's really possible for you to make your own decisions and feel comfortable about them regardless of how your family might respond?
- At this point in the interaction, a closed question is not necessary.

   C. You'd like to have your own inner point of reference that would give you a realistic way of determining the value of your accomplishments.
- This is an accurate reflection of what the client has communicated to you.

   D. I see.
- Your response does not demonstrate understanding.

SHORT-ANSWER QUESTIONS

Write your answer for each of the following questions.

1. When should you ask closed questions?
2. What are the problems with starting an interaction by saying, "How may I help you?"
3. If you come to believe that it is necessary to make a suggestion, at what point in the problem-solving process should you offer it?
4. If a client brings up a viable option, what should you do?
5. When first discussing a topic, what is wrong with referring to the circumstances with a word such as "situation," "stuff," or "this?"
6. What is the disadvantage of relying on feeling terms such as "upset," "concerned," or "bothered?"
7. What do you communicate when you ask a question the client already has answered?
8. When should you use qualifiers such as "kind of," "a little," or "sort of?"
9. What is the image you convey when you rely on repetitive phrases?
10. What are you implying when you say that something "makes you feel" or "must have been?"
11. In terms of problem solving, what are the implications of using feeling terms such as "hopeless" and "helpless?"

POSSIBLE ANSWERS FOR SHORT-ANSWER QUESTIONS

The answer-checking procedures remain the same as before.

• For each item, compare your answer to the one we provide.
• If you believe your answer is correct, you are done with that item.
• With any question for which you believe your answer is incorrect, consider our answer and, if needed, review relevant portions of the chapter. Keep your original answer that you now think is incorrect, but add to it a response that you believe would be correct.

1. You should ask closed questions when you would be satisfied with a brief reply, such as a simple "Yes" or "No."
2. An opening like, "How may I help you?" puts the focus on you and implies your role is to solve problems for clients rather than to encourage problem-solving efforts on their part.
3. If you believe a suggestion is necessary, make it at the end of the alternatives phase after first having pulled for options from the client.
4. When a client brings up a viable option you should acknowledge it.
5. You and the client ought to have a shared understanding of the conditions and events you are discussing. In order to achieve such an understanding, you must specifically describe the circumstances, rather than referring to them in vague ways.
6. Almost all clients are "upset," "concerned," and "bothered." Consequently, those terms don't say anything unique about the person you are interviewing.
7. When you ask a question the client already has answered, you communicate the impression that you have not been paying attention to the person.
8. You should use qualifiers such as "kind of," "a little," or "sort of" when you want to decrease the impact of your comment.
9. Using repetitive phrases conveys the impression of being on automatic pilot, rather than encouraging the client to see you as an interested and caring human being.
10. Phrases such as "makes you feel" or "must have been" imply that it is impossible to change the way the client responds to the circumstances.
11. "Hopeless" and "helpless" emphasize the futility of trying to cope with distressing circumstances. Consequently, reflections that use such words may discourage problem solving rather than encourage it.

FILL-IN-THE-RESPONSE QUESTIONS

Listed below are a series of client statements. For each one, write a worker response that you believe would be appropriate.

1. I'm really fed up at work. I've been in the same position for five years, and I've done my job well. In fact, on our last two annual evaluations, I got the highest ratings of anyone on my team. But the promotions were announced this week, and I've been passed over again.

2. This is the third year that I've been eligible to move up. But for two of the people who got promoted, this is the first year of their eligibility, and I know I'm doing better work than either one of them. I'm sure my annual evaluations are higher than theirs. It's not fair.

3. With the injustice of it all, I feel like forgetting about even trying to do a good job. The supervisors obviously don't have a genuine appreciation for the work I do. They give me excellent evaluations, but they don't seem to pay any attention to my ratings when it's time to actually promote someone.

4. I feel they are just using my skills and are taking me for granted. I guess they think that they can promote people for purely political reasons and that I'll just keep on pumping out the work. But I'd like to give them a big surprise.

5. It would be great to quit. That's exactly what they deserve. Let them try to run the operation with the kind of people they're promoting. Eventually their incompetence will do them in, and, when that happens, I'd like to be on the outside just laughing at them.

6. I'm so furious I could leave tomorrow. Although I know that, at least in the short-run, I would be in worse shape than them. Rather than realize what they were losing, they probably wouldn't even care. So I would give up my job and be out of work, while it probably would be months before they noticed that anything was different.

POSSIBLE ANSWERS FOR
FILL-IN-THE-RESPONSE QUESTIONS

For each response opportunity, there are many possible correct answers. We list two, and, as in previous chapters, we suggest you use them in the following manner.

- Look at our two answers and think about them.
- Consider relevant material covered in the chapter.
- Read the client statement again, then immediately read your answer and the two options listed here.
- Write another response that you believe might be an improvement on your first effort.
- Repeat this procedure for each of the remaining items.

1. • It's disappointing not to get the promotion you believe you deserve.
   • Not being promoted has you really discouraged.
2. • The apparent favoritism is frustrating.
   • You're angry that less qualified persons are advancing while you're standing still.
3. • You feel betrayed by your superiors.
   • It's hard to keep plugging away when you think your efforts will go unrewarded.
4. • The promotion process has you so feeling so abused that you're considering some drastic action.
   • What steps are you considering?
5. • You would enjoy seeing them fail.
   • It would be gratifying for them to realize the extent of your contributions.
6. • Although you feel mad enough to leave, you think you would be the one hurt the most by such a move.
   • You're thoroughly disgusted with your supervisors, but you've concluded that quitting now probably would be unwise.

SUMMARY

You can avoid the difficulties discussed in this chapter by keeping four thoughts in mind: use the least amount of authority necessary to accomplish your objectives, demonstrate your understanding of the client, talk in ways that seem natural and unrehearsed, and remember your ultimate purpose is to encourage productive change. The negative sides of those guidelines are the themes around which the chapter's material is organized.

Ways of using too much authority include the following: asking unnecessary closed questions, asking three or more questions in a row without reflecting any of the client's responses, asking "Why" questions, asking multiple questions, repeatedly making reflections into questions, starting the interaction by taking responsibility for solving the client's problems, making judgmental comments, offering general observations about life, giving advice, suggesting options too soon, focusing on someone other than the client, inappropriately changing the topic, interrupting, failing to recognize options generated by the client, making opinionated exclamations, and offering to take actions that the client is fully capable of doing.

Behaviors that fail to demonstrate understanding include the following: using vague words to refer to circumstances you have not specifically reflected; failing to recognize feelings; using amorphous feeling terms; making a statement such as, "Tell me more" without first reflecting what the client has already told you; asking questions the client previously has answered; saying "I see" or "I understand;" using qualifiers that diminish the intensity of your comments when that is not your intent; inappropriately decreasing the importance of an event by using the word "just;" and frequently saying "you know."

Talking in ways that seem artificial and programmed may involve using repetitive phrases or parroting exact words used by the client.

Terms and phrases that can hinder movement toward productive change include saying that something "makes" the client act or feel certain ways and using strong words or phrases without considering their impact.

Chapter 6

ESTABLISHING GOALS, OBJECTIVES, AND PLANS

Often you can judge the impact of your efforts with clients in terms of their progress related to adaptive goals, objectives, and plans. Skill in establishing such targets is an important ability for human service workers to have. Many organizations require that all clients have written targets. Whether they are required or not, written goals, objectives, and plans can provide a focus for sessions, and measurement criteria can help both the client and worker track movement toward targets. But how are realistic targets selected, and how is productive change measured? We address those issues in this chapter.

Let's start with some definitions. Goals are the more broadly stated changes the client would like to accomplish. Objectives are subcomponents of a goal, or changes that may increase the probability of accomplishing the goal. Plans are the concrete actions the client will take in order to work toward achieving the objectives and, eventually, the goals.

If you are helping a client to progress and you want the change to last, the target being worked toward must be one that is valued in the individual's everyday environment. In other words, the change should be maintained by naturally occurring rewards in the real world. For instance, you might select a goal that is commonly reinforced by desirable attention.

If you want the target to be one the person is motivated to work toward, in addition to being something naturally valued, the area selected must also involve experiences the individual really wants to master. For example, you could focus on an ability the person would like to develop. As we mentioned in Chapters 1 and 4, empirical research demonstrates that individuals put more persistent effort into targets which are personally meaningful than into ones where change is motivated by external pressures or by guilt (Sheldon & Elliot, 1999).

So effective targets involve changes that the client is motivated to work toward and that will be valued in the client's everyday life. In addition, we have previously said effective targets are under the client's control. As we discussed in Chapter 4 with regard to problem solving, targets that focus on changes in someone other than the client are likely to be ineffective because the client does not have control over other people. For instance, "get my roommates to help clean the apartment" is not an effective goal because the roommates' behavior is not under the client's control. A more effective goal might be "increase assertiveness with my roommates."

Clients sometimes identify an end-product as something they would like to work toward. For example, students often say they would like to increase their grade point average. Grade point average is a product that is not solely under the control of the individual. On the other hand, studying is something that is under the person's control. Thus setting a goal to "improve study habits" is more likely to result in success. For example, during a particularly challenging semester, a student's grade point average may not increase even with better studying. If the goal was to increase the grade point average, the student may become discouraged. However, if the student set a goal to improve studying, the person still may have a sense of making progress and be more motivated to continue improving study habits.

In summary, targets should focus on changes that are under the client's control, that the client is motivated to work on, and that are valued in the client's environment. In addition, the ways targets are written can be important. Effective targets (1) are written in "continuous" terms and (2) focus on what to increase or improve rather than on what to avoid. Let's take a closer look at those two issues.

Targets can be worded to be either categorical or continuous. When they are worded categorically, the client either meets or does not meet the target. The problem with this approach is that clients may become discouraged and even give up if they don't reach the target. However, if the target is written using continuous terms, even small increases can be identified as improvement, resulting in greater self-efficacy and motivation to continue. So, if a client sets a goal such as "complete class assignments on time" a sense of failure may result if the person does not complete *every* class assignment on time. However, if the goal is to "increase the number of class assignments completed on time," even completing a few additional class assignments in a timely manner can be experienced as a success, which may enhance the client's motivation to work toward greater improvements.

Targets may also be written in terms of what to avoid or what to increase. Let's say a client states a desire to "stop procrastinating." This goal is written in terms of a behavior to avoid. Consequently the behavior the client will increase in order to meet the goal is not clear. Compared to persons who focus more on what to improve or increase, research has indicated that individuals with more avoidance personal goals tend to make less progress toward their goals and may experience a decrease in physical and psychological health (Elliot & Sheldon, 1998; Elliot, Sheldon, & Church, 1997).

Most avoidance goals can be easily reframed in terms of what to increase or improve. For example, a client who wishes to stop procrastinating could be encouraged to set a goal to "increase the number of tasks completed on time." Elliot and Church (2002) found that clients who articulated more increasing/improving goals (and fewer avoidance goals) also reported more problem improvement, higher satisfaction with their worker, and greater increases in subjective well-being.

To give you some practice with the concepts of continuous versus categorical and increasing versus avoidance, let's consider a common New Year's Day resolution that we will initially phrase as "stop being a couch potato." (Before reading the rest of this paragraph, think about what is wrong with that resolution and how to fix it.) The goal of "stop being a couch potato" is stated in categorical terms and in terms of a behavior to avoid. Because it is stated categorically, the person will either stop a sedentary lifestyle or not stop a sedentary lifestyle and may experience a sense of failure if components of a sedentary lifestyle continue. Furthermore, because the goal is stated in terms of what to avoid, the new behaviors to establish in order to stop being a couch potato are not clear. However, the goal can be written in continuous terms and in terms of what to increase. For instance, one could set a goal to "increase my amount of physical activity." This goal is stated in terms of a behavior to increase and is also stated in continuous terms, so even small improvements in physical activity can be experienced as a success, thus enhancing self-efficacy.

A good way to begin the target-setting process is to ask the client, "How would you like things to be different?" It is *not* advisable to start by saying, "I use a process called. . . ." or "What would you like your goal to be?" Comments such as those tend to confuse clients and may make the target-setting process unnecessarily complicated.

In Figures 6.1 and 6.2 we give you a Goals–Objectives–Plans format for recording such targets and an Observation Scales format for measuring progress on goals and objectives. There is no need, however, to provide clients with elaborate explanations of those formats.

After getting an answer to, "How would you like things to be different?" you can summarize the response in a statement, such as, "It seems as though you would like. . . ." If the individual agrees with your comment, you can say, "So a goal for you would be to. . . ." (Since this process is based on the client's descriptions, it is perfectly acceptable to use the client's words and phrasing when describing targets.)

Write down the name of the goal in the Goals column of the Goals–Objectives–Plans record. (See Figure 6.1 for an example of a Goals–Objectives–Plans record.) Then you can ask, "What will you need to change in order to meet that goal?" or "What has kept you from accomplishing that goal in the past?" Responses to those questions will help you and the client establish objectives. You can acknowledge a possible objective with a statement like, "One of the things that you will need to change in order to (name the goal area) is (name the possible objective)." If the client agrees, you can say, "Maybe this is a subgoal, or what we often call an objective," and write it down in the Objectives column of the Goals–Objectives–Plans record. In order to establish additional objectives, you can then ask what else the person will need to change or what other things have kept the individual from achieving the goal in the past. A rule of thumb is that there should be at least two objectives for each goal.

As mentioned earlier in the chapter, an important reason for setting targets is so that you and the client can monitor progress. One of the best known systems for setting goals and measuring change is *Goal Attainment Scaling* (Kiresuk, Smith, & Cardillo, 1994; Schlosser, 2004). With Goal Attainment Scaling there are five levels of attainment (expected outcome, somewhat more than expected, much more than expected, somewhat less than expected, and much less than expected). Thus change indicated by Goal Attainment Scaling is a function of two factors: (1) future reports of the client's behavior and (2) accuracy of the staff member in defining the attainment levels. The latter factor is

Figure 6.1

Name <u>David Williams</u>

Goals	Objectives	Plans
Do better at work	Improve performance at work	Seek constructive feedback and view it as a learning opportunity
		Be responsive to feedback and use it to guide future efforts
		In subsequent meetings, describe examples of seeking feedback and applying it
	Increase work attendance	Set an alarm and get up when it goes off
		When I feel an urge to skip work, remind myself of the reasons for improving work attendance
		Use scheduled days off to accomplish what had been taking place on missed work days
		Reward myself at the end of the week if I've attended work each day that week
		As needed, discuss attendance challenges and ways of coping with them

so crucial that Goal Attainment Scaling experts recommend at least a year of direct-service experience in a relevant setting before one seeks the 14 hours of training necessary to implement the technique (Cardillo, 1994; Smith, 1994). Clearly, there are few, if any, readers of this book who meet those experience and training criteria.

Goal Attainment Scaling experts also recommend that a minimum of three goals be established for each client and that subsequent rating interviews be conducted by uninvolved third parties. Because those procedures cost both time and money, Goal Attainment Scaling primarily has been used as a means of program evaluation rather than as a regular aspect of interventions. For example, in a time-limited service delivery format, a typical strategy is to use the procedure with every fifteenth client (Kiresuk & Choate, 1994).

In our opinion, though, setting targets and measuring progress toward them can have important therapeutic benefits for clients. So we offer an approach we call Observation Scaling. (We recommend that you keep Figures 6.2 through 6.6 handy for easy reference during the remainder of this chapter.) If our system is used for program evaluation, then as with Goal Attainment Scaling, the sponsoring entity must make adequate time and funding available for the setting of at least three targets and for the subsequent rating interviews to be conducted by uninvolved third parties.

We believe, however, that setting targets and measuring progress can become a standard part of interventions, even when there is not time for setting three targets and when the subsequent ratings will not be done by uninvolved third parties. And rather than new staff members waiting a year before incorporating target setting into their work, as is the case with Goal Attainment Scaling, we believe such persons should be able to use target setting with the first clients they see. Immediate use of our system is possible because of the way we define the attainment levels. Unlike Goal Attainment Scaling, in which attainment levels are defined by an experienced *worker's predictions* of future behavior, the attainment levels in Observation Scaling are defined by the *client's self-observations* from the past and present. Consequently, it is possible for novice workers to learn and to use Observation Scaling. (You will find the basic form in Figure 6.2 and examples of two targets in Figure 6.3. Those two targets might be seen as objectives relating to the goal of "Do better at work" from Figure 6.1.) Observation Scaling can be used in conjunction with Goals–Objectives–Plans records so that human service organizations requiring such records can easily incorporate Observation Scaling into already established procedures.

Figure 6.2
Observation Scales

Name _____

Attainment Level	Target 1	Rated Level	Target 2	Rated Level	Target 3	Rated Level
Further from Target						
No Change						
Normal Level of Success						
Improved Level of Coping						

Figure 6.3
Observation Scales

Name David Williams

Attainment Level	Target 1 Improve performance at work	Rated Level	Target 2 Increase work attendance	Rated Level	Target 3	Rated Level
Further from Target	Generally fail to meet minimum performance standards		Call in sick more than 6 times a month			
No Change	Generally do only the minimum to get by	KF 1-19-06	Call in sick 4 - 6 times a month	KF 1-19-06		
Normal Level of Success	Generally surpass minimum performance standards	KF 5-25-06	Call in sick 1 - 3 times a month			
Improved Level of Coping	Generally do substantially better than minimum performance standards		Go a month or more without calling in sick	KF 5-25-06		

When using Observation Scaling, the first step is to specify a target (either a goal or an objective) and its attainment levels. This endeavor requires attention to five considerations.

1. ***Who develops the targets?*** The staff member and the client collaborate in defining the targets.
2. ***When are targets established?*** Targets can be established at almost any time. If you are doing problem solving with an individual, you can discuss targets at the end of the exploration phase or later.
3. ***What do the attainment levels contain?*** You must write the target scales so that both the client and another staff member could ascertain the levels of attainment. In other words, the descriptions of the attainment levels should enable the collection of information that clearly indicates the current degree of success. To the best of your ability, make sure of the following: the attainment levels are concretely described; the levels do not overlap; nothing could fall between two adjacent attainment levels; the levels are defined in terms of ranges rather than specific points; the scale describes only one dimension of behavior; and the levels focus on areas that are clearly under the *client's* control.
4. ***How many attainment levels are there?*** In Observation Scaling there are four possible outcomes. Ability to cope can deteriorate, remain unchanged, return to a normal level of adjustment, or expand. The attainment levels on the Observation Scales form represent each of those possibilities: Further from Target, No Change, Normal Level of Success, and Improved Level of Coping.
5. ***How many targets are there?*** For program evaluation efforts, Goal Attainment Scaling experts recommend establishing at least eleven possible steps in order to produce a summary change score that is reliable (Cardillo & Smith, 1994). If that psychometric issue is of interest to you, the minimum number of targets is three (containing a total of twelve possible steps). It is our experience, however, that setting even one target can have a positive influence by helping to focus your efforts on desired change.

If you are going to use Observation Scaling to measure progress toward objectives for different goals, you may want to complete a separate Observation Scales form for each goal. You can begin with the first objective by writing the name of it in the Target 1 box and then asking, "Right now how would you say you are doing with regard to (name the objective) . . . ?" Once you have a clear picture of current conditions, summarize the information and enter it in the box for the *No Change* level of Target 1.

Next, you can say, "Things would be worse if (describe circumstances worse than current conditions)." Enter the description in the box for *Further from Target* for Target 1.

Now say, "Within the recent past (or you may define a relevant time period) what is the best you've been able to do with regard to (name of objective)?" (Throughout the discussion be sure to use the objective's name, rather than referring to it as "this objective.") Summarize the individual's answer and enter the range (from current to very best) in the box for *Normal Level of Success* for Target 1.

At this point say, "Things would be better if (describe circumstances above the best the client has achieved)." Write the information in the box for the *Improved Level of Coping* for Target 1.

After you have defined all of the attainment levels for the target, review with the person the information you have collected. To do this, name the objective, then describe (1) the *No Change* level by saying, "Right now. . . . ," (2) the *Further from Target* level by stating, "Things would be worse if. . . . ," (3) the *Normal Level of Success* by saying, "The best you've been able to do in the past was to. . . . ," and (4) the *Improved Level of Coping* by stating, "An improved situation would involve. . . ."

(Those steps also can be used if you are developing attainment levels for a goal rather than for an objective.)

With regard to pulling for information needed to establish a target and its attainment levels, here are the sorts of initial phrasing we have recommended. (Items 1, 2, and 4 require the client to provide answers, which you should clarify or summarize. Items 3 and 5 are defined by you, based upon the adjacent attainment level.)

1. *Name of Target* "How would you like things to be different?"
2. *No Change* "Right now how would you say you are doing with regard to (name of target)?"
3. *Further from Target* "Things would be worse if (describe circumstances worse than current conditions)."

4. ***Normal Level of Success*** "Within the recent past (or specify a time period), what is the best you've been able to do with regard to (name of target)?"
5. ***Improved Level of Coping*** "Things would be better if (describe circumstances above the best the client has achieved)."

When it is time for you to review all of the elements for a target, we have suggested the following kinds of phrasing.

1. ***Name of Target*** "You would like to (say the name of the target)."
2. ***No Change*** "Right now you are (describe the *No Change* level)."
3. ***Further from Target*** "Things would be worse if (describe the *Further from Target* level)."
4. ***Normal Level of Success*** "The best you've been able to do in the recent past (or other time period) has been to (describe the *Normal Level of Success*)."
5. ***Improved Level of Coping*** "An improved situation would involve (describe the *Improved Level of Coping*)."

The preceding target-setting strategy helps clients focus their energy; it does not confuse them. But you *are* likely to make the process confusing if you sidetrack the interaction with technical terms by asking questions such as, "What is your normal level of success?" or by making statements like, "Your improved level of coping would be. . . ." Rather than reading the Observation Scaling labels to the client, use phrasing that will make sense to a person who has no knowledge of this target-setting procedure.

Recall our "stop being a couch potato" scenario. We redefined that goal as "increase my amount of physical activity." Let's imagine you are working with a client who set this target, and she has described three ways she could work toward the goal: go out more often with friends, exercise, and develop an active hobby. The two of you select "go out more often with friends" as an objective on which to assign attainment levels. On an Observation Scales form (Figure 6.2) you write "Go out more often with friends" in the *Target 1* box, and then you ask, "Right now, how would you say you are doing with regard to going out more often with friends?" Based on the client's comments you summarize her current condition, then write "Go out with friends 2 to 3 times a month" in the *No Change* box for Target 1. Right away you go on to define the lower level yourself by suggesting, "Things would be worse if you went out with friends less than twice a month." The client agrees, so you write "Go out with friends less than 2 times a month" in the *Further from Target* box for Target 1. You continue mapping out levels by inquiring, "Within the past year, what is the best you've been able to do with regard to going out with friends?" The client describes the best she has done with regard to socializing. After summarizing her remarks, you jot down her best performance in the *Normal Level of Success* box for Target 1. In this case it reads "Go out with friends 4 to 6 times a month." The range begins with four because that is the next step up from the *No Change* definition without leaving any space between the levels. Six is the very best she has been able to do in the last year, so that defines the cap for this level of attainment. The final level of coping is described next as you explain that, "Things would be better if you go out with friends more than six times per month." The client nods agreement, and in the *Improved Level of Coping* box for Target 1 you write "Go out with friends more than 6 times a month."

At this point you review everything for Target 1 by saying the following. "With regard to increasing your amount of physical activity, one objective is for you to go out more often with friends. Right now you go out with friends about two to three times a month. Things would be worse if you went out with friends less than twice a month. The best you've been able to do within the past year has been to go out with friends four to six times a month, and an improved situation would involve going out with friends more than six times per month." Provided the person concurs with your synopsis, you now have a concrete and specific measure by which you and the client can chart progress toward the objective "Go out more often with friends."

Take a moment to consider again where Observation Scaling fits into the bigger picture of a helping interview. If you and the client have set targets at the end of the exploration phase of a problem-solving interaction, it may be appropriate to move to the alternatives phase of problem solving by saying, "In order to (name of a target) you have (summary of what you have learned about past coping attempts). We could talk about some of those possibilities in greater detail or we could discuss other things you have attempted or considered with regard to (name of that target)?" Using our previous example, the transition may sound something like, "In order to increase your physical activity, you have gone out with friends occasionally, thought about starting an exercise program, and made plans to try an outdoor hobby. We could talk about some of those possibilities in greater detail or we could discuss other things you have attempted or considered with regard to increasing your physical activity?" Often ideas mentioned by the client can be recorded in the plans column of the Goals - Objectives - Plans record. It may also be helpful to write down plans that could be carried out in future meetings with the client. For example, if the person is unable to generate options to foster progress toward an objective or generates far more options than could be addressed in one session, you could write something like, "Explore possible plans with worker."

After writing down a target and its attainment levels on the Observation Scales form, enter the date and your initials in the box at the top of the *Rated Level* column in the *No Change* row for that target. During each subsequent measurement of the target, enter the date and your initials in the *Rated Level* column next to the attainment level the client is at that day.

Progress can be monitored as frequently as you and the client wish. Knowing that desired change has taken place provides both of you with a sense of satisfaction. Conversely, on those occasions when lack of progress becomes evident, you can help the individual consider what might be done to get things moving forward.

If you want to use Observation Scaling as a truly objective measure of outcome, follow-up interviews for this purpose should be conducted by a third party. The less investment the follow-up worker has in the outcome, the more unbiased the rating is likely to be.

So far in this chapter we have considered ways of establishing goals, objectives, and plans, but we have not given much attention to what might constitute important targets to address. As we discussed in Chapter 1, David Barlow and his colleagues have suggested that in situations involving recurring negative emotions, there appear to be three commonly appearing areas in need of change: action tendencies, improving a sense of control and predictability, and reducing self-monitoring of unwanted internal states (Barlow, Allen, & Choate, 2004). By focusing thoughts and behaviors on adaptively dealing with real environmental challenges, desirable control increases and undesirable self-absorption decreases. So when selecting targets, you may want to encourage clients to focus on increasing or improving positive actions and thoughts that enhance their sense of control. That is exactly what all of the targets in this chapter do.

The following dialog provides an example of an interaction that identifies goals, objectives, and plans. At the end of the dialog you will find a Goals–Objectives–Plans record and Observation Scales forms that are based on the information gathered during the interaction.

Worker: What's on your mind today?

Sue Clark: I'm having some trouble at work that is really starting to bother me. I'm a registered nurse, and six months ago I was hired onto a new unit to be a nurse consultant. I'm to do counseling and teaching with postoperative patients. I was hired basically because of my background as a preoperative nurse and my knowledge of surgical procedures. But since I have been working there, I have found that I'm not being allowed to do what I was hired to do.

Worker: Mmhmm.

Ms. Clark: The unit is very understaffed, and frequently the other staff members see me as just another RN. Quite often they ask me to do activities such as taking orders off charts, making beds, and so forth, and I'm having a really hard time saying "No." I see how short-handed they are, and I'm unable to stand up for myself and say, "This is really not what I was hired for."

Worker: When you started your job on this unit, you were under the impression that you would do a lot of teaching activities with the patients to help them cope with their postoperative conditions. But you find yourself being asked to take on other duties. Although you are frustrated, you really haven't stuck up for yourself.

Ms. Clark: Well, yeah. They are really short-staffed, and when they ask me to do something like change a dressing, or empty a catheter bag, how can I say "No"? I have the skills to do those types of things. But what I really want to do is what I was hired for, and that is to get in there and talk with patients and answer their questions about their surgery and find out how their recuperation is progressing. But I just can't do that as often as I would like. And my head nurse is not the type of person I would feel comfortable sitting down with and talking to about this problem.

Worker: So you have been keeping your thoughts to yourself, and now they are building up inside. You're feeling very unhappy about the way things are going.

Ms. Clark: I'm really feeling frustrated because this is not what I wanted to do. If I had wanted to be a staff nurse, I could have easily just gotten a staff nurse position. I've tried to drop little hints to the other staff that I need to be counseling patients. But if they really need my help in making a bed, I'll do it. Then I sort of just huff and puff around, hoping that they will get the message. But they don't. And I don't know how to come right out and say, "Hey, this is not what I was hired to do, and I am only going to do my own job."

Worker: You're disappointed about the extra demands on you. And you've made some efforts at trying to do what you would prefer to be doing, but so far, they haven't worked out as well as you would like.

Ms. Clark: No, they haven't. I think that if I had more confidence, I could just go and talk to my head nurse. I described the situation to some of my friends, but really there's nothing that they can do about it. I would like to have the confidence to just sit down and talk with my supervisor, but I don't. I guess what I really should have done was get a contract. That way it would be in writing, and it would be enforceable. But we don't have a union where I work, so that was out of the question.

Worker: One thought you've had is that you would like to speak with your head nurse, even though you don't have a job description in writing.

Ms. Clark: Yes. I'd like to sit down and say to her that when I was hired, I was under the impression that I was to be doing post-op teaching, and not actual hands-on nursing. But I'm really afraid to rock the boat. I'm a new employee. I've only been there six months, and I really need this job. I'm afraid that if I start complaining, she may just show me the door.

Worker: So, confronting your supervisor is something you're having misgivings about. You also mentioned similar difficulties with some of your coworkers.

Ms. Clark: Right. If there are other nurses, or orderlies, or nursing assistants, or anyone who needs help, I will go and help them even if there are other things that I need to be doing. I really have a hard time saying "No" to anyone. I wish I could stand up for myself more.

Worker: At work you tend to give in to other people when they ask you to do something. With regard to responding to requests when you are busy, how are things outside the work setting?

Ms. Clark: It's basically the same outside of work too. With my family and friends, if I want to do something, everyone else comes first. I'm taking a class right now, and if I'm in the middle of doing an assignment for school and a friend calls and says she needs help doing something, I will drop what I'm working on and go help her. And when that happens, I get really angry inside. But I just can't say "No." I have a real hard time taking care of myself first.

Worker: What led to our meeting today was your dissatisfaction with the amount of patient counseling you've been allowed to do. But as we talk, you are discovering that you fail to stick up for yourself at the hospital, as well as in other areas of your life.

Ms. Clark: Yes, I guess so.

Worker: Let's imagine that we work together. It's now several weeks or months down the road, and we have done everything that we set out to accomplish. How do you hope that things will be different as a result of us working together?

Ms. Clark: Well, I would like to be able to say "No" to people without hurting anyone's feelings and without making waves. I would like to be able to tell people that I will do what they request of me when I am finished with my own responsibilities. But I don't know if there will ever be a way for me to learn to do that.

Worker: Saying "No" is how you're describing it, but when you talked about sharing your concerns with your supervisor, you expressed it in a positive way. Asking to be allowed to do the patient counseling seems to be more than just saying "No." How about describing what you want as, "Sticking up for my own needs?"

Ms. Clark: But that sounds selfish to me.

Worker: You believe it is inappropriate to stick up for yourself?

Ms. Clark: No, it just sounds hard to do. Sometimes I'm afraid that I should be doing what people ask rather than sticking up for myself.

Worker: You think that there might be other things you will need to accomplish before you feel comfortable being more assertive.

Ms. Clark: Yes. Maybe it's a confidence issue. I would like to develop more confidence in myself. If I have more confidence, then maybe I can stick up for myself.

Worker: So you would like to be more assertive and stick up for yourself when it seems appropriate, and you're thinking that you may feel more comfortable being assertive if you increase your self-confidence?

Ms. Clark: Yes.

Worker: OK, how about if we name the goal "Increase assertiveness" and we say that one objective in helping to reach that goal is to "increase self-confidence?"

Ms. Clark: That sounds good.

Worker: So "Increase self-confidence" will be an objective that we work on together. I'm going to jot that down. (Pause while writing on the Goals–Objectives–Plans record and on the Observation Scales form.) How would you describe your self-confidence right now?

Ms. Clark: Pretty low. I wake up most mornings wondering what is going to go wrong and how my day is going to get screwed up. I feel sure I'm going to get shot down; I just don't know who is going to do it.

Worker: Generally, you believe your ideas are going to fail.

Ms. Clark: That's right.

Worker: But there are a few times when you think you will succeed.

Ms. Clark: Yes.

Worker: OK, I'm going to jot that down. (Pause while writing on the Observation Scales form.) So, things would be worse if you were to almost always believe your own ideas were going to fail. (Pause while writing on the Observation Scales form.) Now, within the last six months or so, I would like you to focus on a time when you felt the most confident in that entire six months.

Ms. Clark: Well, I think it was when I first got this job. When I saw the advertisement for the nurse consultant position, I knew it would be something that I could do. I had the skills and the background they were looking for. So when I applied for it and when I went for my interview, I felt pretty sure that I had a good shot at getting the position. That's the most recent time that I felt confident.

Worker: During that period of time, how would you describe your self-confidence?

Ms. Clark: I started the job thinking I would do fine. But I quickly learned that I was wrong. So I guess I just stopped trying with regard to a lot of things.

Worker: There was a time when you generally believed you would succeed. But when you encountered setbacks you tended to give up.

Ms. Clark: Right.

Worker: In terms of encountering setbacks, seeing them as learning experiences and adjusting your efforts in response to them might represent an improvement over giving up when faced with difficulties.

Ms. Clark: Yes. I guess I would like to keep on trying rather than cave in.

Worker: Let me write that down. (Pause while writing on the Observation Scales form.) Now I'd like to review what we've decided. The objective you set is to increase self-confidence. Right now you generally believe your own ideas will fail. Your self-confidence would be lower if you almost always believed your own ideas would fail. The best you have been able to do in the recent past is to generally believe your own ideas will succeed, but then tend to give up when faced with setbacks. And an improved level of self-confidence would be generally believing your own ideas will succeed, while seeing setbacks as learning experiences and adjusting your efforts in response to them.

Ms. Clark: Yeah.

Worker: When we were discussing assertiveness or sticking up for yourself, you also mentioned that you sometimes doubt whether your needs should come before the requests of others.

Ms. Clark: Yes. I guess I don't give my own responsibilities a high priority.

Worker: You're thinking you would be more likely to be assertive if you placed a high priority on your responsibilities?

Ms. Clark: Yes. If I recognized the importance of my own responsibilities I wouldn't feel as bad about telling people what I need.

Worker: Is increasing the priority of your own responsibilities a second objective that you would like to work on?

Ms. Clark: Yes.

Worker: OK. I'm going to jot that down. (Pause while writing on the Goals–Objectives–Plans record and on the Observation Scales form.) When was the last time, either at home or at work, that you gave your responsibilities a high priority?

Ms. Clark: Well, at work it was a few months ago, right after I started this job. I was working with a patient who had just had abdominal surgery two days earlier. I was teaching him deep breathing exercises and how to sit up in bed without putting excess strain on his incision. Right in the middle of our talk, a doctor interrupted and wanted me to drop what I was doing and change a dressing with him. I told the doctor I would be there to assist him as soon as I was finished with the patient I was currently working with. That was really difficult for me, and I probably did not finish the talk with my patient in the same way as I would have completed it if I hadn't been interrupted by the doctor. But that episode was several months ago.

Worker: That was the most recent time at work when you put your own responsibilities first?

Ms. Clark: Yes. When that happened, the doctor was really upset with me. I didn't want to risk having that happen again, so I think that's part of the reason why I'm now in the situation that I'm in.

Worker: What about at home?

Ms. Clark: Well, at home it is easier with the kids. But if it's my husband or another family member, again I have a hard time saying "No." So it's been awhile. If my husband says jump, I jump. But if the kids say jump, I say hold on, I'll jump when I'm finished.

Worker: So we are really talking about adults.

Ms. Clark: Yes.

Worker: I'm going to add something to your objective so that it reads, "With adults, give my responsibilities a high priority more often." Including your husband and other adults, when was the last time you gave your responsibilities a high priority?

Ms. Clark: Well, two weeks ago I was in the middle of making supper, and my husband wanted me to come into the garage to help him with something on the car. I told him that I was in the middle of fixing supper and that I could help him after supper, so he would either have to wait or do it himself. Well, that led to a major argument. But what was I to do?

Worker: It's been about two weeks since you stuck up for yourself then?

Ms. Clark: Yes.

Worker: In the past month, what was the total number of times that you stuck up for yourself?

Ms. Clark: Well, that time with my husband was the one I remember best.

Worker: Were there others?

Ms. Clark: Maybe two other times.

Worker: So, during the last month you have given yourself a high priority and stuck up for yourself once for sure, and maybe three times.

Ms. Clark: Yes.

Worker: (Pause while writing on the Observation Scales form.) What I wrote down was, "Give self a high priority one to three times a month" is how things are going right now. The situation would be worse if you gave yourself a high priority less than once a month. Since you started your new job, what's the best month you've had in terms of sticking up for yourself?

Ms. Clark: Probably my first month. At that time I really felt I knew what my job was, and I actually spent my time fulfilling those responsibilities. But I think once people got to know me, they found out that if they asked me to do something, I would do it.

Worker: OK, including home and work, how many times did you stick up for yourself during that month?

Ms. Clark: Oh, maybe five times.

Worker: Five times?

Ms. Clark: Yeah. Five or six.

Worker: Possibly six? What I have jotted down is that within the recent past, the best that you have been able to do as far as giving yourself a high priority has been from four to six times a month. Do you believe that it would be appropriate to be prepared to be assertive more than six times a month?

Ms. Clark: That would be great.

Worker: OK, let's review what you have said. The name of this objective is, "With adults, give my responsibilities a high priority more often." Right now you give your responsibilities a high priority one to three times a month, including work and home. Things would be worse if you gave yourself a high priority less that once a month. In the recent past, the best you have been able to do is to give yourself a high priority from four to six times a month. And things would improve if you were to give yourself a high priority more than six times a month.

Ms. Clark: Right.

Worker: And you're thinking that you will be better prepared to be assertive if you increase your self-confidence and you more often put a high priority on your needs.

Ms. Clark: That's right.

Worker: What else would you like to be different as a result of our work together?

Ms. Clark: Well, I guess I would like to sleep better. Now when I get in bed, I usually take a real long time before I get to sleep. Then often I wake up early, so that I'm only getting about four and a half hours of sleep a night—give or take fifteen minutes. So I feel tired during the day, and that makes it really difficult for me to function.

Worker: Meeting the day's challenges is hard after you've had a rough night.

Ms. Clark: Yes, it's tough.

Worker: So, we could have a goal called "Improve sleep." How would that be?

Ms. Clark: It sounds good.

Worker: (Pause while writing on the Goals–Objectives–Plans record.) You said that one of your difficulties regarding sleep is that it takes you a while to get to sleep.

Ms. Clark: That's right. It seems that lately it's been taking me about an hour to fall asleep. I get frustrated because I'm not falling asleep and that just makes it even harder to fall asleep.

Worker: Maybe one of your objectives toward improving sleep, then, is to go to sleep sooner after getting into .bed.

Ms. Clark: Yes. I think that would help.

Worker: (Pause while writing on the Goals–Objectives–Plans record and beginning a new Observation Scales form for the objectives of this second goal.) And you said that lately you've been falling asleep about an hour after you go to bed. Things would get worse if it took you longer than that to fall asleep?

Ms. Clark: Yes.

Worker: Since you started your current job, what is the least amount of time it has taken you to fall asleep after you've gone to bed at night?

Ms. Clark: There have been a few nights when I've fallen asleep about 40 minutes after laying down, but I still was frustrated that it was taking so long to fall asleep.

Worker: (Pause while writing on the Observation Scales form.) The soonest you've fallen asleep lately, then, is about 40 minutes after getting into bed. And you would feel better if you could fall asleep sooner.

Ms. Clark: That's right.

Worker: (Pause while writing on the Observation Scales form.) I've written down that your objective is to fall asleep sooner after going to bed. Right now it is taking you about 50 to 70 minutes to fall asleep and things would be worse if it took you longer than that to fall asleep. The soonest you've fallen asleep recently is 40 minutes–give or take about 10 minutes–and it would be better if you could fall asleep sooner than that after going to bed.

Ms. Clark: Yeah.

Worker: You also mentioned that you tend to wake up early, so you end up getting less sleep than you'd like.

Ms. Clark: That's right. I tend to wake up early in the morning because of noise. Then I start worrying about the things I need to do at home and work, so I can't fall asleep again.

Worker: One objective for improving your sleep might be to sleep longer into the morning.

Ms. Clark: Yes, that would help.

Worker: (Pause while writing on the Goals–Objectives–Plans record and Observation Scales form.) When we started talking about sleep, you said that right now, you are sleeping four and a-half hours–plus or minus fifteen minutes.

Ms. Clark: Correct.

Worker: (Pause while writing on the Observation Scales form.) Things would be worse if you got less than four and a-quarter hours sleep a night.

Ms. Clark: That's true.

Worker: Since you started your current job, what is the best night's sleep you've had?

Ms. Clark: I guess about five and a-half hours. But that still didn't feel like enough. I would like to be back to getting about six hours a night, that's what seems right for me.

Worker: (Pause while writing on the Observation Scales form.) So the best you've done recently is five and a-half hours of sleep. And you would like about six hours of sleep.

Ms. Clark: Yeah.

Worker: Let me go over what I've written down. "Sleep longer" is the objective. Right now you sleep from four and one-quarter to four and three-quarters hours a night. Things would be worse if you slept less than that. The best you have done recently is to sleep up to five and one-half hours. And your sleep would be better if you slept more than five and one-half hours.

Ms. Clark: Yeah.

Worker: Let's go on to what some of your options might be and to how you can start moving toward your objectives of increased self-confidence, higher priorities for your own responsibilities, falling asleep sooner, and sleeping longer. Since you started working, you have made some efforts to stick up for yourself. Think about the positive aspects of those endeavors and tell me what comes to mind.

Ms. Clark: Well, when I was able to stick up for myself and do what I was hired to do, I completed my tasks. That in itself was rewarding.

Worker: Mmhmm.

Ms. Clark: When I see my patients improving and doing the things that I have taught them, it's a very positive experience.

Worker: It's reinforcing to counsel patients and to see them using what you've worked on together. In order to get the time you need with patients, what have you done in the past that might work again?

Ms. Clark: Well, when I was going to be with a patient, I've said to my coworkers that I'm not to be disturbed during that period of time.

Worker: So in the past you have been able to make a prediction as to how long it will take you to do a certain task, and you've asked not to be interrupted during that interval. You did that for a while, and then you stopped.

Ms. Clark: Yeah. Like I said, my coworkers figured out that I would come to help them, no matter if I was tied up or not.

Worker: Initially you talked about your time restraints, but people would keep at you and you would give in. Now you are saying that you're willing to make another try at being persistent and sticking up for yourself?

Ms. Clark: Yes. It may shock some people at first, but I'm going to have to do it.

Worker: Let's have an experiment. Think about an occasion in the week ahead when you might tell your coworkers that you need a certain amount of time with a patient.

Ms. Clark: Well, I know that there will be patients this week that I will need to spend time with. So I can just tell my coworkers that during such and such a time, I will be with Mr. Jones or whomever, and don't interrupt me during that time.

Worker: OK.

Ms. Clark: Maybe part of the problem is that they don't understand what my job is. Maybe they just see me as someone who floats around the halls. If I were to explain what it is that I want to accomplish with a certain patient and why, maybe they would have a better understanding and respect for what it is that I'm trying to do. Then they might be less likely to disturb my patient interactions.

Worker: So you plan on explaining your role, then stating the time that you need.

Ms. Clark: Yes.

Worker: I would like you to keep a diary of how things go. When you get home after one of your efforts and you have a few minutes of free time, I would like you to write down what you tried, as much as you can remember of what you actually said, how you felt as you were saying it, how the other person responded, and how it worked out. When we see each other next week, we can review your diary and see how things went.

Ms. Clark: OK, I can do that.

Worker: Maybe one of the things we can discuss when we review your dairy is how confident you felt when you were letting others know the priority or importance of your role and responsibilities.

Ms. Clark: I think that would be helpful. I'd like to start feeling more confident about telling others what I need.

Worker: You've mentioned a number of plans for increasing the priority you place on your responsibilities and for increasing your self-confidence. I've written those plans down. Related to increasing your self-confidence, I have that you will keep a diary regarding your steps toward assertiveness which we will review in future meetings. I also wrote that we could discuss self-confidence, as needed, in future meetings. Regarding giving yourself a high priority more often, I have that you will describe to others the time you need for particular responsibilities, that you will explain your role to coworkers, and that we will talk about other options as needed. How does that sound?

Ms. Clark: Good.

Worker: Another area you want to work on is improving your sleep. What have you tried to get to sleep?

Ms. Clark: Well, what really used to work for me was reading a novel until I got tired, then getting in bed and falling asleep. But I guess I've gotten away from doing that.

Worker: Would novel reading be worth a try again?

Ms. Clark: Probably so.

Worker: So, what might you do?

Ms. Clark: Well, I could get one of the novels that I've bought but never read. And I could read in it until I get sleepy. Then I could get in bed.

Worker: Your plan would have three parts: getting ready for bed, reading outside of bed until you're sleepy, then getting in bed to go to sleep.

Ms. Clark: Yes.

Worker: You would also like to sleep longer. What have you tried in the past to keep from waking up early in the morning?

Ms. Clark: Well, I bought one of those machines that blocks out noise. It was working for a while, but I stopped using it because my youngest child was in a crib and I wanted to make sure I heard her if she cried.

Worker: Would you feel comfortable using the machine now?

Ms. Clark: Yes. All of my children are old enough now to get out of bed and wake me up if they need something.

Worker: You would feel comfortable trying the white noise machine again now that your children are older. What other things have you thought about doing to lengthen the amount of time you sleep?

Ms. Clark: I've thought about trying to darken the room so that I don't wake up when it starts getting lighter outside.

Worker: How might you do that?

Ms. Clark: I could buy some of those room-darkening shades and see if they work.

Worker: You've mentioned that you'd like to improve your sleep by reading a novel before bed and then going to bed after you get sleepy, and by using a white noise machine and room-darkening blinds. We could also discuss other options, if needed, in future meetings. How does that sound?

Ms. Clark: Those plans sound helpful.

Worker: OK. I'll write them down. (Pause while writing on the Goals–Objectives–Plans record.) So tell me what your homework is for the coming week, with regard to sleep and with regard to work.

Ms. Clark: Well at night, I will get ready for bed, read a novel until I'm sleepy, then I'll get into bed. I'm also going to try the noise machine and room-darkening blinds. At my job, I'm going to first explain to my coworkers what it is that I actually am to do at work. And once they understand that, I will tell them that I have this period of time that I will be with a patient, and I am not to be disturbed during that time. And if others do come and interrupt me while I'm with a patient, I will stick up for myself and remind them of my role. Then when I get home, I will write in my diary how the interactions went.

Worker: At work you will explain your job tasks to your coworkers, so they can appreciate what it is that you will be doing, and then you will tell them when you are not to be interrupted. At home, you will keep a diary of your efforts. As a strategy for getting to sleep, your plan is to get ready for bed, read in a novel until tired, then get in bed to go to sleep. You'll also try a noise machine to block disturbing sounds and blinds to darken the room.

Ms. Clark: Yes.

Worker: Well, I look forward to hearing how things turn out. Let's plan to meet again at the same time next week.

Ms. Clark: OK, I'll see you then. Thank you very much.

In this interaction the worker talked slightly more than the client in order to complete the target-setting process. During subsequent sessions the staff member would return to the practice of talking less than the client.

The interaction began with the exploration stage of problem solving in which the worker initially relied on reflections that recognized feelings such as frustration, unhappiness, and disappointment. Having encouraged the airing of those emotions, he then focused on desired changes by using factual reflections.

After a reflection/open question combination and a brief summary, the worker led into target setting by asking, "How do you hope that things will be different as a result of us working together?" Ms. Clark expressed her thoughts on the topic, but she rejected the goal of "Sticking up for my own needs," as being too selfish. Following further discussion, she chose "Increase assertiveness" as a goal. The worker then assisted her in identifying an objective to help with meeting that goal by reflecting that she would feel more comfortable being assertive if she increased her self-confidence. With this objective established, the worker began to gather Observation Scaling information for the *No Change* level by asking, "How would you describe your self-confidence right now?" After defining the *No Change* level as, "Generally believe own ideas will fail," the worker defined the *Further from Target* level as, "Almost always believe own ideas will fail." Then he moved to the *Normal Level of Success* by saying, "Now, within the last six months or so, I would like you to focus on a time when you felt the most confident in that entire six months." Eventually the worker defined the *Normal Level of Success* range as, "Generally believe own ideas will succeed, but tend to give up when faced with setbacks." Next he described the *Improved Level of Coping* as, "Generally believe own ideas will succeed; see setbacks as learning experiences and adjust effort in response to them." With the final level now established, the worker reviewed the objective and its four attainment levels.

The worker then helped Ms. Clark identify a second objective related to increasing assertiveness by reflecting her belief that she would be more likely to be assertive if she increased the priority she places on her own responsibilities. In order to determine the *No Change* level for the Observation Scales form, the worker explored when the last time was that she had given her responsibilities a high priority at work and at home. This discussion led the objective's name to be changed to, "With adults, give my responsibilities a high priority more often," and it resulted in defining the *No Change* level as, "Give self a high priority one to three times a month." The worker defined the *Further from Target* level as, "Give self a high priority less than once a month." Next he moved the discussion to the *Normal Level of Success* by asking, "Since you started your new job, what's the best month you've had in terms of sticking up for yourself?" After arriving at the number six, he defined the Normal Level of Success by saying ". . . within the recent past, the best that you have been able to do as far as giving yourself a high priority has been from four to six times a month." Once verifying that Ms. Clark wanted to be assertive more than six times a month, the worker defined the *Improved Level of Coping* as, "Give self a high priority more than six times a month." He then reviewed the second objective and its attainment levels.

When asked, "What else would you like to be different as a result of our work together?" Ms. Clark described sleep difficulty. The worker reflected her frustration and named the goal "Improve sleep." He then helped her establish two objectives to assist with meeting that goal.

One objective was to fall asleep sooner after getting into bed and the other was to sleep longer. They also worked together to establish four attainment levels for each objective regarding sleep.

We can consider how realistic Ms. Clark's goals and objectives were by thinking about whether they involved experiences (1) that were naturally reinforced in the environment, (2) that she really wanted to improve, and (3) that were under her control. Those maintenance and motivation issues fare well with regard to her selections.

Ms. Clark's first goal was to increase assertiveness, and it involved objectives related to increasing self-confidence and placing priority on her responsibilities. Progress in those areas had the potential to be maintained since, as Albert Bandura (1997) has noted, possessing such confidence is associated with characteristics that are reinforced by society. Consequently, her first two objectives met the criterion of having naturally occurring reinforcers that encourage the maintenance of changes commonly associated with the goals. When an individual is self-confident and assertive, the person tends to engage in certain actions, and others typically reward a variety of those endeavors, including the following: hard work, perseverance on tasks, welcoming new challenges, and a willingness to accept and use feedback resulting from mistakes.

Ms. Clark's initial goal and objectives also made sense in terms of her motivation to work toward them because, as Bandura (1997) has documented, confidence often breeds enjoyment and success. Persons tend to be successful when they work hard, stick with tasks, try new endeavors, and learn from their mistakes. And when they approach life in this way, people tend to enjoy experiences rather than fret about them.

The goals and objectives also focused on areas under Ms. Clark's control. She did not set a goal to get her coworkers to stop asking her to take on extra responsibilities. Instead, the goal and objectives focused on changes in her that may improve her experiences at work and home. She has more control over herself, and so she is more likely to experience success by focusing on how she can change than if she were to focus on changing others.

Her second goal of improved sleep focused on a change that was under her control and was likely to be reinforced by feeling better during the day. Consequently, motivation to work on it also was likely to continue.

In addition, all of Ms. Clark's goals and objectives were written in continuous terms and in terms of what to increase. Words such as "improve" were used to create continuous targets, thereby making it possible for small changes to indicate movement toward the target. Words such as "improve" also resulted in specifying what to increase instead of what to avoid. For example, rather than setting a goal to "stop giving in to coworkers" which would necessitate total change and focus on behavior to avoid, Ms. Clark set a goal to "increase assertiveness."

Having completed the goal-setting process, the worker moved the interaction to the alternatives phase of problem solving. Since Ms. Clark said she wanted to try being more assertive, the worker suggested an experiment in which she would attempt to be assertive during the coming week. With her positive reaction to that idea, the discussion progressed into clarifying the specifics of the plan on which she would work. Although she earlier had expressed a desire to confront her supervisor, Ms. Clark's ideas for being assertive focused on her coworkers, and the worker accepted her choice not to involve the head nurse in her initial efforts. Once she had developed a plan for interacting with other staff members, the worker turned the focus to improved sleep. After considering options and developing plans for the objectives related to sleep, he asked Ms. Clark to review her plans. He then summarized them himself, expressed interest in the outcome, verified when their next meeting would be, and ended the session. (Ms. Clark's completed Goals–Objectives–Plan record is shown in Figure 6.4 and her Observation Scales forms are shown in Figures 6.5 and 6.6.)

Figure 6.4

Name <u>Sue Clark</u>

Goals	Objectives	Plans
Increase assertiveness	Increase self-confidence	Keep diary of assertiveness attempts
		Review diary in future meetings
		Discuss self-confidence in future meetings as needed
	With adults, give my responsibilities a high priority more often	Describe to others amount of time needed to particular responsibilities
		Explain work role to coworkers
		Discuss other options as needed
Improve sleep	Fall asleep sooner after getting into bed	Read novel before bed until sleepy
		Go to bed when sleepy
		Discuss other options as needed
	Sleep longer	Use white noise machine
		Darken room with blinds
		Discuss other options as needed

Figure 6.5
Observation Scales

Name Sue Clark

Attainment Level	Target 1 Increase self-confidence	Rated Level	Target 2 With adults, give my responsibilities a high priority more often	Rated Level	Target 3	Rated Level
Further from Target	Almost always believe own ideas will fail		Give self a high priority less than once a month			
No Change	Generally believe own ideas will fail	KF 1-10-06	Give self a high priority 1 - 3 times a month	KF 1-10-06		
Normal Level of Success	Generally believe own ideas will succeed, but tend to give up when faced with setbacks		Give self a high priority 4 - 6 times a month			
Improved Level of Coping	Generally believe own ideas will succeed; see setbacks as learning experiences and adjust effort in response to them		Give self a high priority more than 6 times a month			

Figure 6.6
Observation Scales

Name Sue Clark

	Target 1 Fall asleep sooner after getting into bed	Rated Level	Target 2 Sleep longer	Rated Level	Target 3	Rated Level
Attainment Level						
Further from Target	Fall asleep more than 70 minutes after getting into bed		Sleep less than 4.25 hours a night			
No Change	Fall asleep 50 - 70 minutes after getting into bed	KF 1-10-06	Sleep from 4.25 hours, up to as much as 4.75 hours a night	KF 1-10-06		
Normal Level of Success	Fall asleep 30 - 49 minutes after getting into bed		Sleep more than 4.75 hours, up to as much as 5.5 hours a night			
Improved Level of Coping	Fall asleep sooner than 30 minutes after getting into bed		Sleep more than 5.5 hours a night			

MULTIPLE-CHOICE QUESTIONS

Items 1-15 are with one client, and items 16-22 involve a different individual. Your instructions are the same as in the previous chapters.

- For each of the following client statements, choose the response or responses you believe would be appropriate. (Several items have more than one correct answer.)
- Indicate your selection in writing.
- Read the discussions of all four options.
- If you are correct, go to the next item.
- If you are incorrect, think about the explanations and, if necessary, review relevant portions of the chapter; then, once you better understand the issues, proceed to the next question.

For the client in items 1-15, you are meeting with the person for the first time, and you have spent about 20 minutes exploring thoughts and feelings. Much of what you have discussed relates to the person's shock, disappointment, and guilt concerning the client's son being assigned to a special class due to his disruptive behavior. At this point in the interaction, you want to engage the person in target setting.

1. Worker: Let's imagine that we work together. It is now two or three months down the road, and we have completed what we set out to do. How do you hope that things will be different as a result of our efforts?

   Client: I want Michael to feel good about going to school. I don't want him to think that he is being labeled or set apart. I don't want him to view himself as an outsider. Also, I don't want this decision to follow him into future grades. I don't want him stuck with a label that limits his opportunities and keeps him from advancing.

   A. You are very worried about both the short-term and long-term implications of your son's new classroom assignment.
   B. So, in three months you would like him to be enjoying school, and you would like his potential to be undiminished.
   C. What changes in your behavior might increase the chances of Michael getting the most out of school?

D. What does Michael's school need to do in order for him to have a good educational experience?

Discussion of options.

A. You are very worried about both the short-term and long-term implications of your son's new classroom assignment.
  • You have accurately reflected the client's comment, but it is time to focus the interaction on target setting.
B. So, in three months you would like him to be enjoying school, and you would like his potential to be undiminished.
  • Your response describes the desirable state of affairs portrayed by the client. But those conditions relate to the son, not to the individual with whom you are speaking.
C. What changes in your behavior might increase the chances of Michael getting the most out of school?
  • This open question recognizes the client's desires for Michael, and it also focuses the interaction on identifying areas in which the *client* might change.
D. What does Michael's school need to do in order for him to have a good educational experience?
  • Michael's school is not your client. In target setting, your focus should be on the person with whom you are talking.

2. In order for him to do better in school, I guess he needs some kind of assistance, but I don't know what I should do. I want to give him what he needs, but I'm not sure what that is.
  A. Helping him improve his performance is something you would like to do.
  B. You believe he could use some extra support. What might be your role in that?
  C. So, you're really pretty lost in terms of knowing what you want to be doing.
  D. You could talk with his teachers and ask for their suggestions.

Discussion of options.

A. Helping him improve his performance is something you would like to do.

- Your reflection focuses on a possible target the client could work toward.

B. You believe he could use some extra support. What might be your role in that?
  - By making a combination response with a reflection followed by an open question, you communicate understanding while also calling for discussion of what the client might do.

C. So, you're really pretty lost in terms of knowing what you want to be doing.
  - This is an overly negative reflection of what the client has communicated to you.

D. You could talk with his teachers and ask for their suggestions.
  - Your advice does not facilitate target setting.

3. Maybe if I could help him learn some things that he could use at school, he might be able to get along better there.
   A. So, we could name your goal, "Improve Michael's academic learning."
   B. It's usually best to leave the teaching to the teachers. I think you should be working on improving Michael's compliance to requests from adult authorities.
   C. Let's set some attainment levels for your goal.
   D. What is a school-related skill you could encourage him to develop?

Discussion of options.

A. So, we could name your goal, "Improve Michael's academic learning."
  - There are two problems with this comment. First, it is too soon to name the goal. Second, the goal is not defined in terms of your client's behavior.

B. It's usually best to leave the teaching to the teachers. I think you should be working on improving Michael's compliance to requests from adult authorities.
  - Your judgmental response is inconsistent with supportive helping. Rather than letting the client select the goal, you are negating the person's views and attempting to impose your own opinions.

C. Let's set some attainment levels for your goal.
   • In addition to your response being premature, it uses a term ("attainment levels") that probably will confuse the client.
D. What is a school-related skill you could encourage him to develop?
   • Your open question calls for the client to identify a specific area on which to work with Michael.

4. I think completing his homework is something that he needs to do a better job of and is something that I might be able to help him with.
   A. What have you done in the past to help him complete his homework?
   B. Developing ways of encouraging him to do his homework would be of interest to you.
   C. What might be some appropriate ways for you to encourage Michael to do a better job of completing his homework?
   D. Providing effective homework supervision could be an endeavor for us to tackle.

Discussion of options.

   A. What have you done in the past to help him complete his homework?
      • Your open question is moving the interaction toward considering alternatives and developing a plan. But right now it is better to stay with the task of setting a goal.
   B. Developing ways of encouraging him to do his homework would be of interest to you.
      • This accurate reflection facilitates the task of selecting a goal.
   C. What might be some appropriate ways for you to encourage Michael to do a better job of completing his homework?
      • As with the A option, this problem-solving question is out of place. For now, keep the interaction focused on establishing a goal.
   D. Providing effective homework supervision could be an endeavor for us to tackle.
      • You support the goal-setting process with this response.

5. If I could become better at encouraging him to complete his homework each day, I would feel that I was making progress.
   A. I believe your focus is too narrow. We need to be working toward something more global than helping your son complete his homework.
   B. What should we name this goal?
   C. What if we set a goal for our efforts and name it, "More frequently encourage completion of homework?"
   D. What if we set a goal for our efforts and name it, "Have Michael complete his homework?"

Discussion of options.

   A. I believe your focus is too narrow. We need to be working toward something more global than helping your son complete his homework.
   • While a more general goal certainly would be possible, feeling positive about encouraging Michael to do his homework is the goal that the client seems to favor, and there is really nothing wrong with it.
   B. What should we name this goal?
   • Your question is not bad, but you probably have enough information to go ahead and propose a name for the goal.
   C. What if we set a goal for our efforts and name it, "More frequently encourage completion of homework?"
   • In an understandable way, you introduce the term "goal." And you suggest a name for the goal that uses the client's ideas and phrasing to focus on her own behavior.
   D. What if we set a goal for our efforts and name it, "Have Michael complete his homework?"
   • The first part of your comment is fine, but the goal is defined in terms of Michael's actions rather than in terms of your client's behavior.

6. That sounds good. I really want to encourage him more, but sometimes I don't say anything to him about homework because I'm not sure I'm going to be able to do any good.
   A. You would like to work on more frequently encouraging Michael to complete his homework, and you think in order to meet that goal you may need to become more confident about your efforts.

B. You're afraid that encouraging him won't do any good.

C. What do you think you could do better to encourage him?

D. Maybe we should think about a different goal.

Discussion of options.

A. You would like to work on more frequently encouraging Michael to complete his homework, and you think in order to meet that goal you may need to become more confident about your efforts.
  - This response reflects agreement with the goal and moves toward setting an objective.

B. You're afraid that encouraging him won't do any good.
  - This reflection moves her away from target setting and may encourage pessimism.

C. What do you think you could do better to encourage him?
  - This questions rushes into developing a plan before completing the work on a goal and objectives. It also fails to reflect her desire for more confidence.

D. Maybe we should think about a different goal.
  - The client said she likes the goal.

7. Yes. That's right.

A. So how about if we call that objective, "Decrease self-doubt about encouraging completion of homework?"

B. So how about if we call that objective, "Become self-confident?"

C. So how about if we call that objective, "Become more confident in ability to encourage completion of homework?"

D. So what do you think we should call that objective?

Discussion of options.

A. So how about if we call that objective, "Decrease self-doubt about encouraging completion of homework?"
  - This objective focuses on what to avoid rather than on what to improve or increase.

B. So how about if we call that objective, "Become self-confident?"
  - This objective is categorical rather than allowing for levels of

change. It also fails to specify the area in which she would like to be more confident.

C. So how about if we call that objective, "Become more confident in ability to encourage completion of homework?"
  • This objective allows for levels of improvement and focuses on the experience (confidence) to be increased.
D. So what do you think we should call that objective?
  • This question will get the client involved in the target-setting process, but you already have plenty of information to set the objective.

8. That sounds fine to me.
  A. When was the last time you felt confident about the way you were encouraging him to do his homework?
  B. Did you feel confident about the way you encouraged him to do his homework yesterday?
  C. What would be the "No Change" level of attainment for your goal?
  D. Since the school year started, what is the best you've been able to do in terms of encouraging Michael to do his homework?

Discussion of options.

  A. When was the last time you felt confident about the way you were encouraging him to do his homework?
  • Your question effectively calls for information that will help in specifying the *No Change* level of attainment.
  B. Did you feel confident about the way you encouraged him to do his homework yesterday?
  • This closed question is much too narrow. Consequently, it is an inefficient response to use at this point.
  C. What would be the "No Change" level of attainment for your goal?
  • Your question uses terminology that probably is unfamiliar to the client and may confuse the person.
  D. Since the school year started, what is the best you've been able to do in terms of encouraging Michael to do his homework?
  • This question is intended to gather information relevant to the *Normal Level of Success*. But we suggest that you first

describe the *No Change* and *Further from Target* levels before moving to the *Normal Level of Success.*

9. I guess there were one or two times last week when we were working on a special project.
   A. Right now, it might be fair to say that Michael completes his homework approximately once or twice every two weeks.
   B. Right now, it might be fair to say that you feel confident about homework encouragement approximately once or twice every two weeks.
   C. Doing that once or twice every two weeks might describe the "No Change" level of attainment.
   D. Things would be worse if that happened less than once every two weeks.

Discussion of options.

   A. Right now, it might be fair to say that Michael completes his homework approximately once or twice every two weeks.
      • This comment focuses on Michael rather than on your client.
   B. Right now, it might be fair to say that you feel confident about homework encouragement approximately once or twice every two weeks.
      • Your comment serves to define the *No Change* level of attainment.
   C. Doing that once or twice every two weeks might describe the "No Change" level of attainment.
      • Unless the client is already familiar with Observation Scaling, don't use attainment-level terminology.
   D. Things would be worse if that happened less than once every two weeks.
      • Defining the *Further from Target* attainment level is your purpose in making this comment, but it is not time for that yet.

10. That's right.
    A. Things would be worse if you went longer than two weeks without feeling confident regarding encouragement of homework.
    B. So, going longer than two weeks without feeling confident

regarding encouragement of homework would be the "Further from Target" level of attainment.

C. How might you go about changing that?

D. There's a lot of room for improvement in terms of how you feel about your efforts toward encouraging Michael to complete his homework.

Discussion of options.

A. Things would be worse if you went longer than two weeks without feeling confident regarding encouragement of homework.
   - Your comment is a logical extension of what the client has said, and you have now defined the *Further from Target* attainment level.

B. So, going longer than two weeks without feeling confident regarding encouragement of homework would be the "Further from Target" level of attainment.
   - Don't confuse your client by using attainment-level terminology.

C. How might you go about changing that?
   - For now, stay with objective setting rather than moving to the alternatives or plan stages of problem solving.

D. There's a lot of room for improvement in terms of how you feel about your efforts toward encouraging Michael to complete his homework.
   - Your reflection is accurate, but it does not enhance forward movement of the target-setting process.

11. Yeah, I guess that's true.

A. Looking ahead at the rest of the school year, what do you think would be the best you could do in terms of feeling confident about encouraging Michael to do his homework?

B. Looking ahead at the rest of the school year, what do you think would be the best Michael could do in terms of completing his homework?

C. Since the school year started, what has been the very best two-week period in terms of Michael completing his homework?

D. Since the school year started, what has been the very best two-week period in terms of you feeling confident about encouraging Michael to do his homework?

Discussion of options.

A. Looking ahead at the rest of the school year, what do you think would be the best you could do in terms of feeling confident about encouraging Michael to do his homework?
   - Your question is an inefficient way of attempting to gather information on the *Improved Level of Coping*. It is much easier to define the *Normal Level of Success*, and then to describe a logical extension of that level in order to define the *Improved Level of Coping*.

B. Looking ahead at the rest of the school year, what do you think would be the best Michael could do in terms of completing his homework?
   - Like option A, this question is an attempt to generate information relevant to the *Improved Level of Coping*. It also focuses on Michael.

C. Since the school year started, what has been the very best two-week period in terms of Michael completing his homework?
   - As with the B option, this question relates to the son's behavior rather than to the behavior of your client.

D. Since the school year started, what has been the very best two-week period in terms of you feeling confident about encouraging Michael to do his homework?
   - Your question fosters progress toward defining the *Normal Level of Success*.

12. I guess at the very start of school, I felt pretty confident about interacting with him when he got home.
    A. And you would like to have those positive feelings again.
    B. What were you doing at the beginning of the year that seemed to be working for you?
    C. During the first two weeks of school, on how many days did you feel confident about encouraging him to do his homework?
    D. So, were there more than two days when you felt confident about encouraging him to do his homework?

Discussion of options.

A. And you would like to have those positive feelings again.
   - Your comment does not facilitate the task of target setting.

B. What were you doing at the beginning of the year that seemed to be working for you?
- This is a good problem-solving question, but right now it is better to keep the interaction centered on the task of establishing an objective.

C. During the first two weeks of school, on how many days did you feel confident about encouraging him to do his homework?
- This question helps you progress toward defining the *Normal Level of Success.*

D. So, were there more than two days when you felt confident about encouraging him to do his homework?
- Your closed question is inefficient. There is a better option listed in this group.

13. I guess I felt confident in those interactions on about five of the ten days.
A. So, the best you have been able to do this year is to feel confident about encouraging Michael to do his homework on five days out of ten.
B. So, the best Michael has been able to do is complete his homework on five days out of ten.
C. The "Normal Level of Success" would be from one good day every two weeks, up to five good days every two weeks.
D. The "Improved Level of Coping" would be more than five good days every two weeks.

Discussion of options.

A. So, the best you have been able to do this year is to feel confident about encouraging Michael to do his homework on five days out of ten.
- Your reflection is accurate and it serves to specify the upper limit of the *Normal Level of Success.*
B. So, the best Michael has been able to do is complete his homework on five days out of ten.
- This response focuses on Michael, rather than on your client.
C. The "Normal Level of Success" would be from one good day every two weeks, up to five good days every two weeks.
- Avoid using attainment-level terminology that may confuse your client.

D. The "Improved Level of Coping" would be more than five good days every two weeks.
- Your comment unnecessarily uses attainment-level terminology, and it moves to the *Improved Level of Coping* before you have fully described the *Normal Level of Success.*

14. Yes.
- A. Well, let's move on to considering what you might do to feel more confident about encouraging Michael to complete his homework.
- B. So, things would be better than the best they have been this year, if you felt confident about encouraging him to do his homework on more than five days during a two-week period.
- C. What do you think would be the best you could do in terms of encouraging Michael to complete his homework?
- D. Do you think you could do any better in terms of encouraging Michael to complete his homework?

Discussion of options.

- A. Well, let's move on to considering what you might do to feel more confident about encouraging Michael to complete his homework.
  - Your comment is premature. Finish the objective-setting procedure before you return to problem solving.
- B. So, things would be better than the best they have been this year, if you felt confident about encouraging him to do his homework on more than five days during a two-week period.
  - Your comment is a logical extension of what the client has said, and by making it, you have described the *Improved Level of Coping.*
- C. What do you think would be the best you could do in terms of encouraging Michael to complete his homework?
  - This question is not necessary in order for you to define the *Improved Level of Coping.*
- D. Do you think you could do any better in terms of encouraging Michael to complete his homework?
  - Your closed question does not facilitate target setting.

15. That's right.
    A. Now that we have set a couple of targets and decided on how to measure progress, let's consider what we might do to help you go forward with making some changes.
    B. Let me review what we have just decided. Your goal is for your son to complete his homework. Right now, about once or twice every two weeks Michael does his homework. Things would be worse if he did it less than once every two weeks. The best he has been able to do this year is doing his homework three to five times in two weeks. And things would be better if more than five days in two weeks he completed his homework.
    C. Let me review what we have just decided. Right now, about once or twice every two weeks you think you are meeting your goal. Things would be worse if you felt that way less than once every two weeks. The best you've been able to do this year is meeting your goal three to five times in two weeks. And things would be better if more than five days in two weeks you met your goal.
    D. Let me review what we have decided so far. A goal you set is to "More often encourage completion of homework." Related to that goal is an objective of, "Feel more confident about ability to encourage completion of homework." Right now, about once or twice every two weeks you feel confident about encouraging Michael to complete his homework. Things would be worse if you felt that way less than once every two weeks. The best you've been able to do this year is to feel confident about the homework issue three to five times in two weeks. And things would be better if on more than five days in two weeks you felt confident about encouraging Michael to complete his homework.

Discussion of options.

    A. Now that we have set a couple of targets and decided on how to measure progress, let's consider what we might do to help you go forward with making some changes.
       • Before moving on to considering alternatives and developing a plan, you should summarize what you have accom-

plished during target setting. In addition, it is best to have at least two objectives for each goal.

B. Let me review what we have just decided. Your goal is for your son to complete his homework. Right now, about once or twice every two weeks Michael does his homework. Things would be worse if he did it less than once every two weeks. The best he has been able to do this year is doing his homework three to five times in two weeks. And things would be better if more than five days in two weeks he completed his homework.
   • Your summary inaccurately describes your target-setting conclusions in terms of Michael's behavior.

C. Let me review what we have just decided. Right now, about once or twice every two weeks you think you are meeting your goal. Things would be worse if you felt that way less than once every two weeks. The best you've been able to do this year is meeting your goal three to five times in two weeks. And things would be better if more than five days in two weeks you met your goal.
   • This summary does not specifically describe the targets selected by your client.

D. Let me review what we have decided so far. A goal you set is to "More often encourage completion of homework?" Related to that goal is an objective of, "Feel more confident about ability to encourage completion of homework." Right now, about once or twice every two weeks you feel confident about encouraging Michael to complete his homework. Things would be worse if you felt that way less than once every two weeks. The best you've been able to do this year is to feel confident about the homework issue three to five times in two weeks. And things would be better if more than five days in two weeks you felt confident about encouraging Michael to complete his homework.
   • This is an accurate description of the goal, an objective related to the goal, and the objective's attainment levels.

The remaining multiple-choice items help to show how some of the concepts discussed earlier in the chapter can be viewed in different ways. (Difference #1) Items 16-22 involve a client for whom you have proceeded to the point of naming an objective to, "Become more assertive when I need to stick up for myself." In the interview with Sue Clark, "Increase assertiveness" was a goal (Figure 6.4). Determining what are goals and what are objectives is unique for each person. What is a goal for one individual may be an objective for another person. In the following items, improving assertiveness will be an objective rather than a goal. (Difference #2) Unlike Sue Clark's objective of, "With adults, give my responsibilities a high priority more often" (Target 2 in Figure 6.5) for which all attainment levels involved the counting of events, the attainment levels for the objective in items 16-22 will be defined by verbal descriptors (e.g., "occasionally" and "almost never"), as well as by indicators of frequency (e.g., "more than half of the time"). (Difference #3) With Sue Clark, the worker did not define assertiveness. Instead he helped her to set up an experiment in which she would be "assertive" and keep a diary of her efforts. Subsequent discussions of her diary would provide an opportunity to consider the concept of assertiveness more fully. With the client in items 16-22 the worker is taking a different approach and wants to offer a definition of assertiveness.

16. Worker: What if we name this objective, "Become more
                assertive when I need to stick up for myself"?
    Client: That would be fine.
    A. Being assertive can be thought of as involving three steps. The first one is describing another person's problematic behavior. The second one is saying how you feel about it. And the third one is stating what you want to happen. Can you remember the last time you behaved that way?
    B. Being assertive can be thought of as involving three steps. The first one is describing another person's problematic behavior. The second one is saying how you feel about it. And the third one is stating what you want to happen. How many times have you behaved that way during the last three months?
    C. Being assertive can be thought of as involving three steps. The first one is describing another person's problematic behavior. The second one is saying how you feel about it. And the third one is stating what you want to happen. When was the last time you described another person's problematic behavior, said how you felt about it, and stated what you wanted to happen?

D. When was the last time you were assertive?

Discussion of options.

A. Being assertive can be thought of as involving three steps. The first one is describing another person's problematic behavior. The second one is saying how you feel about it. And the third one is stating what you want to happen. Can you remember the last time you behaved that way?
  • You might be setting yourself up to receive a "No" to this closed question.
B. Being assertive can be thought of as involving three steps. The first one is describing another person's problematic behavior. The second one is saying how you feel about it. And the third one is stating what you want to happen. How many times have you behaved that way during the last three months?
  • Since the time span you specify is so large, the client probably will have difficulty responding to your question.
C. Being assertive can be thought of as involving three steps. The first one is describing another person's problematic behavior. The second one is saying how you feel about it. And the third one is stating what you want to happen. When was the last time you described another person's problematic behavior, said how you felt about it, and stated what you wanted to happen?
  • This question provides a definition of the term "assertive" and asks when the last time was that the client acted in that manner. Consequently, you are moving toward a specification of the *No Change* attainment level.
D. When was the last time you were assertive?
  • Since for this client you want to move forward with the person having in mind a particular definition of what it means to be "assertive," it is better to provide a description of that definition.

17. I guess it was today.
    A. Tell me what happened.
    B. So, right now you are assertive about once a day.
    C. How were you assertive?
    D. What is the best day you've had in terms of assertiveness?

Discussion of options.

   A. Tell me what happened.
- The response to your probe is likely to clarify whether the client's behavior was assertiveness or some other type of response.

   B. So, right now you are assertive about once a day.
- Your reflection moves too rapidly toward defining the *No Change* attainment level. Rather than progressing quite so quickly, it is better to make sure that you and the client both have the same concept of assertiveness.

   C. How were you assertive?
- This question probably will elicit details that reveal the nature of the client's actions.

   D. What is the best day you've had in terms of assertiveness?
- It is too soon to address the *Normal Level of Success.*

18. I was in a staff meeting explaining a project I'm working on, and, like he usually does, Bill started talking over me. So I shouted at him to shut up and let me finish.
   A. In a provocative way, your response to Bill communicated what you wanted to happen, but it did not describe his behavior or how you felt about what he did. So, I'd like you to tell me about a time when you not only stated your desires, but you also identified the troubling behavior and how you felt about it.
   B. So, being assertive once a day is where you are now.
   C. Remember, we've decided that being assertive is describing the other person's behavior, stating your feelings about it, and saying what you would like to happen.
   D. Remember, we've decided that being assertive is describing the other person's behavior, stating your feelings about it, and saying what you would like to happen. So, the episode today probably was not an example of assertiveness. Using the definition I've just described, I want you to make another try at describing the last time you were assertive.

Discussion of options.

   A. In a provocative way, your response to Bill communicated

what you wanted to happen, but it did not describe his behavior or how you felt about what he did. So, I'd like you to tell me about a time when you not only stated your desires, but you also identified the troubling behavior and how you felt about it.

- Productive discussion is likely to result from your combination of a low-key critique of the client's response and a clearly stated request for an appropriate example.

B. So, being assertive once a day is where you are now.

- The episode described by the client is not an example of assertiveness as you have defined it.

C. Remember, we've decided that being assertive is describing the other person's behavior, stating your feelings about it, and saying what you would like to happen.

- This comment is accurate, but it is not very efficient in terms of target setting because it provides no direction as to what the client should discuss next.

D. Remember, we've decided that being assertive is describing the other person's behavior, stating your feelings about it, and saying what you would like to happen. So, the episode today probably was not an example of assertiveness. Using the definition I've just described, I want you to make another try at describing the last time you were assertive.

- Your response provides corrective feedback to the client and supplies guidance in terms of what needs to be discussed.

19. It probably was last weekend when my roommate made a big mess in the kitchen without cleaning it up. I said that when dirty dishes were left I felt taken advantage of and that, unless we have some other agreement ahead of time, the person who makes the mess should clean it up.

A. So by identifying the problem behavior, expressing your feelings about it, and describing what you believed should happen, you were assertive with your roommate.

B. What you have described would be an example of assertiveness. In a typical week, how often are you assertive when you need to stick up for yourself?

C. When needing to stick up for yourself, how do you think you could increase the number of instances in which you assertively express yourself, as you did with your roommate?

D. How could things get worse?

Discussion of options.

A. So by identifying the problem behavior, expressing your feelings about it, and describing what you believed should happen, you were assertive with your roommate.
  - Your reflection is accurate, but it provides no guidance as to where the client should go now with regard to the task of objective setting.

B. What you have described would be an example of assertiveness. In a typical week, how often are you assertive when you need to stick up for yourself?
  - By using a combination response that recognizes the client's account as an appropriate example and then asks a realistic question about how often the behavior occurs, you facilitate movement toward specifying the *No Change* attainment level.

C. When needing to stick up for yourself, how do you think you could increase the number of instances in which you assertively express yourself, as you did with your roommate?
  - At this point, stay with objective setting, rather than attempting a return to problem solving.

D. How could things get worse?
  - Before trying to address the *Further from Target* attainment level, make sure you have defined the *No Change* level.

20. Although there are exceptions, I'm usually not assertive when I need to be.

A. Right now, when you need to stick up for yourself, occasionally you are assertive. Within the last couple of months, what do you think the best week has been in terms of your assertiveness?

B. Right now, when you need to stick up for yourself, occasionally you are assertive, and things would be worse if you weren't assertive at all during the week. Within the last couple of months, what do you think the best week has been in terms of your assertiveness?

C. Right now, when you need to stick up for yourself, occasionally you are assertive, and things would be worse if you were almost never assertive. Within the last couple of months, what do you think the best week has been in terms of your assertiveness?

D. Right now, when you need to stick up for yourself, occasionally you are assertive. What would be the best you think you could do in terms of being assertive?

Discussion of options.

A. Right now, when you need to stick up for yourself, occasionally you are assertive. Within the last couple of months, what do you think the best week has been in terms of your assertiveness?
   • Your comment defines the *No Change* level, and then moves the focus to the *Normal Level of Success.* Before going to the *Normal Level* we suggest that you first define the *Further from Target* attainment level.

B. Right now, when you need to stick up for yourself, occasionally you are assertive, and things would be worse if you weren't assertive at all during the week. Within the last couple of months, what do you think the best week has been in terms of your assertiveness?
   • This comment appropriately defines the *No Change* level, but the description of the *Further from Target* level is faulty. If the client is *almost* never assertive, what attainment level has the person achieved? The client's behavior would fall between the *No Change* and *Further from Target* attainment levels since it would not meet the criteria for either one.

C. Right now, when you need to stick up for yourself, occasionally you are assertive, and things would be worse if you were almost never assertive. Within the last couple of months, what do you think the best week has been in terms of your assertiveness?
   • You have provided workable descriptions of the *No Change* and *Further from Target* levels, and you have begun to address the *Normal Level of Success.*

D. Right now, when you need to stick up for yourself, occasionally you are assertive. What would be the best you think you could do in terms of being assertive?
   • Your description of the *No Change* level is good. But we recommend that you first address the other two levels before concentrating on the *Improved Level of Coping.*

21. Although people seem to walk all over me an awful lot, I probably haven't had a week where I was assertive more than half the time I needed to be.
    A. In the recent past the best you've been able to do, when needing to stick up for yourself, is to be assertive most of the time.
    B. In the recent past the best you've been able to do, when needing to stick up for yourself, is to be assertive up to half the time. So things would be better if you were able to be appropriately assertive more than half of the time.
    C. In the recent past the best you've been able to do, when needing to stick up for yourself, is to be assertive up to half the time. So things would be better if you were able to be appropriately assertive all of the time.
    D. In the recent past the best you've been able to do, when needing to stick up for yourself, is to be assertive up to half the time. So things would be better if you were simply able to be assertive whenever it is necessary.

Discussion of options.

A. In the recent past the best you've been able to do, when needing to stick up for yourself, is to be assertive most of the time.
   • You inaccurately describe the *Normal Level of Success.*

B. In the recent past the best you've been able to do, when needing to stick up for yourself, is to be assertive up to half the time. So things would be better if you were able to be appropriately assertive more than half of the time.
   • This response correctly describes the *Normal Level of Success* and the *Improved Level of Coping.*

C. In the recent past the best you've been able to do, when needing to stick up for yourself, is to be assertive up to half the time. So things would be better if you were able to be appropriately assertive all of the time.
   • According to the way you have defined the levels, there is a gap between the *Normal Level of Success* and the *Improved Level of Coping.*

D. In the recent past the best you've been able to do, when needing to stick up for yourself, is to be assertive up to half the time. So things would be better if you were simply able to be assertive whenever it is necessary.

• Your statement is true, but it fails to clearly indicate an attainment level for the *Improved Level of Coping.*

22. That's correct.
    A. Now that we have defined an objective and decided how to measure progress towards it, let's consider what you might do to become more assertive.
    B. So, your objective is to be appropriately assertive whenever it is necessary.
    C. So, we have named the objective, "Become more assertive when I need to stick up for myself." In terms of being assertive when needing to stick up for yourself, right now you are not doing it very often, and you would be doing better than your previous best if you became able to be appropriately assertive more than half of the time.
    D. So, we have named the objective, "Become more assertive when I need to stick up for myself." In terms of being assertive when needing to stick up for yourself, right now you are occasionally doing it, and things would be worse if you almost never did it. In the last couple of months, the best you've been able to do is to be appropriately assertive up to half the time. And things would be better if, when needing to stick up for yourself, you were assertive more than half of the time.

Discussion of options.

A. Now that we have defined an objective and decided how to measure progress towards it, let's consider what you might do to become more assertive.
    • Before returning to the task of problem solving, you should review the specifics of what you have accomplished with regard to objective setting.
B. So, your objective is to be appropriately assertive whenever it is necessary.
    • This comment is true, but it does not provide a review of what you have achieved in terms of objective setting.
C. So, we have named the objective, "Become more assertive when I need to stick up for myself." In terms of being assertive when needing to stick up for yourself, right now you are not doing it very often, and you would be doing better than your

previous best if you became able to be appropriately assertive more than half of the time.

- Your remarks include a partial description of the attainment levels. Rather than skipping so many details, it would be better to provide more complete coverage so that the client could have a better idea of what has been decided.

D. So, we have named the objective, "Become more assertive when I need to stick up for myself." In terms of being assertive when needing to stick up for yourself, right now you are occasionally doing it, and things would be worse if you almost never did it. In the last couple of months, the best you've been able to do is to be appropriately assertive up to half the time. And things would be better if, when needing to stick up for yourself, you were assertive more than half of the time.

- You provide a specific description of what has been decided with regard to the objective and its attainment levels.

SHORT-ANSWER QUESTIONS

Write your answer for each of the following questions.

1. List several possible goals focusing on changes that might be generally valued in one's everyday environment. Be sure to name goals that are under the person's control and that focus on what to improve rather than on what to avoid or decrease.
2. Choose one of the goals you listed in item 1 and identify at least two possible objectives that could assist in meeting the goal. Be certain that the objectives are under the person's control, focus on what to increase or improve, and are generally valued in one's everyday environment.
3. Ask a friend to role play a client who is interested in setting a goal or an objective. With your "client," implement the Observation Scaling procedure described in the chapter. Use the blank Observation Scales form (Figure 6.2) to name one target and to specify its four attainment levels. After completing the exercise, write down your thoughts about the process.

POSSIBLE ANSWERS FOR SHORT-ANSWER QUESTIONS

The answer-checking procedures remain the same as before.

- For each item, compare your answer to the one we provide.
- If you believe your answer is correct, you are done with that item.
- With any question for which you believe your answer is incorrect, consider our answer and, if needed, review relevant portions of the chapter. Keep your original answer that you now think is incorrect, but add to it a response that you believe would be correct.

1. Goals valued in one's everyday environment might include the following: increasing school and work attendance, expressing interest in others more often, and effectively fulfilling one's roles more often (such as parent, supervisor, student).
2. Possible objectives for the goal to, "Increase school and work attendance" include the following: improve time management, increase participation in enjoyable activities at school and at work, and increase sleep.
3. You should have an Observation Scales form completed for one goal or objective, and you should have several sentences that describe your thoughts about implementing the procedure.

FILL-IN-THE-RESPONSE QUESTIONS

Listed below are a series of client statements. For each one, write a worker response that you believe would facilitate Observation Scaling.

Up to this point in the chapter, Observation Scaling has been used to set attainment levels for objectives. In the following exercise, the focus will be on using Observation Scaling to set attainment levels for a goal.

1. You asked what I would like to be different in my life as a result of us working together. As I mentioned, I seem to be losing my temper a lot lately. Sometimes I just flip out. I don't want to keep on doing that. I want to be able to control myself.

2. A goal of doing something about my anger sounds good. I know I've got to make some changes. I usually don't seem to go longer than three or four days without having a tantrum.
3. I guess two weeks ago I went Sunday through Friday without blowing up.
4. That's right.
5. Yes, I would like to turn things around like that.

POSSIBLE ANSWERS FOR
FILL-IN-THE-RESPONSE QUESTIONS

For each response opportunity, there are several possible correct answers. We list two, and, as in previous chapters, we suggest you use them in the following manner.

- Look at our two answers and think about them.
- Consider relevant material covered in the chapter.
- Read the client statement again, then immediately read your answer and the two options listed here.
- Write another response that you believe might be an improvement on your first effort.
- Repeat this procedure for each of the remaining items.

1. • So, not letting irritating situations get the best of you is something you would like to strive for. What if we have that as a goal and name it, "Control anger more often?"
   • It sounds like you're talking about doing something other than lashing out when you are frustrated. How would you feel about having that as a goal and naming it, "Improve temper control?"
2. • Right now you usually can control your anger for three or four days, but that's generally about as long as you go. So things would be worse if during a week you were able to control your anger for less than three days in a row. Thinking back over the last two months, what is the longest you've been able to control your anger?
   • These days a typical week involves controlling your temper for three or four days before having a blowup. Matters would be worse if you were able to control your temper for only two days

or less. During the last couple of months, what has been the most number of days in a row you have had in which you controlled your temper?

3. • In the recent past, you've been able to control your anger for more than four days, but six days has been your maximum.
   • Six days has been the longest stretch of controlling your temper that you've had recently.
4. • And things would be better if you were able to control your anger for more than six days in a row.
   • So there would be improvement if you were to control your temper for a week or longer.
5. • Let's review what we have decided. The name of your goal is, "Control anger more often." Right now, you are able to control your anger for about three or four days in a row. Things would be worse if you started being able to control your anger for less than three days in a row. The best you've been able to do in the recent past is to control your anger for more than four days, up to a maximum of six days. And matters would be better if you were able to control your anger for more than six days.
   • Let me summarize what we've just done. The name of the goal is, "Increase temper control." You usually are controlling your temper for three or four days before having an outburst. Things would be worse if you controlled your temper for two days or less before having another blowup. The best you've done recently is control your temper for up to six days, and things would be better if you could maintain control for a week or more.

SUMMARY

Lasting improvement becomes more likely when you focus on changes that are naturally reinforced and when clients believe the targets seem worth working toward. Although it is possible to simply name an area in which progress is desired, setting written goals, objectives, and plans can be helpful if there will be ongoing meetings with the client. The Goals–Objectives–Plans record offers a format for specifying targets, and Observation Scaling provides a method for describing relevant levels of target attainment and measuring progress on those attainment levels.

Chapter 7

COMMUNICATING NONVERBALLY

Sometimes, the most important communication information arises out of what individuals do rather than out of what they say. Consequently, it is recognized that effective helping requires attention to nonverbal communication (e.g., Geller, Lehman, & Farber, 2002).

CHANNELS OF INFORMATION

Nonverbal communication is transmitted through several channels. Those include smell, touch, sight, and sound.

Smell

Although generally not a very informative channel, how clients smell can have some significance. Examples include emitting a strong body odor and having breath that smells of alcohol. Hopefully, this is a one-way channel when it is relevant, so that how you smell will never be a concern to your clients.

Touch

This is the most problematic channel of information for two reasons. First, the meaning of a touch can be misunderstood. And second, erotic contact always involves this channel.

Let's first consider potential misunderstandings. What does it mean when one is hugged, patted, or rubbed? The person initiating the hugging, patting, or rubbing may have one intent, and the individual receiving it may perceive a very different message. This can be disastrous when workers initiate physical contact they view as supportive but clients perceive as sexual. Such perception is especially likely when overly warm workers initiate the physical contact.

Unfortunately, there are times for some workers when the meaning of their physical contact is intended to be sexual. When such interactions occur, they are abusing their power and are behaving in a way that is clearly unethical.

How does one preclude the possibilities of misunderstood touch or actual erotic contact? There are many views on this issue (e.g., Smith, Clance, & Imes, 1998). Our opinion is a conservative one. We believe that, if you wish, it can be appropriate to shake hands with a client. Otherwise, our position is that workers should not touch adult clients. With regard to children, we believe that when a child initiates socially appropriate physical contact, there are times when reciprocation can be in the best interests of the child. For example, a child may become confused if a well-meaning hug is not returned by the worker. Touching children is a complex area, though, with many considerations to keep in mind. For an insightful discussion of nonerotic touch with children, we recommend the article by Fawn McNeil-Haber (2004) listed in the references.

Sight

This is a crucial channel of information. Vision provides you with a vast amount of data, including messages communicated through gestures, posture, facial expressions, clothing, hair style, and jewelry. And, of course, clients are able to note the same sort of information about you.

A bit later we will consider the meaning of some visual data. But for now, let's examine client reception of visual information from you as it relates to two areas: eye contact and your appearance.

How much eye contact on your part is appropriate? The answer, regardless of your cultural background or setting, is always less than 100 percent. You do not want to stare down your client. Consequently, the seating arrangement should be at an angle, rather than head-on, so that it is possible for you to comfortably look away and break eye contact. Looking at the person 70 to 90 percent of the time is appropriate for clients who feel comfortable with frequent eye contact. Two of the factors affecting such comfort are the person's cultural background and gender. Generally, men tend to desire less eye contact than women, and Asian Americans, Latino Americans, Native Americans, and African Americans tend to prefer less eye contact than Americans with European heritage.

On the issue of appearance, take your cues from coworkers or professional peers. Notice the range of clothing, hair styles, etc. that they display and stay within that range. Employ a style with which you are comfortable and which gives the sort of impression you wish to convey.

Sound

This is the primary source of information during the interaction. Most of what you learn will be communicated to you by what clients say and how they say it. Interpretation of auditory material is addressed in the next section.

MEANINGS OF NONVERBAL BEHAVIOR

Unfortunately, there is no dictionary of nonverbal behavior that reliably and validly translates the meaning of such signals. Consequently, in attempting to assign meaning to nonverbal events, a worker should consider what preceded the behaviors, what occurs with them, and what follows the actions. In most cases, the greatest significance is found in departures from the client's normal ways of talking and moving. Focusing on such departures, rather than on nonverbal traits, may be especially important if you are working with a client who has a cultural background different from your own. Rather than assigning clinical meanings to behaviors that occur throughout the interaction (for example, amount of eye contact), you may be more accurate if you reserve those interpretations for changes in the client's usual nonverbal demeanor.

Compared to verbal comments, nonverbal communication is less susceptible to both conscious subterfuge and unconscious editing. As a result, it often provides information that clients do not realize they are communicating. Although they understand the words they are saying, most individuals do not realize what they are doing nonverbally as they speak. Consequently, clients may convey messages that they have no intention of sending and that they are unaware of having given.

Although interpretation must be tentative and must be considered within the context of the interaction, there are some frequently occurring ways in which common messages are communicated nonverbally.

Anxiety

Speech Behavior
- faster speech and less silence
- repeating phrases
- frequent changes in train of thought and not completing sentences
- shifting voice volume
- stuttering

Body Messages
- more gesturing
- increased sweating and face flushing
- frequent shifting of seating position
- rapid repetitive behaviors (such as foot or finger tapping)

Anger

Speech Behavior
- fast and loud speech
- short durations with brief pauses

Facial Expressions
- frowning
- tensed lips
- chin and head thrust forward
- wide eyes

Grief, Sadness, and Depression

- slow speech
- frequent pauses

- sighing
- crying

Control

- increase in speed or volume of speech when the worker tries to talk
- increase in speed or decrease in volume of speech when discussing embarrassing topics
- when the worker is speaking, the individual purposefully appears disinterested or disdainful (such as rolling eyes, looking away, turning away, or demonstrative sighing)

Coldness and Distance

- not smiling
- little or no eye contact
- removing corrective glasses or wearing sunglasses
- closed posture (leaning back, arms folded across chest, or legs crossed high up)

Warmth and Openness

- smiling
- making eye contact
- removing sunglasses
- open posture (leaning forward, uncrossed legs, and arms not folded)

Interest and Attention

- timely "Mmhmms"
- appropriate head nods (Both "Mmhmms" and head nods work best when done occasionally. They become distracting when done too much.)

MULTIPLE-CHOICE QUESTIONS

Items 1-5 are with one client; questions 6-10 are with a second person; items 11-17 involve a third client; and questions 18-20 are with a fourth individual. Your instructions are the same as in the previous chapters.

- For each of the following client statements, choose the response or responses you believe would be appropriate. (Several items have more than one correct answer.)
- Indicate your selection in writing.
- Read the discussions of all four options.
- If you are correct, go to the next item.
- If you are incorrect, think about the explanations and, if necessary, review relevant portions of the chapter; then, once you better understand the issues, proceed to the next question.

1. Two months ago my husband got a great job opportunity in another state. We were all excited about it, sold our house, moved into a wonderful new home, got the kids settled in, enrolled them in school . . . then "poof," it was all gone. The company made cutbacks; my husband lost his job; we moved back here; and now we're living with my husband's parents.
A. There have been a few alterations in your lifestyle.
B. Boy, it sounds like you've been busy!
C. In a short period of time you've been through a lot of changes.
D. You must be devastated.

Discussion of options.

A. There have been a few alterations in your lifestyle.
- Characterizing the major transitions the client has experienced as "a few alterations in lifestyle" does not accurately reflect the magnitude of her situation.
B. Boy, it sounds like you've been busy!
- This response is unlikely to help the client engage in problem solving.
C. In a short period of time you've been through a lot of changes.
- Without any verbal or nonverbal expression of feeling, your factual reflection is the most appropriate response.

D. You must be devastated.
  • The person does not *have to* be anything, and until you receive some verbal or nonverbal expression of emotion, it is best not to assume you know how the client feels.

2. Having to live with my husband's parents is the most difficult part of this whole mess. I can't stand it there! But until he finds a new job, we're stuck. Oh I'm grateful, really, for a place to stay . . . if only he hadn't taken that stupid job! But I know it's not his fault. I can't hold him responsible for all that's happened, although I don't see why we have to live with *his* parents. But I'm not mad . . . really! (As the client was speaking she became louder and louder, began to lean forward, widened her eyes, and had a frown on her face.)
A. It's difficult for me to believe you're not angry with your husband because you look and sound pretty angry to me.
B. You don't want to blame your husband, but living with your in-laws is very hard for you.
C. Things certainly didn't turn out the way you had hoped, did they?
D. You're trying not to be angry with your husband, but deep down inside, you're furious.

Discussion of options.

A. It's difficult for me to believe you're not angry with your husband because you look and sound pretty angry to me.
  • A confrontational remark so early in the interaction is inappropriate and may evoke a hostile response from the client.
B. You don't want to blame your husband, but living with your in-laws is very hard for you.
  • Your empathic response will help create the supportive atmosphere this client needs to freely express her feelings.
C. Things certainly didn't turn out the way you had hoped, did they?
  • If rephrased as a reflection, this leading question would have been an appropriate response to the person's earlier statements but not to her most recent remarks.
D. You're trying not to be angry with your husband, but deep down inside, you're furious.

• Judging from the client's nonverbal behavior, your assumption may be right. She, however, may not agree with you. Since you are just getting to know this person, your underlying feeling comment is unnecessarily risky.

3. I just don't know how long I can go on this way. My husband's parents are nice people, but they interfere when I try to discipline my kids. And since his folks are retired, I can never be alone at their house. More and more I've been making excuses to run errands and be away. But sometimes I get so exasperated with the whole situation, I feel like I'm going to explode!
   A. As long as you're at your in-law's house your situation will be unbearable.
   B. You've mentioned leaving the house for short durations as one way of coping with your living arrangements. What else have you tried?
   C. The daily frustrations of a shared household are becoming harder to take.
   D. You're finding it more and more difficult to cope with the aggravation of living in someone else's home.

Discussion of options.

A. As long as you're at your in-law's house your situation will be unbearable.
   • You have exaggerated the client's circumstances, and because of your response, she may feel even worse about her situation.
B. You've mentioned leaving the house for short durations as one way of coping with your living arrangements. What else have you tried?
   • The client is just beginning to express her emotions and explain the details of her problem. You have cut off her efforts with this premature transition to the alternatives phase.
C. The daily frustrations of a shared household are becoming harder to take.
   • Your accurate reflection encourages further exploration.
D. You're finding it more and more difficult to cope with the aggravation of living in someone else's home.

• Focusing on the person's emotions will encourage her to continue disclosing her true feelings.

4. For now we're stuck at my in-laws until my husband gets a good job. If he doesn't find one soon, I don't know what's going to happen to us. We're getting so mixed-up as a family. The other day my little girl asked for a cookie before dinner. Simultaneously I said "No," and her grandmother said "Yes." She was so confused. My own daughter doesn't know who's in charge of her anymore. (Throughout these comments, the client paused often to sigh, and spoke slowly.)
What feeling does the client's present behavior most resemble?
A. Grief.
B. Anxiety.
C. Sadness.
D. Frustration.

Discussion of options.

A. Grief.
  • The person does exhibit some of the nonverbal signs for grief, but the conversation's verbal content does not indicate that she is grieving.
B. Anxiety.
  • An anxious person's speech pattern tends to be rapid with little silence and with frequent shifts in volume. These vocal behaviors are not present in the client's voice.
C. Sadness.
  • You have accurately interpreted the client's nonverbal activity as indicating sadness, which is a likely emotion in light of what she is saying.
D. Frustration.
  • Frustration is a feeling similar to anger and anxiety, both of which tend to include fast speech with few pauses. These elements are not present in the client's nonverbal behavior.

5. Sometimes I think things will never be the way they used to be. I just want to be a family again . . . my husband, the kids, and me, in our own place, taking care of our own needs. But I don't see

how that can happen anytime soon. (Nonverbal behavior continues as in item 4.)
A. At times you feel discouraged about being able to restore your family's traditional style of living.
B. The way things are now really angers you.
C. A moment ago you looked as if you might cry.
D. You really don't like your in-laws.

Discussion of options.

A. At times you feel discouraged about being able to restore your family's traditional style of living.
   • This reflection clearly captures what the client expressed.
B. The way things are now really angers you.
   • Although the person nonverbally conveyed anger earlier, she does not indicate feeling that way now. Instead, she seems to reveal sadness in her most recent verbal messages and nonverbal behavior.
C. A moment ago you looked as if you might cry.
   • Your remark fails to acknowledge what the individual just shared. She may conclude you have not been listening.
D. You really don't like your in-laws.
   • The heart of the client's message is not reflected in this response.

The next five items deal with a different woman.

6. Some stuff has been going on at work, uh, and it hasn't been, well, I don't know what to think about everything that's been going on at work. It's, it's . . . do you think this talking is going to help? Because once I had a friend who saw a counselor, and, well never mind. Anyway . . . is it?
The person's speech behavior best fits which description?
A. Controlling.
B. Distant.
C. Depressed.
D. Anxious.

Discussion of options.

A. Controlling.
- You don't have enough information about the client's non-verbal behavior to assume that she is trying to control the interaction. To make such an assessment, you would need to observe her voice volume and rate of speech when you try to speak or when she discusses a sensitive topic.

B. Distant.
- Nonverbal behaviors associated with coldness and distance are not suggested in this person's behavior.

C. Depressed.
- The nonverbal signs of depression, such as sighing, crying, slow speech, and frequent pausing, are not being displayed by the client.

D. Anxious.
- The individual's repetition of phrases, shifts in train of thought, and incomplete sentences, suggest that she is experiencing anxiety.

7. Well, of course it's going to help. I mean why else would people come to you, right? I guess I should get to the point. I'm really nervous at work . . . it's my boss. He's kind of been giving me trouble. Unless I start going out with him, he won't give me the raise I really need and deserve.

A. You seem concerned about the effectiveness of our interaction. What exactly are the circumstances that you hope we can work on together?

B. Unless you go out with him, he won't give you a raise?

C. You're feeling stressed by his unfair request.

D. Due to the conditions your boss has attached to getting a wage increase, you have grounds for a sexual harassment case.

Discussion of options.

A. You seem concerned about the effectiveness of our interaction. What exactly are the circumstances that you hope we can work on together?

- The client feels nervous and is having difficulty describing her problem to you. Asking her to get to the point while ignoring what she has already shared is not likely to develop the trust and rapport necessary for her to feel comfortable speaking with you.

B. Unless you go out with him, he won't give you a raise?
- There are two problems with this response. It fails to use fresh words, and it is an unnecessary question.

C. You're feeling stressed by his unfair request.
- You have accurately summarized the person's message. And by ignoring her anxious remarks about the value of talking to you, you have focused the interaction on the client and on her reason for coming to see you.

D. Due to the conditions your boss has attached to getting a wage increase, you have grounds for a sexual harassment case.
- Filing sexual harassment charges is not an option that the client has suggested. Consequently, this response reflects your opinion rather than hers.

8. It all started when I turned him down for a date. Ever since then, he's been pushing me to go out with him. And now that it's time for my annual review, he's been hinting that my chances for a raise would be better if I would be more "cooperative." He's such a perverted pig!

A. The way your boss has tried to coerce you really disgusts you.
B. The boss keeps badgering you despite your efforts to discourage him. What might be some reasons for his continued persistence?
C. You would never go out with someone like your boss, regardless of the benefits it would bring.
D. It's clear you don't want your boss to bother you anymore. What have you tried so far to get him to back off?

Discussion of options.

A. The way your boss has tried to coerce you really disgusts you.
- The way you've characterized the person's attitude toward her boss matches the intensity of her comments. Consequently, she is likely to continue sharing her feelings.

B. The boss keeps badgering you despite your efforts to discourage him. What might be some reasons for his continued persistence?

- Your initial reflection is good, but your question requires the person to guess what's going on in her boss' mind. The client may also interpret your probe as an accusation that she is doing something to provoke her boss' advances.

C. You would never go out with someone like your boss, regardless of the benefits it would bring.

- This judgmental response does not reflect the client's remarks and is unlikely to facilitate the problem-solving process.

D. It's clear you don't want your boss to bother you anymore. What have you tried so far to get him to back off?

- The client has just begun to express how she feels about what is going on at work. You should explore these emotions and circumstances before concentrating on options.

9. What type of Neanderthal chauvinist creep would do something like this? I shouldn't have to deal with his kind of attitude. You know he actually told me once that he was my only hope for a successful career? (The client expressed these thoughts in short bursts with brief pauses. Her lips were tense, her eyes were wide, and her head was thrust forward.)

What feeling does the person appear to be experiencing?

A. Control.

B. Sadness.

C. Anger.

D. Anxiety.

Discussion of options.

A. Control.

- The individual has not displayed indications of attempting to control the interaction.

B. Sadness.

- There are no nonverbal or verbal suggestions of sadness coming from the client.

C. Anger.

- Her nonverbal messages suggest she is angry. This possibility is even more likely when you consider what she is saying.

D. Anxiety.

- Earlier the client displayed characteristics associated with anxiety, but the clarity of her speech and other nonverbal signals hint that currently she does not feel tense or nervous.

10. There are three people on the review board, and as far as I can tell, my boss is the only one who might say anything negative about me. If the other two supervisors say it's OK, I get the raise. But even if I get the extra money, I'm still stuck with this boss who won't leave me alone. I don't think I can keep putting up with his harassment...it's hard just going to work anymore, knowing what I have to face.

A. Whatever happens with your raise, you dread the thought of continued pressure from your boss.

B. The wage issue is likely to be resolved in a positive way despite your boss, but you still face the difficulty of dealing with him on a regular basis.

C. Your chance for getting a raise is still pretty good, since the decision doesn't rest solely on your boss.

D. Life is coming to a standstill for you. Even the routine things, like going to work, have become a struggle.

Discussion of options.

A. Whatever happens with your raise, you dread the thought of continued pressure from your boss.

- You have made an appropriate reflection.

B. The wage issue is likely to be resolved in a positive way despite your boss, but you still face the difficulty of dealing with him on a regular basis.

- This productive response focuses the interaction on an area within the client's control, in this case her response to the boss's behavior.

C. Your chance for getting a raise is still pretty good, since the decision doesn't rest solely on your boss.

- You've pointed out a likely possibility with regard to the raise. Because this issue probably will work itself out (unlike the relationship with her boss), focusing the interaction on her salary is not the most efficient way to help your client.
D. Life is coming to a standstill for you. Even the routine things, like going to work, have become a struggle.
  - Since the person has made the effort to speak with you, she is not at a "standstill." And as far as you know, it is only her job, not everything, that is difficult.

Multiple choice questions 11-17 involve a different client.

11. (The following person is a 15-year-old sent to see you because of an angry outburst directed toward his teacher. In response to your greeting, he remains silently seated with his arms crossed and his eyes fixed on the floor.)
Your first impression of this teenager is that he is. . . .
A. Controlling.
B. Anxious.
C. Sad.
D. Cold and distant.

Discussion of options.

A. Controlling.
  - Without hearing his nonverbal speech patterns, you do not have the information necessary to make this conclusion.
B. Anxious.
  - The client is not expressing any of the nonverbal indicators that suggest anxiety.
C. Sad.
  - Because no sighing, crying, or slow speech is being demonstrated, nonverbal indicators of sadness are not being displayed.
D. Cold and distant.
  - The person's lack of eye contact, closed posture, and refusal to respond imply a cold and distant attitude.

12. Keeping in mind the young man's reluctance to talk and the nonverbal message he is sending, which worker comment is most likely to get a response?

A. How are you today?

B. You seem distant and aloof.

C. What are you feeling right now?

D. Did you have any trouble finding my office?

Discussion of options.

A. How are you today?
  - Judging from the client's reaction to your greeting, it is unlikely that this question will produce a response.

B. You seem distant and aloof.
  - This insightful observation will probably have no effect on the teenager's present disposition.

C. What are you feeling right now?
  - The person was unwilling to return your greeting. Consequently, it is doubtful that he will divulge his emotional state before developing some rapport with you.

D. Did you have any trouble finding my office?
  - Asking a simple closed question, to which the client knows the answer, has a good chance of eliciting a response. Even a minimal reply from the young man would be progress from his present silence.

13. The client shakes his head and mumbles "No" under his breath.

A. I'm glad you got here without any problems. Who sent you to see me?

B. Good, that's a start. Now tell me what brings you to see me today?

C. I take it that's a "No." It's important that you speak up next time if we are to communicate clearly.

D. So you made it here without any difficulty. Were you sent by your teacher?

Discussion of options.

A. I'm glad you got here without any problems. Who sent you to see me?
  - Your first comment suggests that you are listening and that you care. The second part of your remark is an easy ques-

tion that the young man should be able to answer, but it purposefully requires an intelligible response.

B. Good, that's a start. Now tell me what brings you to see me today?
  • Because the client has yet to give you a clear verbal reply, it is unlikely that you will receive an answer to your question.
C. I take it that's a "No." It's important that you speak up next time if we are to communicate clearly.
  • The person doesn't appear to want to communicate at all, much less clearly. Thus your request will probably be ignored and may be taken as being provocative, since he has made it verbally and nonverbally obvious that he doesn't wish to talk.
D. So you made it here without any difficulty. Were you sent by your teacher?
  • By recognizing the individual's response and by asking an easily answered closed question, you increase the chances of receiving a productive reply.

14. The principle, Mr. Jones, told me I had to come.
  A. What do you think are the reasons for Mr. Jones wanting us to talk?
  B. Did Mr. Jones tell you what he wanted us to talk about?
  C. You probably don't want to be here then, if Mr. Jones forced you to see me.
  D. I'm sure he had a good reason for sending you over. What do you think that purpose might be?

Discussion of options.

  A. What do you think are the reasons for Mr. Jones wanting us to talk?
    • If you believe that you can get a reasonable response by asking this open-ended question, it is worth a try. You may be rewarded with a productive answer.
  B. Did Mr. Jones tell you what he wanted us to talk about?
    • If you suspect the student is not quite ready to open up, asking this closed question is appropriate.
  C. You probably don't want to be here then, if Mr. Jones forced you to see me.

• By putting the focus back on the client's reluctance to talk, you are reminding him to be uncommunicative with you.
D. I'm sure he had a good reason for sending you over. What do you think that purpose might be?
• Your first statement implies you are taking sides on the issue, against the student and for Mr. Jones.

15. I got into some trouble with Mr. Kirby in math class.
   A. So the two of you aren't getting along. Tell me what happened.
   B. The reason you were so distant when we began talking is because you were sent here as a disciplinary measure.
   C. You and Mr. Kirby are having some difficulties. (Pause.) What's going on between you?
   D. You're having problems with Mr. Kirby. What other teachers do you have a hard time getting along with?

Discussion of options.

   A. So the two of you aren't getting along. Tell me what happened.
   • This combination of a reflection and a probe is likely to generate an informative response.
   B. The reason you were so distant when we began talking is because you were sent here as a disciplinary measure.
   • Your analysis is an inappropriate and unhelpful response.
   C. You and Mr. Kirby are having some difficulties. (Pause.) What's going on between you?
   • By reflecting the person's short explanation, you demonstrate that you're listening, and by pausing, you allow him the opportunity to respond. When he chooses not to reply, you effectively follow up with a question that should increase the amount of communication taking place.
   D. You're having problems with Mr. Kirby. What other teachers do you have a hard time getting along with?
   • Your question about the client's relationship with other teachers may sidetrack the interaction away from the incident with Mr. Kirby, which is the issue the student has been sent to discuss. Later, you may find a need to look for a behavior pattern involving other teachers, but for now you should address the topic at hand.

16. This morning, while I was sitting at my desk, I tried to throw a piece of garbage away, and it landed on the floor. I didn't pick it up 'cause I'd get in trouble for leaving my seat. Then Mr. Kirby walked over and said, "Why did you just leave that on the floor?" I tried to tell him, but he wouldn't listen. He just said, "Pick that up right now, young man . . ." just like my father.

   A. Mr. Kirby wouldn't hear your side of the story. Even though it was just an honest mistake on your part, you got in trouble with him anyway.

   B. Because of the similarities between the two men, you responded to the teacher as you would to your father.

   C. What led you to believe that getting up and putting the garbage in the trash would get you into trouble?

   D. The garbage on the floor was an accident, but you felt it was better to leave it there than to get up from your chair. When Mr. Kirby got on you about it, you were reminded of your dad.

Discussion of options.

   A. Mr. Kirby wouldn't hear your side of the story. Even though it was just an honest mistake on your part, you got in trouble with him anyway.
   • Stressing the unfairness of the person's circumstance may increase his hostility toward the teacher, and such heightened anger is unlikely to help the client.

   B. Because of the similarities between the two men, you responded to the teacher as you would to your father.
   • This response contains too much analysis. In order to facilitate exploration, you should stick to the content and feelings the person communicates verbally and nonverbally.

   C. What led you to believe that getting up and putting the garbage in the trash would get you into trouble?
   • The young man has finally made an effort at communicating, but because your question asks him to explain his decision in Mr. Kirby's class, he is more likely to defend his actions than to continue exploring his thoughts and feelings.

   D. The garbage on the floor was an accident, but you felt it was better to leave it there than to get up from your chair. When

Mr. Kirby got on you about it, you were reminded of your dad.
- You summarize the client's story, then focus on a potentially important area—the similarity the young man sees between his teacher and his father.

17. My dad *always* tells me what to do. He never listens. He just yells at me all the time. I can never do anything right for him, no matter what I do. I hate him. (In addition to speaking loudly through tensed lips, the student makes frequent eye contact and uncrosses his arms. He also rests his elbows on the chair's arms to support his forward lean.)
What attitude is the client taking with regard to you?
A. Anger.
B. Openness.
C. Anxiety.
D. Coldness and distance.

Discussion of options.

A. Anger.
- This emotion is probably the way the young man feels towards his father, and his nonverbal message is consistent with that feeling.
B. Openness.
- The client's verbal self-disclosure is consistent with the openness that his nonverbal behavior portrays.
C. Anxiety.
- The client is not giving nonverbal signs associated with anxiety.
D. Coldness and distance.
- The involvement that the person is showing, both verbally and nonverbally, suggests he no longer is trying to be unfeeling and indifferent. Consequently, coldness and distance do not describe his current attitude.

The remaining multiple-choice items focus on a different person.

18. My husband is obsessed with his ex-wife. No matter what I do it's never enough because she would have done it better. I'm sick of

being compared to her. If she's so great, why isn't he with her now?

A. You're tired of being measured against your husband's former wife.
B. Although he's married to you now, you think you would be better off if he still was with his previous wife.
C. Your husband thinks you're inferior to his ex-wife.
D. There is no way for you to please your husband as much as his other wife did.

Discussion of options.

A. You're tired of being measured against your husband's former wife.
  • You have accurately reflected both the client's feelings and the circumstances.
B. Although he's married to you now, you think you would be better off if he still was with his previous wife.
  • This response is an unsubstantiated interpretation of what the person has said.
C. Your husband thinks you're inferior to his ex-wife.
  • You are focusing on the husband rather than on your client.
D. There is no way for you to please your husband as much as his other wife did.
  • Concentrating on the person's inability to fulfill her spouse's expectations is overly pessimistic.

19. I just don't know what my husband expects from me. He's constantly bringing her up, talking about the things *she* would do or say. I'm beginning to wonder if he really loves me. He does this all the time, and I don't want to hear it anymore.
A. He's constantly bringing her up, and you don't want to hear it anymore.
B. The way your husband repeatedly brings up his ex-wife really annoys you. Tell me about a recent incident when that occurred.
C. Based upon his behavior towards you, you've concluded that your husband doesn't love you.
D. Your husband carrying on about his ex-wife saddens you.

Discussion of options.

A. He's constantly bringing her up, and you don't want to hear it anymore.
- This remark does not use fresh words.

B. The way your husband repeatedly brings up his ex-wife really annoys you. Tell me about a recent incident when that occurred.
- Your reflection and your request for an example constitute an appropriate combination response.

C. Based upon his behavior towards you, you've concluded that your husband doesn't love you.
- The client said she was unsure about her husband's love. But her uncertainty is not reflected in your comment.

D. Your husband carrying on about his ex-wife saddens you.
- You do not have enough indicators to conclude that she is sad.

20. A recent incident. . . . Well . . . um . . . I guess it was last week sometime. I had gone shopping, and he had come home from work while I was out. As soon as I walked in the door he started yelling at me, saying that when he gets home from work I should be waiting for him . . . like his ex-wife used to do. I was so fed up, I just slammed the door and stomped out of the room. (As the client spoke, her voice became louder, her lips tensed, and her eyes widened.)

What does the person's nonverbal behavior communicate?

A. Anxiety.

B. Warmth.

C. Anger.

D. Distance.

Discussion of options.

A. Anxiety.
- The client's nonverbal messages suggest she is feeling something other than anxiety.

B. Warmth.
- Warmth is not being communicated by the person's nonverbal activity.

C. Anger.
  • The client's loud speech and facial expressions indicate she is angry.
D. Distance.
  • Her demeanor does not suggest coldness or distance.

SHORT-ANSWER QUESTIONS

Write your answer for each of the following questions.

1. Name four channels of nonverbal communication.
2. Create a scenario in which a client is sending a nonverbal message by the way she smells.
3. Invent a situation involving a person whose appearance communicates important information.
4. How should professional workers present themselves in terms of their appearance?
5. Name some of the speech patterns and body language associated with anxiety.
6. Give several ways that individuals nonverbally express grief, sadness, or depression.
7. State two clues that may suggest a client is trying to control the interaction.
8. Cite some behaviors that might imply a person is feeling cold and distant towards you.
9. Name some nonverbal ways you can demonstrate interest and attention to clients.

POSSIBLE ANSWERS FOR SHORT-ANSWER QUESTIONS

The answer-checking procedures remain the same as before.

• For each item, compare your answer to the one we provide.
• If you believe your answer is correct, you are done with that item.
• With any question for which you believe your answer is incorrect, consider our answer and, if needed, review relevant portions of

the chapter. Keep your original answer that you now think is incorrect, but add to it a response that you believe would be correct.

1. Nonverbal messages can be transmitted through smell, touch, sight, and sound.
2. A young woman enrolled in a program to quit smoking smells distinctly of tobacco while proudly reporting that she has not smoked, or been anywhere near smokers, in over two weeks. The cigarette odor in her clothes, hair, and breath suggests that perhaps she is not being honest.
3. A young boy, whose mother is being accused of child neglect, plays on his swing set during a surprise visit to his home. He appears clean, and his energetic activity suggests he is in good health. His hair is brushed and was cut recently enough so that it does not hang in his eyes. His fingernails are also neatly trimmed. The jacket he wears is the right size and is appropriate to the weather conditions. His shoes are worn (but have no holes), seem to fit, and are tied with double knot bows. He wears a pair of pants durable enough for outdoor play, and when he smiles his teeth appear clean and healthy. Overall, the little boy's appearance suggests that someone is adequately meeting his physical needs.
4. Workers should dress in similar ways to their peers and should avoid extremes in attire and hairstyles while on the job.
5. When anxious, individuals often talk quickly with few breaks, repeat themselves, and frequently switch both volume levels and topics. They may perspire, increase gesturing, move their sitting postures, and engage in nervous foot or finger tapping.
6. If they are feeling down, people may sigh and cry often, have slow speech, and pause frequently when talking.
7. If a client increases volume when the worker tries to speak and talks faster or quieter when discussing an embarrassing topic, the individual probably wants control of the interaction.
8. You might infer someone is cold and distant when the person doesn't smile, won't make appropriate eye-contact, continues to wear sunglasses, or maintains a closed posture.
9. Attentive and interested workers occasionally say "Mmhmm," make appropriate eye-contact, and at times, nod their heads while their clients are speaking.

FILL-IN-THE-RESPONSE QUESTIONS

Listed below are a series of client statements. For each one, write a worker response that you believe would be appropriate.

1. (The client is on the edge of her chair, has wide eyes, and talks through tightly clenched teeth.) Last night when I came home to the apartment that my boyfriend and I share, there it was . . . all my stuff stacked up outside. Then when I tried my key, I realized the lock had been changed. On the door was this note that said, "It's over." I was shocked! How could he do this to me?

2. The more I think about it, the more upset I get. I don't know why he broke it off, and I can't believe the way he did it! You would think that after being together for two years, he could at least have the decency to tell me in person. The whole thing makes me furious.

3. I guess I'm hurt more than anything. I really thought he loved me. He told me he could never get along without me. I don't know if he was lying to me the whole time, or if . . . if he's met someone else. (The person's speech has become quiet and slow, and her last remarks were interrupted by deep breaths.)

4. I know I should hate him for this, and sometimes I do. But. . . . (The client begins to cry and, for the moment, is unable to continue.)

5. I'm so mixed-up. I don't know where to go from here. Everything is a mess . . . my life, my future, my feelings, everything! Nothing seems right anymore.

6. It just hurts so bad . . . to lose everything we had together. The hopes and the dreams we shared . . . gone, changed overnight. We talked about getting married! So much for "happily ever after," huh?

POSSIBLE ANSWERS FOR
FILL-IN-THE-RESPONSE QUESTIONS

For each response opportunity, there are many possible correct answers. We list two, and as in previous chapters, we suggest you use them in the following manner.

- Look at our two answers and think about them.
- Consider relevant material covered in the chapter.
- Read the client statement again, then immediately read your answer and the two options listed here.
- Write another response that you believe might be an improvement on your first effort.
- Repeat this procedure for each of the remaining items.

1. • You're outraged at his lockout.
   • It's infuriating to be treated so shabbily.
2. • Your anger goes off the scale when you consider the manner in which your boyfriend cut off the relationship.
   • You're very angry and also mystified about your boyfriend's actions.
3. • Separating from your boyfriend is painful for you.
   • You're unsure why your boyfriend broke up with you, but, whatever the reason, you still ache inside.
4. • (You place a tissue box near the client before responding. After a brief pause, you make the following comment.) At other times you feel differently.
   • (After putting a tissue box within the person's reach, you allow the silence to continue so she can compose herself enough to go on.)
5. • There are so many feelings and so many changes, that you're not sure what step to take next.
   • Things aren't turning out the way you planned.
6. • Right now, you feel devastated.
   • You're grieving the loss of a future that until yesterday you had envisioned with anticipation and joy.

SUMMARY

There are occasions when you can learn from the nonverbal behavior of your clients. For example, they may reveal something to you by the way they smell or because of how they look. At the same time, you are also *sending* nonverbal messages. Your appearance, for instance, gives information about how you wish to be perceived. And as a worker, your goal should be to look professional within the range of styles employed by your colleagues.

In addition to sight and smell, communication can also occur through the nonverbal channel of touch. Since touching can be easily misunderstood, it is our position that you should not touch your clients except to shake hands or to reciprocate touch from a child.

Another nonverbal source of information is sound. You often can learn a great deal by paying attention to how words are said.

Since nonverbal messages usually are uncensored, they may allow you to develop additional insights regarding clients. But your interpretations of nonverbal signals may not always be accurate. Consequently, evaluations of nonverbal messages should be done tentatively, taking into account the nature of the interaction and the client's usual patterns of communication.

While recognizing the limitations on understanding nonverbal signals, there are some fairly consistent nonverbal patterns associated with specific feelings. Examples include: anxiety, anger, grief, sadness, depression, coldness, distance, control, warmth, openness, interest, and attention.

Chapter 8

SCHEDULED APPOINTMENTS

Recognizing that supportive helping is used in a variety of human service settings, we would like to address considerations that arise before, during, and after scheduled office appointments. All of the topics in this chapter relate to such interactions, and many of the following observations also have applications to other sorts of contacts with clients.

BEFORE THE APPOINTMENT

Prior to the appointment time there are several factors to be considered. They include scheduling of the interaction, worker preparation for the session, arrangement of the physical setting, initial client expectations, and potential client fears.

Appointment Scheduling

Both you and the client should have the same understanding of when the appointment is to begin and how long it is expected to last. If the length of your interaction has not been discussed with the person prior to your meeting, you ought to describe the anticipated duration at the start of the contact.

Scheduled appointments should be set at times that are convenient for clients and for you. Failing to do this can have several negative effects. (1) The clients may not show up. (2) You or your clients may be late. (3) If the meetings do take place, participants may become distracted during the interactions. Clients may find themselves focusing on worries such as repercussions for missing work, transportation difficulties, or unsatisfactory child care arrangements. And you may find yourself absorbed with thoughts of unfinished work, ongoing events that should involve you, or time pressures following the interaction. If you or your clients feel stressed by poor timing of interactions, it is difficult to remain fully focused on the tasks at hand.

When the appointed time arrives, the expectation is that you will meet. Even if you have done your best to schedule the interaction for a convenient time, the client may be late or may fail to appear at all. If you wish to decrease such occurrences, you should have a relevant, agency-approved appointment policy that you share with clients. The policy can be included with other written information that you may provide.

As suggested above, sometimes it is the worker who is not available when the appointment time arrives. That may result from any number of situations. Regardless of how valid the reasons may be, not starting an appointment on time suggests to clients that other priorities are more important to you. When those demands on your time lead to chronic lateness, clients frequently respond by coming late themselves. Once that begins to occur, you have lost control of your schedule.

Although there are many possibilities with regard to setting appointment times, here is our position. Take a realistic look at your responsibilities and schedule clients at times you actually will be available to see them. Keep to your schedule. If a crisis should arise, your clients will understand. But recurring "crises" mean you must redesign your schedule.

Worker Preparation

If you know an appointment is scheduled, you have an opportunity to prepare for it. One common preparatory activity is to read your written report on the preceding meeting. Other possibilities include reviewing the following sorts of material: previously established goals, objectives, and plans; data from other professionals or organizations; assessment information; and professional literature regarding topics that are relevant to the case.

Having examined appropriate material, you can prepare an interview format. There are many ways to do that, but here is our preference. At the top of the page enter the client's name, the session number, and the date. If it is the first session, also enter the person's date of birth and age. Down the left side of the page, write words or brief phrases (skipping a couple of lines between each entry) to indicate topics to be covered during the session. When done in this way, the interview format fulfills two functions. First, it serves as a plan for structuring the interaction, thereby enhancing your confidence as you begin the interaction. Second, it provides a method of organizing what you record during the interaction, so that your notes are entered next to the topics to which they relate.

The interview format can provide an anticipated structure, but it should be used with flexibility. For example, if the client is in the midst of unexpected stress, such as the sudden serious illness of a family member, you may discard the anticipated topics and focus on issues associated with the new situation. On the other hand, if the client continually brings up alternative topics that prevent you from addressing crucial issues, it may be necessary to discuss the consequences of not dealing with the areas being avoided.

Arrangement of the Physical Setting

Arranging the physical setting may largely be outside of your control. Nevertheless, here are some issues to keep in mind, and, to the extent possible, you may wish to implement some of these practices.

Auditory and visual distractions should be eliminated or reduced to their minimum. For example, it may be possible to cover interior windows that open onto other rooms. To mask disturbing sounds, "white noise" can be helpful. Often such masking noise is provided by air conditioners, fans, heaters, computer components, or other devices. If there is a need for additional sound masking, another possibility is using a "white noise" machine (a device with a small fan inside that makes a constant sound).

If you meet with clients in an interviewing room or private office that has a door, there should be a way of indicating to others that you are not to be interrupted. In some settings that may simply mean having the door shut, while in other circumstances you may need a "session in progress/do not disturb" sign. If in a nonemergency situation someone should knock on the door or enter the room, you ought to assertively explain that you are speaking with a client, and you should politely ask the person to leave. Later, you can tell the individual that, unless there is an emergency, you are not to be disturbed when you are with clients.

If there is a telephone in the room, others in the organization should understand that during a session you are only to be called when there is a serious emergency that requires *your* attention. If these interruptions are frequent, you and your colleagues must plan alternate ways of handling such "emergencies."

For the unfortunate arrangement in which there is a phone in the interviewing room that can be activated directly by any caller, there may be a distinctive sound that indicates the call is from an outside line. When you hear that signal, you have the choice of answering the phone or letting it ring. We let it ring.

Another aspect of your physical setting is how you keep track of time. It is helpful if there is a clock in the room that is easy for you to observe in an unobtrusive manner. Being able to easily check on the time allows you to pace the interaction as needed. Awareness of time becomes especially important with regard to ending the interaction, which is a topic addressed later in the chapter.

If there is a desk in the room, the bulk of it should not be between you and the client. Acceptable alternatives include the following: you and the client sitting around a corner of the desk, putting the desk to the wall so that it is impossible to sit on the opposite side from you, or arranging seats so that no one is at the desk. Whether or not there is a desk, you should avoid facing your client straight on and opt instead for sitting at an angle. This allows you to break eye contact in a natural and comfortable way.

Generally, men prefer greater physical distance than women. Whether or not this is true for the particular men and women you work with, a choice of seating options allows clients to select the arrangement with which they feel most comfortable.

Another consideration with regard to physical arrangements is your safety. Clients sometimes assault workers, and your organization must anticipate that possibility. If you cannot immediately summon effective assistance by yelling for help, there should be a help button in the room or on a device that you carry. Pushing that button should result in trained individuals immediately coming to your aid.

To the extent possible, the room should be free of objects that could be used as weapons. Letters openers, note spindles, and scissors ought to be taboo. And other objects that can be thrown or used to strike, such as lamps and clocks, often can be secured to the floor or wall.

Thus far, we have been considering preappointment events from your perspective. But clients also have their own issues relating to anticipated appointments. For ongoing clients you usually know what those are, so let's limit our attention to factors that can influence the first appointment.

Initial Client Expectations

If the client is seeking assistance, where does this interaction fall in that effort? When the contact with you is the first attempt to get help, the person may be fairly optimistic. On the other hand, when the individual has been to many professionals and has struggled for some time, pessimism may be the predominant attitude.

Another influence on client expectations is how the person came to contact your organization. If there was a referral or if word of mouth resulted in the appointment, what did others tell the client about you or about your organization? Such information can have a profound impact on the person's expectations.

Finally, what has been the nature of the individual's previous interactions with your organization? For example: What was the time period between requesting the appointment and seeing you? If the person has interacted with other staff members in the organization, what was the quality of those contacts? If the client has been in a waiting room just prior to seeing you, how was that experience? All of those factors can contribute to the individual's expectations and demeanor when you meet for the first time.

Potential Client Fears

Sometimes clients fear what may happen when they first come to see you. They may feel inadequate, fear rejection, or be worried about losing control over decisions that affect them. An excellent way of responding to such concerns is to communicate empathy, warmth, and genuineness. Through your words and actions you can convey understanding, respect, acceptance, and straightforward honesty. When clients see you as an empathic and caring person who can be trusted, they are less likely to feel incompetent, judged, or powerless.

Another concern that clients sometimes have is confidentiality. They may wonder who will learn about what they are telling you.

Consequently, how that information will be handled is an area you should be prepared to address.

Breaking confidentiality can be appropriate if such action is necessary to protect the client or others from clear danger. In addition, human service professionals typically are required to report cases of child abuse. So, if you must choose between maintaining confidentiality or preserving life, the appropriate action is to preserve life.

Generally, those who seek service are the clients of your organization and not of its individual staff members. If that is the view at your setting, it always is proper (1) to keep case records that are the property of the organization and (2) to seek consultation on the case from other appropriate staff members in the program.

When you need confidential information from resources outside of your organization or when such resources need confidential information from you, your organization should have a release-of-information procedure for you to follow. That usually involves the client (or guardian) signing a release-of-information form. Such a practice then allows for communication between professionals, as specified in the release.

On the other hand, it is never appropriate to discuss identifiable clients in the presence of persons outside the organization who are not involved in the case. Consequently, you should not talk about clients in the following settings: restaurants and other eating facilities, public modes of transportation, and informal social gatherings such as parties and outings. In our experience, staff members discussing clients in those settings is the most common ethical violation by human service professionals.

DURING THE APPOINTMENT

During the interaction itself there are several issues to keep in mind. They include setting the stage, range and depth of topics, transitions, responding to client questions, silence, note taking, and ending the interaction.

Setting the Stage

If this is your initial contact with the client, establishing a tone for the interaction is important. Since it is a professional relationship, we recommend that you call adults by their last name with an appropriate prefix, such as Mr., Ms., Mrs., or Miss. When clients express a desire for a different form of address (for example, using the person's first name), you should comply with that preference.

In settings where there is a waiting room, you can go to that area, introduce yourself, shake hands (if you wish), and show the person to the room you will be using. After entering that room and offering the person a seat, you may want to help the client become acclimated to the situation by engaging in some light social conversation that focuses on the person's experience regarding some nonthreatening issue. For example, you might say, "How was it finding our building?" or "What is the weather like?" (Of course, you would only ask the latter question if you do not have ready access to an outside window.)

After the individual has had a chance to adjust to the surroundings, you may need to explain your role and/or the purpose of the interaction. If either of these is necessary, you should provide the information in a straightforward and noncondescending way.

When the client has had a chance to take in the situation and when you believe the person understands your role and the purpose of the interaction, it is time to initiate the body of the interview. You can do that by stating an open probe or question, such as, "Tell me your reason for contacting us" or "What brings you in today?" (As mentioned in Chapters 4 and 5, we recommend that you do not use words such as "problem" or "difficulty" in your opening. Such phrasing unnecessarily begins the body of the interview with a negative tone.)

The beginnings of subsequent interactions tend to be simpler for several reasons. Because you now know each other, your waiting room greeting may be briefer. Since the client is now familiar with what to expect, the trip to the session room probably requires little or no explanation. Once seated there, you may not need to discuss your role or the purpose of the interaction, and there may be less need to spend time on social conversation.

Range and Depth

As we have emphasized, supportive helping addresses (1) the circumstances described by individuals and (2) the emotional reactions of clients to those situations. You address both of those areas each time you engage in supportive helping. Time is precious though, and you want to obtain the maximum benefit out of the minutes available.

Fortunately, your helping skills allow you to cover a wide range of material, while also enabling you to focus the interaction on particular subjects. Deciding when to slow down and when to move along is a crucial aspect of being an astute worker.

Each term in his helping skills class, K.F. used to tell the following metaphorical story about range and depth. While doing his predoctoral internship at the University of Florida, he enjoyed occasional trips to Cross Creek (the site of author Marjorie Kinnan Rawlings' former home and the setting for much of her writing). In recent years the creek has dried up, but it was a stream that linked Lochloosa Lake and Orange Lake when he made his visits. He would rent a kayak or a canoe and spend the afternoon fishing. Although he usually had some limited success, he marveled at the fishing skills displayed by some of the local inhabitants.

Several fish-eating hawks usually could be seen in the skies above the lakes. After cruising for awhile and surveying events, a hawk would spot a noteworthy activity. At that point the bird would begin to dive toward the action in the water. Sometimes circumstances became less promising and the hawk would pull out of the dive. Many times though, the hunter continued down until hitting the water, often coming up with a fish as a result of the foray.

The hawks of Cross Creek know about the efficient application of range and depth. And you, as a skilled helper, should also be familiar with those concepts and should use them for the benefit of your clients. Just as a hawk cannot survive without diving, a supportive helper must go for depth. But the hawk also knows that staying at the water's surface would severely limit future rewards, so the hunter climbs back into the sky. Likewise, you must help your clients cover sufficient ranges of topics so that they do not miss out on important opportunities for change.

During the parts of an interaction in which wide coverage is your intent, an effective style is to rely on factual reflections and on reflection-interrogation combinations that end with broad open questions. Such efforts communicate attention, and they also suggest that you are interested in additional information. Consequently, clients tend to move quickly along as they focus on descriptions of events.

On the other hand, when you want to explore an issue more closely, you can use feeling reflections and you can request specific examples. Such actions tend to slow the pace as the person examines the area in greater depth. You now are covering less ground, but the material addressed tends to be significant. For example, one of us had an initial meeting with a rehabilitation client in which the first few minutes of the interview addressed the following subjects: being unemployed, details of an injury-causing automobile accident, rehabilitation experiences, and no longer being head of the household. Reflection of feelings arising out of the recent role reversal led to powerful expressions of loss and regret, and the pace of the interview slowed as that transition was explored in greater detail. Eventually the interaction moved to additional issues: family members who had died from heart attacks, and the client's fear of dying from a heart attack. When the worker reflected emotions associated with this last area, the tempo again slowed as the client shared terrifying premonitions regarding the imminent end of his life.

Sometimes you reflect a feeling and the client responds with new unemotional descriptions of events. When that happens, it usually is most productive to be like a hawk that pulls out of a dive. Activity has calmed, and it normally is safe to continue with factual reflections and broad open questions. But if you reflect an emotion and the client responds by elaborating on that feeling or by discussing additional emotions, then it may be time to slow down and cover that area in greater depth.

Transitions

When the interaction moves from one topic to another you are making a transition. Such shifts can come about for a number of reasons, including a need to address additional topics in the time remaining, the diminishing productivity of the current discussion, or a need for more background information before an issue can receive proper attention.

On those occasions when the client initiates the transition, you have the option of going with the change or immediately bringing the person back to the topic at hand. Although you must judge each interaction on its own merits, our preference is usually to go where the client leads.

If the abandoned area requires more attention, you can return to the topic once you discover where the client wants to go. For example, during an intake interview conducted by one of us, in response to the question, "Have you ever received any counseling or psychotherapy?"

the client launched into a description of physical rehabilitation experienced by his father. Since a description of previous mental health treatment was required by the agency, the worker listened to the father story for a short time, gave a factual reflection regarding it, then brought the client back to the question about previous psychotherapy.

If you are the one initiating the transition, you have two fundamental choices in terms of phrasing. You can link the present and future topics, or you can keep them independent.

Let's say you are in an initial interaction with a young mother who is having problems with her children and with her husband. So far, the interview has centered on her difficulties with the children, but now you want to change the focus to her marital relationship. You could link the two topics by summarizing the initial material, then saying, "The disobedience of your children has you at your wits end. Another source of frustration is the relationship with your husband. I'd like you to tell me how things are going with him." The key in formulating such a link is to find a bridge that will lead from the old topic to the new one. In this example, the bridge was the client's feeling of frustration.

It also is possible to make a transition in which the two topics remain separate. With the preceding client, the worker might summarize the initial information, then say, "You have described your concerns with regard to your children. Let's now turn to the relationship with your husband. Tell me how things are going with him."

When compared to transitions that do not relate preceding and future subjects to each other, link transitions are generally smoother and feel better in the interaction. On the other hand, relating two topics takes more work than simply letting them remain independent, and there may be times when an idea for a bridge does not come to you. Nevertheless, looking for bridges is probably to your benefit since link transitions may contribute to the client's perception of you as a skilled professional.

When the Client Asks You Questions

When confronted with client questions, many workers reply with a pat response such as, "We're not here to talk about me, we're here to talk about you" or "What I think isn't important, it's what you believe that matters." Unfortunately, such responses often detract from the genuineness of the worker and suggest that the staff member is merely playing a role rather than being sincere with the client.

If you feel comfortable with the client's question, it is often easy to provide a brief answer, then return the focus to the person. For instance, if the client asks, "If you were facing what I'm dealing with at work, would you quit your job?" you could say, "I might look for another job, but I probably would be reluctant to leave my old one until I actually had a new position. But you are the one who must decide whether you can continue awhile longer with your present employer. Let's take a look at the pros and cons of quitting."

Sometimes there may be a hidden message in a client's question. If that is the case, you may want to look below the surface and formulate a reply that addresses what the person really may be asking. For example, if the individual says, "How long have you worked here?" the real question may be, "Can you help me?" Consequently, you might offer a response such as, "This is my first month here. Although I'm new with this organization, I've had previous experience in similar settings. At those places I worked with a number of clients who dealt with issues like the ones you are confronting, and most of those individuals made substantial progress in coping with the challenges facing them."

Silence

When a client is silent, there may be several reasons for the person not talking. Here are some possibilities:

- nothing else to say on the topic;
- deciding what to say next;
- considering the validity of something you have said;
- feeling anxious about what is happening in the interaction;
- trying to get a response from you;
- being uncooperative.

The best clue to the meaning of clients' silence is what was going on just before the silence began. Depending on what has been happening, your response to silence could be one of the following:

- "Mmhmm" (if the silence has been only a few seconds);
- a reflection of the client's last remark;
- if a question of yours preceded the silence, rephrasing your question;

• a summary of the topic you have been discussing;
• a reflection of the silence, such as, "You're finding it hard to talk;"
• a comment regarding the silence, such as, "I wonder what the reason is for your silence."

At times the person choosing to be silent may be you, rather than the client. There can be occasions within an interaction when it is appropriate to use silence as an ambiguous stimulus. Employed in this way, worker silence puts pressure on the client without giving any direction as to what the person should discuss. But in order to have such an effect, you must convey the impression that you are comfortable with the silence and that you clearly are waiting for the *client* to speak.

Note Taking

Most human service interactions involve note taking, and there is some empirical evidence that indicates this activity can have an adverse effect on the interaction (e.g., Hartley, 2002). In order to minimize possible detrimental influences, we offer several considerations to keep in mind.

If you are using an interview format as described earlier in the chapter, you can employ the outline as a guide for note taking. Next to each entry you and the client discuss, write down key words or short phrases that will remind you of what transpired. In most instances, the purpose of your writing is simply to jog your memory rather than to create a verbatim transcript of what the person said.

While taking notes, you should keep your attention centered on the client. Continuing to focus on the client is possible if the notes you record are sparse. You will find that you can make brief notations without looking at what you are writing and still be able to read the material after the interview is over.

When a worker takes copious notes, it is impossible to attend fully to the client as the person is speaking. Consequently, the staff member may stop taking notes during intense episodes of the interaction, then return to detailed writing when the client moves to less crucial material. If that is what happens, at the end of the session the worker has a detailed set of notes describing the least important information presented by the person.

Occasionally clients ask what is written on your page. Our way of handling such requests is to hand the paper to the client. If this also becomes your practice, you must follow one guideline: never write anything on the page that you would not be perfectly willing for the person to see. Then, if an individual becomes curious about what is on the paper, you can simply show the material to the client.

We believe there are two times you *must* take notes: (1) when the client provides you with specific information such as names, dates, or addresses; and (2) when you promise that you or your organization will take a certain action. In both of those instances, you need a clear, written record of the material exchanged in the interaction.

Ending the Session

With about ten minutes remaining in your allotted time, you should begin thinking about wrapping up the interaction. You can dampen affect by moving away from feeling reflections and ceasing the exploration of emotions. If the client brings up a new issue that deserves attention but is not urgent, you can state that it will be a topic for your next session. (Be sure to jot it down in your notes.) When a recap of the current meeting seems appropriate, you can summarize what has been accomplished by reviewing decisions made, insights developed, and questions or issues that require additional discussion.

Recall from Chapter 4 that when plans have been negotiated, you should ask the client to describe the tasks that are to be accomplished. Although it is acceptable for you to summarize the plan, having the *client* do it is essential. When the client summarizes, you can verify that the person accurately understands what is to be done. If misunderstandings become evident, you and the client can correct them, so that by the end of the session you have a shared view of actions to be taken.

AFTER THE APPOINTMENT

Immediately after the client leaves, you should write a report of the interaction. We believe your job as a worker is not over until you produce a written account of the contact, and others agree with this opinion (e.g., Prieto & Scheel, 2002). Consequently, we recommend that you discourage interruptions during your report-writing time. Also keep in mind that if you routinely let yourself become sidetracked by additional activities, too much time will pass before you write your account. When you finally sit down to do it, you may produce a faulty report. Potential problems include omitting information, incorrectly describing events, and confusing one client with another.

In most settings, clients have a legal right to your reports. If this turns out to be the case where you work, the most prudent policy is to write your account as if the client will see it.

There are a number of approaches to writing session notes (e.g., Prieto & Scheel, 2002). The format for reports varies from one program to another. Some organizations leave the report style up to the individual staff member, while other programs have specific guidelines that must be followed.

An example of a procedure that involves a medium amount of structure is the SOAP style of progress note writing (e.g., Cameron & Turtle-Song, 2002). With this approach there are four paragraphs, one for each of the following topics: Subjective, Objective, Assessment, and Plan.

Within each of these paragraphs, you can also order the information according to past, present, and future. Arranging the material in a chronological sequence is optional. If you do choose to order the material from past to future, a particular time frame is included only if there is relevant information regarding that period.

In outline form, here is a way information can be organized in a SOAP report.

SUBJECTIVE (S)–the story told to the worker by the client and
 others
 Past–account of the past
  (e.g., how the problem started)
 Present–account of the present situation
  (e.g., how things are now)
 Future–account of expectations and goals
  (e.g., career aspirations, marriage intentions)
OBJECTIVE (O)–factual information
 Past–known past facts based on written documentation
  (e.g., employment history, previous treatment, grades)

Present—known present facts
 (e.g., behavior during the interaction)
Future—known future probabilities
 (e.g., scheduled court date, resumption of school)
ASSESSMENT (A)—your evaluation
 Past—evaluation of past behavior
  (e.g., development of the problem)
 Present—evaluation of present behavior
  (e.g., the client's condition now)
 Future—evaluation of likely future behavior
  (e.g., prognosis, probability of treatment compliance)
PLAN (P)—relevant action
 Past—past plans
  (e.g., plans developed in previous contacts)
 Present—plans for the immediate future
  (e.g., diet, daily activities)
 Future—plans for the more distant future
  (e.g., career change, plans for further education)

Based on our combined 40 years of teaching this format, we know there are two common mistakes that novice workers tend to make. First, they frequently include nonfactual information in the objective paragraph. For example, in this section it is *incorrect* to note that a client was anxious (such a conclusion belongs under assessment). Although it would be *correct* to note that a client tapped his fingers, frequently adjusted his seating position, and displayed a rapid rate of speech. Second, novices often are vague in the plan paragraph when what is needed is a detailed description of intended actions. Dates, times, and places should be specifically mentioned when they are known.

The following example involved a walk-in interaction conducted by a crisis intervention worker. Another staff member had set up the appointment after a brief telephone interaction with the person. While on the phone, the caller had displayed language patterns that suggested the possibility of psychotic thinking. Since referral to a mental health professional was a distinct possibility, the worker planned to assess five areas that such professionals readily understand. Those were: thoughts, perceptions, emotions, behavior, and interpersonal relations. Here are brief descriptions of what the crisis worker was alert for in each of those five areas.

- *Thoughts.* It is possible for an individual to be uncertain about his or her name and location, or about what day and time it is. A disturbed client may be unable to remember recent events. The individual may fail to recognize familiar persons and places. There may be evidence of delusional ideas.
- *Perceptions.* Individuals can experience perceptual distortions involving any of the senses. Auditory hallucinations tend to be most common; for instance, persons may hear voices or it may seem as though their own thoughts come loud to them. Individuals can experience visual hallucinations such as frightening images or other unsettling distortions. It is possible to feel unusual tactile perceptions that are not the result of physical stimulation. Although less frequent, sometimes persons have hallucinations involving smell and taste.
- *Emotions.* Examples of extreme emotions include unresponsiveness and apathy, as well as wildly inappropriate feelings, such as hilarity to circumstances that are not funny or rage at inconsequential events.
- *Behavior.* Individuals sometimes engage in actions that are unusual and disturbing. Examples include the following: prolonged lethargy, periods of extreme agitation, peculiar mannerisms, and self-mutilation. If motor behavior is severely impaired, the person may be unable to perform usual self-care tasks such as dressing, eating, or maintaining normal hygiene practices.
- *Interpersonal relations.* Some individuals develop pronounced difficulties in getting along with others. When clients are reacting primarily to their own internal cues, responding appropriately in any interpersonal situation can be a major challenge.

The crisis worker prepared an interview format that listed the following topics on the left-hand side of the page: thoughts, perceptions, emotions, behavior, and interpersonal relations. After the interaction, the worker used his notes and his recollections of the interview to produce the following report that follows the SOAP format. (The quoted material was jotted down during the interview. When clients' statements have crucial diagnostic significance or relate to suicidal/homicidal lethality, it can be helpful to include direct quotes in your report.)

S The client reported that her difficulties began six years ago when, "I was programmed, and, although I wanted to bite on wood, it felt like I slept for months at a time." She said she arranged for the appointment this evening because a sizzling pain in her stomach was getting worse. In addition to the stomach pain, she reported a variety of other perceptions: sometimes not hearing her own voice when she is talking, the sounds of her coworkers' voices echoing, friends in a neighboring city talking to her (while not using a communication device), overseas radio signals, and arguing voices. She said I would be better able to understand if she could "block it into cubes" for me. When asked if her thoughts came loud to her, she responded, "Yes, like a cheering section." Despite the sizzling stomach and various auditory experiences, she said her difficulties do not interfere with her work as a secretary.

O The 26-year-old client reported that she has lived with her parents since birth and that she has worked as a secretary in a government office for the past five years. According to her, she has never received mental health services. She smiled throughout the interview, and she made frequent eye contact. In her conversation, she quickly moved from one topic to another, and she was so verbal that it was difficult to make a comment without interrupting her.

A Thought disorder was evidenced by the client's thoughts coming loud and by her flight of ideas. Her major complaints related to apparent perceptual disturbances: a sizzling stomach and various auditory hallucinations. The client's smiling through descriptions of sizzling pain and bothersome voices demonstrated inappropriate emotions. In terms of behavior, she did not display any peculiar mannerisms, and her personal hygiene appeared good. Interpersonally, she apparently receives support from her parents, and she seems to have been functioning well enough to maintain a steady job. The preceding information is consistent with a diagnosis of Schizophrenia, Undifferentiated Type.

P The client reported that she wanted medicine in the hope that it would alleviate some of her discomfort. When the mental health office opens tomorrow at 8:30 A.M., a crisis worker will arrange for an emergency psychiatric interview. Once an appointment is obtained, the worker will call the client at the office where she works and tell her when and where she can meet with the psychiatrist.

MULTIPLE-CHOICE QUESTIONS

All of the multiple-choice items involve one client. Your instructions are the same as in the previous chapters.

- For each of the following client statements, choose the response or responses you believe would be appropriate. (Several items have more than one correct answer.)
- Indicate your selection in writing.
- Read the discussions of all four options.
- If you are correct, go to the next item.
- If you are incorrect, think about the explanations and, if necessary, review relevant portions of the chapter; then, once you better understand the issues, proceed to the next question.

1. (You are on the phone talking to a person who wants to arrange an appointment with you. Presently, you have ongoing commitments that end at 3:45 or shortly thereafter.) It's hard for me to leave work during the day. But I get off at 3:00, and a 3:30 appointment would be great for me.
   A. How would 3:30 on Tuesday be for you?
   B. Right now I have other commitments at 3:30, but 3:45 would be OK. How would 3:45 on Tuesday be for you?
   C. Right now I have other commitments at 3:30, but 4:00 would be OK. How would 4:00 on Tuesday be for you?
   D. I already have commitments until late in the day. Right now, it would be best for me if we could arrange an appointment for the mid morning. How would 10:00 on Tuesday be for you?

Discussion of options.

   A. How would 3:30 on Tuesday be for you?
      - By agreeing to meet at 3:30, you run two sorts of risks: (1) shortchanging your ongoing commitment and being preoccupied with that issue at the start of the 3:30 session, or (2) being late for the appointment with your new client.
   B. Right now I have other commitments at 3:30, but 3:45 would be OK. How would 3:45 on Tuesday be for you?

- Sometimes your ongoing commitments can run a bit past 3:45. If that happens on Tuesday, you must cut short your ongoing responsibility, and possibly find yourself thinking of that issue during your 3:45 meeting, or you must be late for your new client.

C. Right now I have other commitments at 3:30, but 4:00 would be OK. How would 4:00 on Tuesday be for you?
  - The 4:00 time is realistic for you and probably will be acceptable to the client.

D. I already have commitments until late in the day. Right now, it would be best for me if we could arrange an appointment for the mid morning. How would 10:00 on Tuesday be for you?
  - From what the client has told you, such a time would be difficult. Consequently, the appointment may be rejected. Even if you get agreement, you may be arranging a no-show. And if the individual does agree and does arrive, the person may be preoccupied with thoughts of work difficulties that will result from the effort.

2. That sounds good. About how long will the appointment last?
   A. It will take at least 20 minutes.
   B. We will plan to talk for about 45 minutes.
   C. I have hourly appointments.
   D. We will take as much time as we need.

Discussion of options.

A. It will take at least 20 minutes.
  - Providing the minimum time is only a partial answer to the client's question.
B. We will plan to talk for about 45 minutes.
  - This is a simple factual response to the client's question.
C. I have hourly appointments.
  - Your response is unclear. One interpretation might be that you spend an hour with each client. But that probably is not true, since you must spend some of the 60 minutes (1) writing an account of the interaction that has just ended and (2) reviewing your preparations regarding the interview that is about to begin.

D. We will take as much time as we need.
  • You have supplied a vague answer. It also is an unrealistic one since you probably have a variety of constraints on your time.

3. (It is now the appointed time on Tuesday. You have greeted the person in the waiting area, and then made your way to the session room, where you both have just taken a seat.)
A. How was it finding our office?
B. Is this time OK with you?
C. This weather has been something, hasn't it?
D. What is on your mind?

Discussion of options.

A. How was it finding our office?
  • Your open question on a nonthreatening topic provides an opportunity for light social conversation. A few moments of such interaction allow the person to become acclimated to the setting.
B. Is this time OK with you?
  • Your closed question can be answered with a simple "Yes" or "No." Consequently, you may be setting the stage for a pattern of brief replies.
C. This weather has been something, hasn't it?
  • You are seeking agreement with your leading question. This is an overly directive way to start the interaction.
D. What is on your mind?
  • By immediately beginning the task of exploration, you give the client little chance to become accustomed to the surroundings before beginning the body of the interview.

4. (You have engaged in some social conversation, and the client has a clear understanding of both your role and the purpose of the interaction. It is now time to begin discussing what led to the appointment.)
A. What can I do for you?
B. Can you tell me what's on your mind?
C. What seems to be the problem?
D. Tell me your reason for coming in today.

Discussion of options.

A. What can I do for you?
- This opening implies that you are going to be the one to solve the client's problems.

B. Can you tell me what's on your mind?
- It is not necessary for you to ask a closed question.

C. What seems to be the problem?
- Although your question is an open one, the word "problem" implies a negative tone.

D. Tell me your reason for coming in today.
- Your open, neutral probe focuses the interaction on the task at hand while also giving the person wide latitude in how to respond.

5. I guess I'm embarrassed about being here. But I really need some help in controlling my 16-year-old daughter. I want to be a better parent, but I don't want other people to know that I'm getting this kind of help.

A. You want to be sure that our discussions will be held in confidence.

B. Our talks will be completely confidential. No one else will ever know about them.

C. The nature of our work together will never be known outside of this organization.

D. Unless you give permission for release of information, the only time we would break confidentiality would be if you or someone else were in danger.

Discussion of options.

A. You want to be sure that our discussions will be held in confidence.
- This reflection is accurate, but now would be a good time to provide appropriate information regarding the issue of confidentiality.

B. Our talks will be completely confidential. No one else will ever know about them.
- Although it is possible that no one else will ever learn of your talks, it also is possible that circumstances will develop so that you do share information with others.

C. The nature of our work together will never be known outside of this organization.
  • As with option B, this statement may be true, but it also is possible that it may turn out not to be true.
D. Unless you give permission for release of information, the only time we would break confidentiality would be if you or someone else were in danger.
  • You have provided a factual response that briefly describes your organization's policy on confidentiality.

6. When would be a time that you would break confidentiality without my permission?
A. That happens so rarely that you really don't need to be concerned about it.
B. There are three times when our organization is required to break confidentiality: in order to prevent suicide, in order to protect someone who is about to be harmed, and in cases of child abuse.
C. Why are you so concerned about this issue of confidentiality?
D. Confidentiality is a complex topic and there really is no simple answer to your question. The best I can say is that our organization follows ethical guidelines and that we maintain case material in confidence unless the guidelines require us to divulge information.

Discussion of options.

A. That happens so rarely that you really don't need to be concerned about it.
  • You are getting the interaction off to a bad start by avoiding the client's question and by telling the person how to feel.
B. There are three times when our organization is required to break confidentiality: in order to prevent suicide, in order to protect someone who is about to be harmed, and in cases of child abuse.
  • Your response describes a straightforward account of your organization's policy on confidentiality.
C. Why are you so concerned about this issue of confidentiality?
  • By asking a "Why" question, you are likely to put the individual on the defensive.

D. Confidentiality is a complex topic and there really is no simple answer to your question. The best I can say is that our organization follows ethical guidelines and that we maintain case material in confidence unless the guidelines require us to divulge information.
- Your response is a smoke screen that attempts to hide the issues that would necessitate breaking confidentiality.

7. I've never been to a place like this before. I hope what you do isn't going to be like some of those magazine articles I've seen where an expert lists five magic steps I'm supposed to take and says that if I follow them, everything will be fine. I don't think that's going to do it. A prepackaged program is not what I want. I need to feel that what we do is going to work in my particular situation.
A. Although you're looking for a source of support that will help you deal with your daughter, you want to feel comfortable with any strategies you attempt.
B. It sounds like you have done some reading on the parenting issues you are facing.
C. Rather than simplistic answers, you want a full airing of issues. And it seems like you also want to be sure you're the one who decides that what you try is really right for you.
D. So, you've thought about what it's going to take in order for your relationship with your daughter to improve. What are some of the possibilities you've been considering?

Discussion of options.

A. Although you're looking for a source of support that will help you deal with your daughter, you want to feel comfortable with any strategies you attempt.
- This summary is on target.
B. It sounds like you have done some reading on the parenting issues you are facing.
- Your reflection is accurate, but it sidetracks the interaction away from the main concern the client is discussing.
C. Rather than simplistic answers, you want a full airing of issues. And it seems like you also want to be sure you're the one who decides that what you try is really right for you.
- You have reflected the essence of what is on the client's mind.

D. So, you've thought about what it's going to take in order for your relationship with your daughter to improve. What are some of the possibilities you've been considering?
   - The first sentence is an accurate reflection, but it fails to address the major thrust of the client's comments. And the open question moves too quickly into considering alternatives.

8. I need some help. But I only want to do things that I feel right about. I've heard about parents being told that they *had* to do this thing or that thing, so I guess I'm hoping that won't happen here. I want to have input in what is decided to be done.
   A. You don't want me to order you to take certain actions with your daughter.
   B. I have a hard time believing that someone in my position actually demanded that a parent behave in a particular way.
   C. You're afraid that I may try to take too much control.
   D. It sounds to me like you want us to discuss important issues, to think about possible options, then to come up with a plan you feel good about. And that is exactly what I would like to help you do.

Discussion of options.

A. You don't want me to order you to take certain actions with your daughter.
   - Although this is an accurate factual reflection, there is a better response in this group.
B. I have a hard time believing that someone in my position actually demanded that a parent behave in a particular way.
   - Your confrontational statement is likely to sidetrack the interaction to an irrelevant debate, which may cost you the opportunity to have a positive relationship with this client.
C. You're afraid that I may try to take too much control.
   - You accurately reflect the client's feelings, but another response in this group is even better.
D. It sounds to me like you want us to discuss important issues, to think about possible options, then to come up with a plan you feel good about. And that is exactly what I would like to help you do.

- Your response correctly reflects the person's concern and also conveys the idea that you want the client to retain decision-making authority.

9. So, I guess I should tell you what's happening with Patti. She seems to be getting wilder by the day. She just got her driver's license, and she is an incredibly reckless driver. Even when I'm in the car, she's squealing around turns and screeching to stops. She never slows down for a yellow light. Instead, she just barrels on through the intersection. It's got me very worried about her safety.
   A. Her driving really scares you.
   B. She has a lot of room for improvement in terms of her driving skills.
   C. You'd like her to be more responsible in her driving.
   D. So, your daughter's driving is *one* area that's troubling you.

Discussion of options.

   A. Her driving really scares you.
      - Your surface feeling reflection is the most appropriate option in this group if you would like more discussion relevant to the issue of driving.
   B. She has a lot of room for improvement in terms of her driving skills.
      - You focus on the daughter rather than on your client.
   C. You'd like her to be more responsible in her driving.
      - This factual reflection is adequate, but there are better options in this set.
   D. So, your daughter's driving is *one* area that's troubling you.
      - Your surface feeling reflection is on target, but it also suggests that you are interested in hearing about other topics that may be of concern to the client. If you want to move the discussion to those other subjects, this is the best option of the four listed.

10. Yeah, her driving is out of control. She's also been staying out too late. Even before she got her license she was missing her curfew. Sometimes she stays out all night, and I have no idea where she is or who she's with. She's starting to hang around with friends I

don't know or I don't approve of. There are guys who call on the phone for her, and when I ask who it is they hang up on me. I don't know what she is getting involved in, but she is developing a very bad temper. And when I confront her about any of this, she just blows up. I'm really upset, and I don't know what I'm going to do.

A. Slow down, I'm having a hard time getting all of this down.

B. So, her staying out too late is another area of friction between you.

C. You're frightened about what she might be getting into with her late hours and her new friends.

D. You shouldn't do anything. It's her own life she's messing up.

Discussion of options.

A. Slow down, I'm having a hard time getting all of this down.
  • Your focus should be on understanding the client rather than on taking notes.

B. So, her staying out too late is another area of friction between you.
  • If you want the client to continue surveying the situation, this is the most appropriate response of the four options offered.

C. You're frightened about what she might be getting into with her late hours and her new friends.
  • By including a feeling component in your reflection, you increase the likelihood of the client continuing to explore the topic under discussion. If such depth of coverage is your intent, this is the best response in the group.

D. You shouldn't do anything. It's her own life she's messing up.
  • Making such a judgmental comment is inappropriate for a supportive helper.

11. I'm very worried. She could easily be killed in an accident because of the way she drives. And with these kids she's hanging around, for all I know she's using drugs and doing who knows what else. I really have no idea what she's getting into. I don't know how serious it is because she won't talk to me. If she were your daughter, what would you do?

A. If she were my daughter, I probably would try to communicate my concern to her, and I might try to use any leverage I had. But what's important for us to do is to figure out what options are realistic for you.

B. It really would be inappropriate for me to discuss what I might do in similar circumstances. Instead, we should be focusing on your thoughts and feelings regarding the situation.

C. The risks she might be running are really terrifying, and it would be comforting to have someone tell you what to do.

D. I would begin by taking the car away from her, and if you want my opinion, I believe that would be a good place for you to start.

Discussion of options.

A. If she were my daughter, I probably would try to communicate my concern to her, and I might try to use any leverage I had. But what's important for us to do is to figure out what options are realistic for you.
   • You have supplied a brief reply to the question and then returned the focus to the client.

B. It really would be inappropriate for me to discuss what I might do in similar circumstances. Instead, we should be focusing on your thoughts and feelings regarding the situation.
   • By evading the client's question it seems as though you are playing a role rather than being genuine with the person.

C. The risks she might be running are really terrifying, and it would be comforting to have someone tell you what to do.
   • This is an accurate reflection that avoids the client's question to you. We believe there is a better response in this group.

D. I would begin by taking the car away from her, and if you want my opinion, I believe that would be a good place for you to start.
   • Your reply is too directive for a supportive helper.

12. Well, the communication between us has really gone down hill. I can't even get her in the house for more than fifteen minutes without her running out the door. If I try to put my foot down and say, "No, you are not going out," she blows up and takes off anyway. On the few occasions that we actually have tried to talk, she just gets defensive, clams up, or makes some excuse that she has to leave.

A. It doesn't look like your efforts are going to have any real effect on her.

B. For us to make progress, I really think I need to see your daughter.

C. It doesn't seem as though she cares very much about what you think or feel.

D. Improved communication with her is something you'd like to achieve, but your recent efforts have been frustrating.

Discussion of options.

A. It doesn't look like your efforts are going to have any real effect on her.
- Your negative comment discourages problem solving.

B. For us to make progress, I really think I need to see your daughter.
- Although your statement may be accurate, it is too soon in the interaction to make such an observation.

C. It doesn't seem as though she cares very much about what you think or feel.
- At this point in the interaction, you should focus on your client rather than on the daughter.

D. Improved communication with her is something you'd like to achieve, but your recent efforts have been frustrating.
- This is an accurate reflection.

13. (You have completed the exploration phase of problem solving with the client, and you now want to begin considering alternatives.)

A. Your daughter's behavior is exasperating for a number of reasons: her possible high-risk activities, the unknown nature of her new friends, her driving, and the difficulty in having a conversation with her. What have you tried with Patti?

B. Your daughter's behavior is exasperating for a number of reasons: her possible high-risk activities, the unknown nature of her new friends, her driving, and the difficulty in having a conversation with her. Let's now take a look at the possibilities for changing your relationship with Patti. Tell me about the efforts you've made.

C. Your daughter's behavior is exasperating for a number of reasons: her possible high-risk activities, the unknown nature of her new friends, her driving, and the difficulty in having a conversation with her. In addition to your attempts to talk with her, what else have you tried with Patti?

D. Your daughter's behavior is exasperating for a number of reasons: her possible high-risk activities, the unknown nature of her new friends, her driving, and the difficulty in having a conversation with her. And it sounds like nothing you've tried has made any difference.

Discussion of options.

A. Your daughter's behavior is exasperating for a number of reasons: her possible high-risk activities, the unknown nature of her new friends, her driving, and the difficulty in having a conversation with her. What have you tried with Patti?
   • This is a transition that keeps the alternatives phase independent from the exploration phase, but in doing so, you fail to recognize the past efforts the client has made.

B. Your daughter's behavior is exasperating for a number of reasons: her possible high-risk activities, the unknown nature of her new friends, her driving, and the difficulty in having a conversation with her. Let's now take a look at the possibilities for changing your relationship with Patti. Tell me about the efforts you've made.
   • You attempt to link the exploration and alternatives phases, but you fail to acknowledge the client's coping attempts that you've already discussed.

C. Your daughter's behavior is exasperating for a number of reasons: her possible high-risk activities, the unknown nature of her new friends, her driving, and the difficulty in having a conversation with her. In addition to your attempts to talk with her, what else have you tried with Patti?
   • Your transition recognizes the client's past efforts and uses them as a bridge for taking the topic in a new direction.

D. Your daughter's behavior is exasperating for a number of reasons: her possible high-risk activities, the unknown nature of her new friends, her driving, and the difficulty in having a conversation with her. And it sounds like nothing you've tried has made any difference.

• The negative tone of your last sentence provides a poor start for the alternatives phase of problem solving.

14. I've tried confronting her, especially when she comes home past her curfew. When I've had no idea who she's been with or what they've been doing, I'll ask her to tell me. But I have to be very careful. There have been times when she's just turned around and taken off again. Recently, I've tried to communicate to her how serious this is by taking away her car keys. But that doesn't seem to matter because she usually can get a ride with one of her friends. I guess mostly I've just tried confronting her.

A. It seems to me that your daughter is out of control.

B. In addition to initiating conversations, two other efforts you've made are speaking with Patti when she arrives home late and taking away her driving privileges. What else have you tried?

C. Think about a recent time when Patti came home late and you confronted her. Tell me how you brought up your concerns and what happened in the interaction.

D. You're disappointed that, so far, your efforts haven't worked.

Discussion of options.

A. It seems to me that your daughter is out of control.
   • There are three problems with this response: it is quite negative and opinionated, it focuses on the daughter, and it returns the interaction to the exploration stage.

B. In addition to initiating conversations, two other efforts you've made are speaking with Patti when she arrives home late and taking away her driving privileges. What else have you tried?
   • You recognize the client's efforts and move the focus to other past attempts. This is the most appropriate response in the group if you want to survey a range of material.

C. Think about a recent time when Patti came home late and you confronted her. Tell me how you brought up your concerns and what happened in the interaction.
   • By asking for an account of a specific coping effort, you may discover something that can be of use as you search for alternatives. Slowing the interaction in this way is appropriate if you are willing to cover the confrontation issue in

greater detail. So if depth of coverage is your intent, this is the best option of the four possibilities listed.

D. You're disappointed that, so far, your efforts haven't worked.
   • This surface feeling reflection is accurate, but it does little to facilitate the consideration of alternatives.

15. (In response to your last comment, the client is silent.)
    A. Mmhmm.
    B. (You remain silent.)
    C. I think that silence tends to be a defense against what your ego believes should not be said. Whatever is happening inside you right now probably relates to an important unconscious issue that we have tapped.
    D. We were talking about your efforts to influence Patti. What are you thinking?

Discussion of options.

A. Mmhmm.
   • Since you were the last person to speak, saying "Mmhmm" does not make sense.
B. (You remain silent.)
   • Some silence on your part can be appropriate. But if both you and the client continue to be silent, the atmosphere will become strained.
C. I think that silence tends to be a defense against what your ego believes should not be said. Whatever is happening inside you right now probably relates to an important unconscious issue that we have tapped.
   • Whether or not your analysis is correct, it is not something a supportive helper would say at this point in an initial inter-action.
D. We were talking about your efforts to influence Patti. What are you thinking?
   • Your first sentence summarizes what you've been discussing, and the second sentence questions the silence. So, in our opinion, this is the best of the four responses provided.

16. I was thinking about difficulties I had with my parents when I was a teenager.

A. Mmhmm.

B. What would your parents do if they were in your shoes now?

C. How does your daughter get along with them?

D. If you like, we can spend some time talking about your own adolescence, but for now, let's concentrate on the relationship between you and your daughter.

Discussion of options.

A. Mmhmm.
  • Your nonverbal expression of interest gives the client complete freedom in deciding where to go with the interaction.

B. What would your parents do if they were in your shoes now?
  • Although this question deals with options, it changes the focus to the client's parents.

C. How does your daughter get along with them?
  • By asking such a question, you shift attention away from your client.

D. If you like, we can spend some time talking about your own adolescence, but for now, let's concentrate on the relationship between you and your daughter.
  • Immediately attempting to bring the client back to the previous topic is a directive response that may cost you valuable information.

17. When you're 16 years old, who do you think should be the boss, you or your parents?

A. Rather than what I think, what's really important is what you believe on that issue.

B. I think that depends in part on the 16-year-old. It seems to me you're wondering if *Patti* is ready to make and to be responsible for her own decisions.

C. The law says the parent is the boss.

D. (You are silent as the client waits for a reply.)

Discussion of options.

A. Rather than what I think, what's really important is what you believe on that issue.
  • This is a pat response that fails to convey genuineness.

B. I think that depends in part on the 16-year-old. It seems to me you're wondering if *Patti* is ready to make and to be responsible for her own decisions.
  • You provide a brief reply to the client's question, and then look behind it to focus the interaction in a productive direction.
C. The law says the parent is the boss.
  • Your response is overly simplistic.
D. (You are silent as the client waits for a reply.)
  • This is not a good place for worker silence.

18. (You have considered alternatives and have developed a plan with the client. It is now near the end of the interaction.)
  A. Review for me one more time the steps you've decided to take.
  B. So, you've decided to take the following steps . . . (you summarize the plan for the client).
  C. It is disheartening to think that your best efforts might not be good enough.
  D. I hope Patti cooperates so that your plan succeeds.

Discussion of options.

  A. Review for me one more time the steps you've decided to take.
    • It is appropriate to ask the client to describe the plan you have negotiated.
  B. So, you've decided to take the following steps . . . (you summarize the plan for the client).
    • Although you may review the plan, it is most important for the *client* to describe it.
  C. It is disheartening to think that your best efforts might not be good enough.
    • Your reflection might be accurate, but it ends the interaction on a pessimistic note with regard to the anticipated efforts.
  D. I hope Patti cooperates so that your plan succeeds.
    • The success of the plan should be judged by what your client does rather than being dependent upon Patti's responses.

19. (The interaction is over, and your client has just left. Which of the following actions is most appropriate?)
  A. You check to see if you have had any phone calls.
  B. You and a colleague begin a conversation about another client.

C. You review material for your next appointment.

D. You write an account of the interaction that has just ended.

Discussion of options.

A. You check to see if you have had any phone calls.
- Retrieving your messages should not be your first priority unless you are in the midst of a crisis situation involving another client.

B. You and a colleague begin a conversation about another client.
- Such consultation is appropriate if the client being discussed is in emergency circumstances. If that is not the case, you have something more pressing to do.

C. You review material for your next appointment.
- You ought to prepare for your next client, but you have something else you should tackle first.

D. You write an account of the interaction that has just ended.
- Barring emergencies, this is what you ought to be doing.

20. (You write an account of the interaction using the SOAP format. Which of the following comments is appropriate for your written SOAP report?)

A. Subjective—The client was within normal limits with regard to thoughts, perceptions, emotions, and behaviors. . . .

B. Objective—The client expressed extreme frustration concerning Patti's driving, choice of friends, high-risk activities, and avoidance of conversation. . . .

C. Assessment—The client was highly motivated to improve interactions with Patti. . . .

D. Plan—We are scheduled to meet again late next week. . . .

Discussion of options.

A. Subjective—The client was within normal limits with regard to thoughts, perceptions, emotions, and behaviors....
- Since this is your evaluation, it belongs in the assessment section.

B. Objective—The client expressed extreme frustration concerning Patti's driving, choice of friends, high-risk activities, and avoidance of conversation. . . .

- Rather than referring to factual information, your comment describes the client's thoughts and feelings. Consequently, this statement belongs in the subjective section.

C. Assessment—The client was highly motivated to improve interactions with Patti. . . .

- It is appropriate for you to put such an opinion in the assessment section.

D. Plan—We are scheduled to meet again late next week. . . .

- The description of your next appointment should include the date and time.

SHORT-ANSWER QUESTIONS

Write your answer for each of the following questions.

1. If you are chronically late for your appointments with clients, what do you risk with regard to your schedule?
2. Your first session with an 8-year-old client and his mother required attention to several pressing issues. The second session is later today. During the previous meeting, the mother said she was wondering whether her son might have Asperger's disorder, and that is one of the topics you want to address today. What do you do to prepare for the session?
3. Describe the physical setting of an ideal session room.
4. Name three sets of influences that may affect a client's initial expectations.
5. While with you in a restaurant, a colleague begins discussing one of your clients. What do you do?
6. Read the sample interview in Chapter 4. Imagine you are the worker and write a set of notes that you may have jotted down during the interaction.
7. Using the SOAP format, write a progress note for the sample interview in Chapter 4.

POSSIBLE ANSWERS FOR SHORT-ANSWER QUESTIONS

The answer-checking procedures remain the same as before.

- For each item, compare your answer to the one we provide.
- If you believe your answer is correct, you are done with that item.
- With any question for which you believe your answer is incorrect, consider our answer and, if needed, review relevant portions of the chapter. Keep your original answer that you now think is incorrect, but add to it a response that you believe would be correct.

1. If you are chronically late for your appointments, you risk losing control of your schedule.
2. Read the accounts of your first meeting, including established goals, objectives, and plans, as well as your progress note. You may want to review the diagnostic criteria for Asperger's disorder, and you may also wish to have relevant resource information available with you during the session. You should prepare an interview format that lists the topics you plan to discuss.
3. White noise from a central air system blocks auditory distractions. A closed door keeps others from interrupting you, and the telephone does not ring. There is a clock you can easily glance at while interacting with clients. The furniture allows you to sit at an angle to clients with no barrier between you. There are very few potential weapons, and there is a help button.
4. A client's initial expectations may be affected by several factors: where the interaction comes in the person's help-seeking efforts, comments by others, and previous interactions with the organization.
5. Suggest to your colleague that the discussion be postponed until you can talk in a private place.
6. Here is a possible set of notes from the Chapter 4 sample interview.

   3 dispatcher
   CI next week
   handle? different, training
   student
   high standards
   time pressure
   check–schedule–post
   check–read at CI
   next–job start
   3-4 10:00

7. The following is a possible SOAP note based on the sample interview in Chapter 4.

S   The client reports being anxious about accepting a position as a crisis worker. Since it is different from her previous employment, she worries about being able to handle the responsibility, and she wonders if the planned training will be adequate. She reports feeling pressured by her job, school, and home responsibilities, and she describes high expectations for herself.

O   She worked for three years as a law enforcement dispatcher, and she recently accepted a job as a crisis worker. Currently she is a college student. During the interview she was verbal, and she made frequent eye contact. She begins the new crisis job next week.

A   The client appears to be a hard-working person who sets high standards for herself. Since the crisis worker position entails so many unfamiliar tasks, she is uncertain about her ability to take on those new duties while continuing to perform at her usually high level.

P   Her plan has two parts. (1) As a means of managing her time, she will develop a schedule and post it so that her roommates can see it. (2) In order to maintain her academics, she will take reading material with her to the crisis job. When we meet again we will discuss her new position with regard to two issues: the nature of the work and the quality of the training. Our next appointment is scheduled for Friday, March 3, at 10:00 A.M.

FILL-IN-THE-RESPONSE QUESTIONS

Listed below are a series of client statements from a 21-year-old woman. For each one, write a response that you believe would be appropriate for worker in a nonmedical human service organization.

1. Are our discussions confidential?
2. I feel really uncomfortable to be seeing you about this, but I have to talk with someone. Right now I feel all alone, and I need some help in figuring out what to do.
3. What do you do with clients? I mean, do you tell people what they should do?

4. (Create two responses to the client's following remarks, one that would promote range and another that goes for depth.) Well I just found out from the doctor yesterday that I'm pregnant. I'm not seeing the father anymore, and I don't know what to do. I can't tell my parents because they would kick me out. I'm still in college, and I'm so afraid. I never thought this would happen to me.

5. (Again, develop two responses. One reply should encourage depth while the other emphasizes range.) I only have one more year to go, and I would have to take time off to have the baby. I don't even want to think about it. It's so unnerving. I just can't deal with it. The father and I kind of ended things in a bad way, so I haven't told him yet. In fact, I don't even know how to get in touch with him or where he is. And I can't tell my parents because they would be so disappointed. They would just tell me that they had wasted their money on my education for the past three years.

6. What do you think I should do?

POSSIBLE ANSWERS FOR FILL-IN-THE-RESPONSE QUESTIONS

For each response opportunity, there are many possible correct answers. We list two, and, as in previous chapters, we suggest you use them in the following manner.

- Look at our two answers and think about them.
- Consider relevant material covered in the chapter.
- Read the client statement again, then immediately read your answer and the two options listed here.
- Write another response that you believe might be an improvement on your first effort.
- Repeat this procedure for each of the remaining items.

1. • Any release of material beyond the organization would be with your consent, unless we would have to share information in order to protect you or someone else from harm.
   • Without your permission to release information, the content of our sessions stays within the organization unless we would have to act in order to keep you or someone else from being harmed.

2. • You're wrestling with a sensitive issue that's hard to talk about.
   • Although it was difficult for you to come here, you know you need to discuss the decisions facing you.
3. • I sometimes tell clients what to do in order to help them get what they decide they want. But clients set their own goals, and I merely assist them in getting to where they want to go.
   • I help clients develop plans, and I may provide information that is relevant to those plans. But the clients are the ones who make the fundamental decisions about what they want to do.
4. • You need some help in dealing with your pregnancy. (This is a factual reflection that would be appropriate if you wish to cover ground rapidly.)
   • You received some surprising news yesterday and aren't sure how to proceed with this interruption to your plans. (This is another "range" response.)
   • It's frightening to face the possibility of having to deal with your pregnancy on your own. (This is a surface feeling reflection that is appropriate if you want depth of coverage.)
   • Your unplanned pregnancy comes as a shock and leaves you feeling isolated and unprepared for this challenge. (This is another "depth" response.)
5. • For the immediate future, you're thinking of coping with being pregnant without involving the father or your parents. (This factual reflection is a "range" response.)
   • You've put off sharing news of the pregnancy with your family and ex-boyfriend. (This factual reflection is also intended to encourage a range of topics.)
   • You hate having to deal with the realities of being pregnant, and for now at least, you're struggling on your own without informing the father or your parents. (This surface feeling reflection is a "depth" response.)
   • The possibilities of putting off graduation, facing your parents, or reestablishing contact with the father all seem overwhelming right now. (This reflection encourages emotional depth.)
6. • Together, I think we should map out the choices you're facing and then take a close look at the pros and cons of the options that seem to be the most promising.
   • I believe you should use our time together to work through some of your fears, identify the best possibilities that you have available, and examine the advantages and disadvantages associated with those options.

SUMMARY

Scheduled contacts involve considerations before, during, and after the appointment. Before the interaction, you should set a convenient time for the meeting and arrange your schedule so that you will not be late. Preparation for the session can include readings in your professional literature, a review of the client's file, and production of an interview format. Physical setting arrangements should do the following: limit auditory and visual distractions, provide unobtrusive observation of a clock, include barrier-free furniture placement that allows natural breaks in eye contact, facilitate your ability to summon emergency help, and reduce access to potential weapons. From the client's perspective, initial expectations may be related to several factors: where the interaction fits in the person's help seeking efforts, comments by others about your services, and previous interactions with the organization. In order to allay potential client fears, you should convey empathy, warmth, and genuineness, and you should maintain appropriate confidentiality.

Activities that set the stage for the interaction include the following: introductions, light social conversation, and clarification of the meeting's purpose. After beginning the body of the session with an open probe or question, you can survey a range of topics while also being ready to cover areas in greater depth. You should be prepared to handle eventualities such as transitions, questions from the client, and silence. As the session progresses, you ought to take appropriate notes, and you should end the interaction with an effective review.

Immediately after the interaction you need to write an account of what happened. The SOAP format is one approach to such reports, although individual organizations often have their own record-keeping expectations.

Chapter 9

RESPONDING TO THE NEEDS OF
VARIOUS CLIENT GROUPS

For the most part, the material discussed to this point is applicable to any client. But we would like to address a few special considerations to keep in mind when working with certain individuals. This chapter presents ideas relating to children, socioeconomic class, aging, psychoses, and long-standing maladaptive behavior.

CHILDREN

Supportive helping is verbal in nature, so when working with children be sure to use an understandable vocabulary. And because of the emphasis on language, the minimum client age for using supportive helping is probably four or five. Below that age you may wish to use techniques similar to those employed in play therapy.

Although it is appropriate to communicate at the child's level, you should not abandon the demeanor of an adult professional. Keep your normal tone and volume of voice rather than using sugary sweet speech or talking overly loud. Also, do not adopt childish patterns of speech, and do not initiate condescending touch, such as patting the child's head, pinching the child's cheek, or tousling the child's hair.

Most other child-related supportive-helping considerations deal with two issues: (1) the fact that children commonly are referred to you by others rather than referring themselves, and (2) the cognitive and emotional development that takes place during childhood. Observations relating to those two themes constitute the remainder of this section.

Referral-Related Issues

In some settings, such as schools or crisis intervention programs, children occasionally may refer themselves. But in most instances, the interaction is taking place because someone other than the child has requested it. The typical scenario of others arranging the interaction means special attention must be given to three areas: establishing yourself as a caring adult who is not taking sides against the child, clarifying the purpose of the interaction, and being straightforward about confidentiality issues.

Establishing Yourself as a Caring, Neutral Adult

If you are about to initiate a one-to-one interaction with a child, assume the young person is going to be cooperative. After introducing yourself, use a positive statement (such as, "We are going to the first room on the left") to direct the child to the place where the interaction will occur. If the young person seems unduly nervous about talking with you, one option is to leave open the door to the session room and say that the child should be the one to shut it when ready to begin your work together. Once you both are seated, you may express appreciation for the individual being there (for example, "Thank you for coming today"), and you may want to engage in some small talk (like, "I see you are wearing a soccer shirt. What position do you like to play?").

During the body of the interview, you can implement the same fundamental strategies that you do with adults: demonstrate understanding of the client and support independent problem solving. For many children, encountering a supportive adult with those goals is a unique experience. What tends to be more typical is for adults to concentrate on their own thoughts and feelings while they simply tell children what to do. But supportive workers don't behave that way. Consequently, once the child discovers that you really are interested in listening and in helping the young person make his or her own decisions, the client may genuinely enjoy the interaction.

Clarifying the Interaction's Purpose

Our practice is to be completely open about the reason for the interview and to explain what led to the interaction. When discussing with the child the adults who initiated the referral, we attribute the adults' actions to concern for the child. Although we may report to the child observations those adults have made, we neither agree nor disagree with that information.

Before the interaction is over, there should be a clear decision as to whether you will meet again. If you know for certain that this will be your only meeting, you should state that at the beginning of the interaction in order to reduce the likelihood of the child feeling rejected. On the other hand, if you know for certain that there will be subsequent sessions, you should state that fact early in the interaction. But on those occasions when the issue of subsequent contacts is a joint decision to be made with the young person, the arrangements are best finalized at the end of the meeting.

Addressing Confidentiality

You should know the rights to information that interested adults (such as parents and teachers) have in your setting, and you should honestly describe to a child circumstances under which others may learn about the nature of your discussions. We believe that it is best for your position on confidentiality to be stated in writing. Such statements can be signed and dated by the interested parties, including the following: the young person, relevant adults (such as one or more of the child's guardians), and you. In Appendix E you will find examples of statements that have been used with regard to consent for psychological assessment and treatment of persons under the age of 18. Both the child's form and the parent's form address the issue of confidentiality. (The Appendix E statements are merely samples. They may not be appropriate for use in your particular setting. The way the child's form has been used has depended upon the age of the client. It has been read to young children; older children have read it out loud; and adolescents have read it silently.)

Providing Structure

Since most children have not reached adult levels of cognitive and emotional maturation, you generally need to provide a fair amount of structure and guidance. We will consider those structuring issues around two themes: gathering information and fostering appropriate behavior.

Gathering Information

You can try to initiate the body of the interview with an open question such as, "How are things going?" But the one-word responses you commonly get, such as "Fine," tend not to be very helpful. Consequently, the funnel style of interrogation usually should be avoided. An approach that often does work, though, is to request specific descriptions of actual events. For example, "Tell me about the fight you were in yesterday" or "What happens when other children in the class are making noise and you are trying to do your work?" Such requests for concrete examples are manageable for most children and often lead to informative discussions.

In Chapter 2 we discussed the problems with leading questions, and those difficulties are magnified when interacting with children. If you wish to obtain an honest response, avoid phrasing questions in ways that suggest an expected answer.

Because children have not yet reached their full cognitive potential, repetition may be necessary in order to accomplish the desired goals of the interaction. When you do need to repeat things, it is important that you remain patient and that you do not appear to be irritated.

Many children have active imaginations. If you come to question whether the child is describing fantasy or reality, you may need to employ mild confrontation in an attempt to ascertain whether the young person is describing something that actually occurred. For example, "Sometimes people talk about things they imagined, and sometimes they talk about things that actually happened. I'm wondering whether what you said about Chris was a pretend story or was something that really happened."

Fostering Appropriate Behavior

Children tend to have shorter attention spans than adults, and they may tire more quickly. Consequently, the total length of the interaction may need to be shorter than your typical interviews with adults.

Young people may also be more restless. Our opinion is that children do not need to remain seated. Instead, it can be acceptable for the child to get up and move around the room as the interaction takes place.

But some young persons may become so active that they disrupt the task at hand. When a child is on the verge of crossing or has crossed the threshold of acceptable behavior, we believe it is appropriate to discuss limits or rules. For example, if foot swinging becomes desk kicking, it probably is necessary to address the behavior by saying something like the following. "It's fine for you to swing your feet, but when you kick the desk, I have a tough time understanding what you're saying. Since I want both of us to hear what the other one has to say, I need for you to stop kicking the desk."

In those instances when the child is persistently uncooperative, our style is to be honest in describing the consequences of such behavior. By calmly explaining the results of nonparticipation and by giving a resistant child the freedom not to participate, we recognize the individual's decision-making ability while also noting the realistic alternatives facing the young person. For example, "The discipline committee has decided that in order to stay in the program, you must work with me. I have asked you three times to tell me about things you like to do, and each time you have shrugged your shoulders and said nothing. I'm going to ask you one more time to tell me about activities you enjoy. If you do not respond by telling me about things you like to do, we will end today's session, I will report to the committee that you chose not to work with me, and you will be out of the program. So, here comes the question. What are some things you enjoy doing?"

SOCIOECONOMIC CLASS

To a certain extent, middle-class and lower-class individuals tend to have different values. And those differences have some implications for workers. We will consider several value dimensions and their effects on supportive helping.

Middle-Class Values

Most middle-class individuals are accustomed to delaying gratification. For example, you are reading this book instead of engaging in other activities you might rather be doing.

Middle-class individuals frequently budget their time. They often plan ahead and set priorities.

For the most part, middle-class persons believe they have a fair amount of control over their lives. They assume they have choices, and they believe that what they do and think actually matters.

Lower-Class Values

Delaying gratification is a luxury available to those with predictable futures. On the other hand, when the future is extremely unpredictable, as it is for many lower-class individuals, immediate gratification is the only approach that makes much sense.

If you are very unsure about what the next day will bring, budgeting your time does not have much value. Although you may plan ahead and set priorities, events can easily sweep away your intentions. Consequently the present, rather than the future, is most important.

Lower-class individuals frequently see their lives as being determined by factors outside of their control. Perceived determinants of one's life may include fate, luck, society, and other entities. When those are viewed as the important influences, one's own choices, thoughts, and actions may seem to have little or no relevance to the direction in which one's life is moving.

Interacting with Middle-Class Individuals

Since delaying gratification is a common experience for middle-class persons, interactions with them may logically focus on courses of action that involve short-term sacrifice in order to achieve long-term benefit. When budgeting time, planning ahead, and setting priorities are familiar activities for the client, it also is easy for these endeavors to be aspects of your work together. And because self-direction tends to be assumed, it makes sense for you to focus on what the person feels, thinks, and does.

Interacting with Lower-Class Individuals

Given the unpredictable nature of the future for many lower-class clients, if a benefit from interacting with you is to be meaningful, that positive result often needs to arrive quickly. But even with short-term objectives there can be pitfalls. If the benefit depends on the client independently planning ahead, budgeting time, and setting priorities, the positive outcome may never accrue. And if during the interaction you focus solely on the client's feelings, thoughts, and actions, the person is likely to perceive that you are out of touch with reality.

In addition to their values influencing the interaction, lower-class clients tend to have some very practical pressures that impinge on them and on their time with you. For example, compared to middle-class persons, they often have fewer resources for child care and for transportation, and they may not have the same amount of freedom to leave work.

Because of the differences in values, in resources, and in freedom, lower-class clients are more likely to be late for appointments and to miss appointments than are middle-class clients. And, as indicated by a meta-analysis of psychotherapy dropout (Wierzbicki & Pekarik, 1993), lower-class clients are more likely to terminate prematurely.

In order to make the most of the time you have with a lower-class client, we make the following suggestions.

- *Demonstrate respect.* When addressing the person, use the individual's last name, with the prefix of "Mr.," "Mrs.," or "Ms." Also, if you are accustomed to shaking hands with clients, here such a gesture could be especially meaningful.
- *Maintain a professional demeanor.* Do not try to adopt the person's speech patterns or other mannerisms that are different from your own.
- *Provide direction as needed.* If necessary, concretely describe the interaction's purpose. Focus on achievable goals that have significance to the client. Although there may be many problematic areas for discussion, you will make the most progress by focusing on endeavors that clients want to work on with you. And while you continue to affirm the capabilities of clients, you should also be willing to provide information and to arrange needed action that is realistic and appropriate.

AGING

A potential feature of advanced age is that individuals may become less concerned about how others view them. If polite social behavior begins to seem less important to them, older persons sometimes become more outspoken, and they may appear to be more stubborn.

But old age can also be a time of increasing isolation. Consequently, although older clients may be more blunt and more cantankerous, they may also hunger for social interaction. So while they sometimes may not care much about the official purpose of the meeting, they are likely to appreciate the fact that the interaction is taking place.

Advancing age also tends to bring increasing physical difficulties. Two of the most relevant areas for workers are hearing loss and low energy. With regard to hearing loss, you should be prepared to speak more loudly if you see nonverbal behaviors such as turning the head to one side or staring at your lips. You may also need to repeat statements. And with regard to energy level, a client lacking stamina may necessitate an interaction that is briefer, slower paced, or in a different setting than what you had originally planned.

PSYCHOSES

As indicated by the SOAP note in Chapter 8, it is possible for you to offer supportive helping to psychotic individuals. For example, when working with persons who have schizophrenia, supportive helping can be a productive component of a comprehensive treatment program, as Carl Rogers (1967) and his colleagues demonstrated. Despite everyone's best efforts, though, psychotic persons may become easily irritated, and they may talk about topics that seem unrelated to your discussion. Consequently, we suggest the following tactics as potential ways of smoothing the interaction.

- Use an even, calm voice.
- Discuss concrete realities on which you both can agree.
- Be willing to provide structure and guidance, but avoid confrontation as much as possible.
- Don't get caught up in flights of fancy. Instead, if you don't understand something, admit your lack of comprehension.

LONG-STANDING ISSUES SUCH AS MISUSE OF ALCOHOL AND OTHER SUBSTANCES[1]

At times, client problems may relate to long-standing patterns of maladaptive behavior, such as the misuse of alcohol or other drugs. When that is the case, supportive workers may want to encourage movement toward new adaptive efforts. One way to do that is to use the basic skills already discussed and to consider ideas associated with two concepts: motivational interviewing and stages of change.

Motivational Interviewing

Psychologists William Miller and Stephen Rollnick (2002) have researched and advocated a style of intervention they call motivational interviewing. Their approach puts the focus on what the person with the difficulty has to say. In fact, *expressing empathy* (which often can be done through reflection) is the first principle of their technique.

Here is an example of empathy with an individual having alcohol-related difficulties. The person says, "My boyfriend and I can't drink around each other. If I drink with him I get very angry. We get in big fights about nothing. One time he called me the wrong name. If I hadn't been drunk, I would have shaken it off. But I really flipped out. I smacked him across the face in front of a lot of people. Then he took me home because I was an embarrassment to both of us." The listener reflects, "Drinking together has led to episodes that you regret."

The second principle is *highlighting differences* between the person's current behavior and the individual's own desires for the future. Two ways of identifying these discrepancies are to reflect remarks that (1) suggest the person recognizes there is a problem or (2) is dissatisfied about how things are going.

Here is an example that focuses on the existence of a problem. The person says, "On Halloween we got dressed up in costumes and went to a party. In the beginning we were having fun. Then I got drunk. I tried to do something with a girl who had a boyfriend. That was a mistake. The next day I said I wasn't going to drink anymore. But that only lasted about a month. Then I started getting drunk again." The listener responds by saying, "There are things you've done when

---

1 Most of this section is taken from *Straight Talk on Alcohol and Other Drugs / a web site for college students* by Kenneth France and Benjamin Dourte (http://www.alcoholandotherdrugs.com).

drunk that you don't want to do again, so you tried to give up drinking."

A second way to highlight differences is to focus on comments that indicate worry or apprehension the individual is having. For instance, a person says, "I've been arrested for underage drinking a few times. Now I'm nineteen, but I can't drive for another year. I have enough money for a car, but I got slapped with another underage drinking charge. If I get arrested again, I won't be allowed to drive until I'm twenty-four. And I really don't want to wait five years until I can drive. My biggest fear right now is getting another underage drinking charge." The listener reflects, "You dread getting arrested again for drinking."

Rolling with resistance is the third principle. Drs. Miller and Rollnick have reviewed the scientific literature on alcohol and other drugs and have concluded that there is no evidence to support the idea that arguing with people helps them to change. On the other hand, there is lots of evidence to support the nonconfrontational approach that motivational interviewing takes. Drs. Miller and Rollnick emphasize that it is the other person's problem and that any decision to change is up to that individual. Consequently, reluctance to change is to be expected, and when it occurs, it is simply acknowledged. Rather than trying to push a course of action, motivational interviewing calls for the listener to encourage the other person to generate options and to explore advantages and disadvantages of those possibilities.

The final principle is *supporting self-efficacy.* The objective here is to encourage the person to develop a realistic belief in his or her ability to handle challenges and to eventually succeed in making a change. Reflection again comes into play as the listener looks for opportunities to highlight comments that communicate (1) intention to change and (2) optimism about making progress.

Here is an example that focuses on intention to change. "Last month I had two friends killed in a car accident caused by alcohol. They weren't drinking. But their car was hit by a guy who had been drinking. He ran a red light and smashed into them. They died in the hospital later that night due to internal injuries. After that I made a pact with myself—I'm never again going to drive after I've been drinking." The listener reflects, "After the deaths of your friends, you became determined not to get behind the wheel when you're under the influence of alcohol."

The idea of reflecting optimism is shown in the following exchange. "I felt like I was spending too much time partying and that I got out of control too often. Now I don't go out during the week, and I work on the weekends. So I don't party that much anymore. I work to make money, but I also do it because it prevents me from being tempted to go out every weekend. I've removed myself from that scene and from the people I was around who did that all the time. When I do go out to have a good time, I don't have to get totally trashed. I can have a couple of drinks and that's it." The listener says, "Your new style feels good, and you believe you can stick with it."

Stages of Change

As just noted, sometimes efforts at changing are successful and sometimes they aren't. Intervenor actions can influence change, but ultimately the most important factor is the person's readiness to change—what Dr. Miller has called "making up one's mind." For a number of years, the topic of how individuals intentionally change aspects of themselves has been the focus of research by psychologists James Prochaska, John Norcross, and Carlo DiClemente (1994; Prochaska & Norcross, 2002) and by social worker Janice Prochaska (Prochaska & Prochaska, 1999). James Prochaska's interest in self-change arouse out of his anger and disappointment at not being able to help a person who was an alcoholic and who was frequently depressed. That person was his father. Mr. Prochaska consistently denied that he had a problem with alcohol. None of his family's attempts to change him were successful, and he refused professional help. When James Prochaska was a junior in college, his father died.

Now, years later, James Prochaska and his colleagues have developed a widely accepted theory of self-change that is relevant to alcohol and other drugs, as well as to many other areas. Regardless of the particular focus of change, the basic elements of the process seem to remain the same. There are stages that individuals tend to go through, and there are different strategies that they tend to use as they pass through the various phases. First, we'll take a look at what Prochaska and his colleagues have to say about the stages of change, and then we'll consider different strategies that can help people to change.

There appear to be six stages of change. Being in one stage does not necessarily mean a person will advance to the next level. When change does occur, though, it usually develops in ways described by the stages.

- **Precontemplation.** Although others may believe that the individual needs to change, a person in the precontemplation stage denies responsibility for those perceived difficulties and intends to continue on the current course. The issues that others see as problems are viewed by the individual as trusted ways of coping and as being under control. Any unwanted patterns that do exist are seen as being caused by others, and they are viewed as being the ones who must change. On occasions when those in the environment successfully pressure the person into new behavior, that change evaporates as soon as the external pressure stops. When others confront the person regarding problematic behavior, the individual may minimize the behavior or may offer rational, but flawed, explanations (although the brighter and more extroverted the person, the more convincing the rationalizing may seem). In addition, negative feelings may be swallowed (internalized)—a trait that is associated with depression. Nevertheless, in the person's mind, the disadvantages of changing outweigh the advantages.
- **Contemplation.** During this stage, the person tries to understand how things got to be the way they are and acknowledges that change is necessary, with the intended effort being in the future. Sidetracking can occur in several ways: requiring certain success before being willing to act, waiting for perfect conditions, or, toward the other extreme, rushing into impetuous action.
- **Preparation.** Now the individual becomes increasingly certain that this is the right decision and makes final arrangements necessary for taking action, including firming up a specific, realistic plan. Before moving to action, though, the person must decrease the number of disadvantages associated with changing and must increase the number of advantages associated with changing, so that the advantages clearly outweigh the disadvantages. (The rule of thumb is two new advantages for every abandoned disadvantage.)
- **Action.** At this time the individual takes public action. Potential difficulties include the following: inadequate preparation, giving up if there is no quick fix, and, at the opposite end of the continuum, maintaining efforts that are only partially successful.

- *Maintenance.* While gaining strength from a successful new style, the person in the maintenance stage also acknowledges a vulnerability to the old ways. Consequently the individual makes the sustained effort necessary to avoid brief lapses and to prevent relapses. When a slip occurs, the person should acknowledge it and should make a plan for remedying the situation that led to it. The individual must prepare for and withstand social pressure from others in the environment who continue to act in the old way.
- *Termination.* The old behavior does not tempt the person, who now has no fear of relapse. The individual is confident and comfortable with the new style. Reaching the termination stage is possible for people who have had difficulties with alcohol or other drugs. Research by Prochaska and his associates (Prochaska, Norcross, & DiClemente, 1994) has shown that 17 percent of former alcoholics and 16 percent of former cigarette smokers are in the termination stage. These individuals now completely abstain from use and are no longer tempted by their old habits.

When a relapse occurs in the action or maintenance stages, most individuals return to contemplation or preparation, rather than going all the way back to precontemplation. Here are some facts about relapse.

- A slip does not constitute a relapse.
- Complications are the norm, rather than the exception.
- Among self-changers, 20 percent or less are completely successful on the first try.
- It is normal to recycle several times.
- It is helpful to see recycling as an opportunity to learn from your mistakes.
- Using available support increases your chances of avoiding subsequent relapses.

Let's consider some of the ways we can integrate (1) the motivational interviewing ideas and (2) the stages of change concepts with (3) the material presented in earlier chapters of this book. The authors of all three of those sources have concluded that developing positive working relationships is crucial for human service workers. As people begin thinking about changing long-standing behavior, they need to believe that they can trust the worker and that the worker understands them. When clients feel ready to change the behavior, they need to consider various ways of bringing about the adjustments. Problem solving can be an effective means for considering options and developing plans. Individuals are more likely to follow through with those ideas if they have been actively involved in developing plans that are consistent with their own needs, values, and preferences.

In Chapter 4 we discussed the importance of not rushing into considering alternatives before fully exploring the client's thoughts and feelings. This is especially important if the person is in the precontemplation or contemplation stage of change. When clients are not yet ready to change, pushing them to adopt new behaviors usually is unsuccessful. In addition, they are likely to feel you don't understand them, which will interrupt the working relationship. As Miller and Rollnick (2002) have explained, it is important to roll with resistance rather than argue about the need for change. You can encourage motivation to change by expressing empathy in a way that highlights differences between the maladaptive behavior and the person's desire for improved well-being.

Exploring possible ways of changing is likely to be successful when the individual is in the preparation stage. Considering options with persons engaging in long-standing maladaptive behavior should include discussing ways of decreasing the disadvantages of changing and increasing the advantages of doing so. The plans that are developed ought to be concrete, and it is particularly important to consider possible obstacles, such as situational variables that might trigger a slip or a relapse. It may be helpful to set written targets that are phrased continuously. Such targets should also focus on behaviors to increase rather than on behaviors to avoid. Persons who set avoidance goals, such as "stop drinking alcohol," may not have identified the actions they need to take in order to achieve those goals. Consequently they may become discouraged and give up if they experience a slip. However, if they set goals such as "increase involvement in sober activities" or "increase the amount of time spent sober," they will have identified behaviors to increase and may experience improvement in self-efficacy as they take even limited steps toward their goals. As clients begin to take action, Observation Scaling can help them progress. When individuals reach the maintenance stage, collaborative efforts can focus on the development of plans for avoiding slips and preventing relapses.

In addition to integrating the motivational interviewing ideas and the stages of change concepts into the skills already discussed in this book, it may also be worthwhile to consider some strategies, outlined by Prochaska and his colleagues, that can be helpful at particular stages of change. Here are brief descriptions of those approaches. The phrase in parentheses is the term that Prochaska and his associates use for the strategy.

Strategies for Bringing About Change

- *Information Gathering.* (Consciousness-Raising) (Used during pre-contemplation and contemplation.) Information gathering involves input from others, such as personal experiences or research findings. It also includes observing, recording, and analyzing your own behavior, thoughts, and feelings. The resulting increased awareness is a prerequisite for meaningful action.
- *Community Involvement.* (Social Liberation) (Used during precontemplation, contemplation, preparation, and action.) Community involvement is tapping public ways in which your environment can be supportive, such as realizing there are others who share similar interests and discovering relevant societal rewards.
- *Expressing Feelings.* (Emotional Arousal) (Used during contemplation and preparation.) Expressing feelings can result from insights you discover, as well as from exposure to real or fictional accounts (movies, television shows, or novels) that touch relevant issues in your life.
- *Acknowledging Your True Values.* (Self-Reevaluation) (Used during contemplation and preparation.) Acknowledging your true values means coming to the heartfelt conclusion that you must change your behavior in order to become the kind of person you want to be.
- *Making a Commitment.* (Commitment) (Used during preparation, action, and maintenance.) Making a commitment involves believing you have what it takes to follow through with the plan you have developed.
- *Using Alternatives.* (Countering) (Used during action and maintenance.) Using alternatives occurs when you think and act in ways that are more productive than your old approach.

- *Dealing With Your Surroundings.* (Environmental Control) (Used during action and maintenance.) Dealing with your surroundings includes the following: identifying challenging situations you must face and preparing to cope with them; avoiding problematic circumstances and people that you can do without; and using physical reminders (notes, lists, or sayings) to help keep you on task.
- *Rewarding Good Effort.* (Rewards) (Used during action and early maintenance.) Ways of rewarding good effort include self-praise and enjoyable consequences that you provide yourself, as well as reinforcers from others.
- *Enlisting Social Support.* (Helping Relationships) (Used during action and maintenance.) Enlisting social support means developing or strengthening relationships with individuals who honestly convey understanding and caring.

MULTIPLE-CHOICE QUESTIONS

Items 1-6 involve a child; questions 7-11 concern a lower-class individual; items 12-16 focus on an older client; questions 17-20 involve an interaction with a psychotic person; items 21-24 deal with a student who has alcohol issues; and questions 25-28 focus on an individual with gambling difficulties. Your instructions are the same as in the previous chapters.

- For each of the following client statements, choose the response or responses you believe would be appropriate. (Several items have more than one correct answer.)
- Indicate your selection in writing.
- Read the discussions of all four options.
- If you are correct, go to the next item.
- If you are incorrect, think about the explanations and, if necessary, review relevant portions of the chapter; then, once you better understand the issues, proceed to the next question.

1. (In the waiting area you have just introduced yourself to a young client you are meeting for the first time.)
   A. Would you like to come with me to my office?

B. Your teacher was hoping we could talk about some of the things that happened in her class recently.

C. You've been here before, haven't you?

D. We're going to talk in my office which is the first room on the left.

Discussion of options.

A. Would you like to come with me to my office?
- Asking a "Would you" question gives the client a chance to say "No." Dealing with a negative reply would take up valuable time, so it is best to avoid questions that set you up for such responses.

B. Your teacher was hoping we could talk about some of the things that happened in her class recently.
- Starting your session in the waiting area is inappropriate. Wait until you are both settled in the interview room and the client is prepared for you to begin.

C. You've been here before, haven't you?
- By asking a leading question you are implying the answer you expect, which suggests that this may be the way you are going to conduct the session.

D. We're going to talk in my office which is the first room on the left.
- You provide appropriate information for directing the child to the session room, and you do so in a firm, cordial way that assumes the client will be cooperative.

2. (After exchanging pleasantries it is time to discuss the matter at hand.)

A. Your teacher asked that we talk. She says she is concerned about you running around and screaming during times when such behavior can be disruptive and dangerous.

B. Why do you think you are here?

C. I met with your teacher yesterday, and she told me that you have been behaving badly in the classroom.

D. Your teacher says you are hyperactive. She believes that you display a lot of off-task behaviors, that you have a short attention span, and that you seem to be lacking in self-control.

Discussion of options.

    A. Your teacher asked that we talk. She says she is concerned about you running around and screaming during times when such behavior can be disruptive and dangerous.
- Using understandable words, you concretely describe the specific reason for the meeting. Your account suggests neither agreement nor disagreement with the referral source, but it does imply that the referring teacher is interested in the student's welfare.

    B. Why do you think you are here?
- As with adults, "Why" questions can be threatening to children and can put them on the defensive.

    C. I met with your teacher yesterday, and she told me that you have been behaving badly in the classroom.
- It appears that you are taking the side of the teacher when you would prefer to be perceived as a friendly, neutral adult. You also do not describe the specific behaviors to be discussed.

    D. Your teacher says you are hyperactive. She believes that you display a lot of off-task behaviors, that you have a short attention span, and that you seem to be lacking in self-control.
- By employing terms such as "hyperactive," "off-task," "short attention span," and "lacking in self-control" you are running two risks. First, the child may not understand what those terms mean. Second, if the student does understand their meaning, they may be taken as negative labels.

3. (Having explained the reason for the meeting, you are ready to solicit comments from the child.)
    A. How are you getting along?
    B. Can you tell me what your teacher might be thinking of in terms of you running and screaming?
    C. Tell me about a time when you were yelling and running around.
    D. Your teacher says she's tired of you creating a commotion in the classroom.

Discussion of options.

A. How are you getting along?
   - You may get a usable response to this open question, but a more likely result is a simple, one-word reply such as "OK."
B. Can you tell me what your teacher might be thinking of in terms of you running and screaming?
   - Asking this closed question invites a brief, negative response.
C. Tell me about a time when you were yelling and running around.
   - By requesting a description of a specific event, you have a fairly good chance of getting a productive answer.
D. Your teacher says she's tired of you creating a commotion in the classroom.
   - You have already established the reason for the client meeting with you. This is an inefficient response.

4. I scream and run around when the other kids are doing the same thing. We do it in class, going to the cafeteria, and on the bus. But I'm the only one who ever seems to get in trouble.
   A. You've named a number of places where it might be important to stay in control. Let's talk about some of them.
   B. So, you get involved with commotion that goes on in several different settings. Tell me about one of those.
   C. You feel you're singled out to take the blame.
   D. It sounds like you've had difficulty in a number of locations. No matter where you go you're getting blamed for things.

Discussion of options.

A. You've named a number of places where it might be important to stay in control. Let's talk about some of them.
   - You start with a factual reflection that casts the issue in the positive light of staying in control, then you give the child an opportunity to choose what to discuss. This is a productive "range" response.
B. So, you get involved with commotion that goes on in several different settings. Tell me about one of those.
   - By combining an accurate reflection with a probe that requests a concrete description of a relevant scene, you move the interaction in a productive direction.

C. You feel you're singled out to take the blame.
   • This comment is an effective "depth" response. The client is likely to elaborate on his feelings about getting into trouble.
D. It sounds like you've had difficulty in a number of locations. No matter where you go you're getting blamed for things.
   • This option takes on an unnecessarily negative tone and leaves little room for helping the client gain a productive perspective.

5. When it's time to go to lunch, they don't line up, they don't get their coats on, and she gets mad. By the time we get to the cafeteria, she's yelling that I will have to go to detention or something like that. Then I get mad at her. While we're waiting to get our food, the other kids play around in line. They act like clowns to get people's attention.
   A. The other kids are misbehaving way more than you.
   B. So, you're in the cafeteria feeling angry, and you're with other students who are cutting up. What are you doing?
   C. It's hard to be good when others are being bad.
   D. Your classmates aren't doing what they're supposed to, and it frustrates your teacher.

Discussion of options.

A. The other kids are misbehaving way more than you.
   • If the client agrees with your factual reflection, it is unlikely he will be motivated to make changes in his own behavior. The risk of this remark clearly outweighs any benefits.
B. So, you're in the cafeteria feeling angry, and you're with other students who are cutting up. What are you doing?
   • You reflect a feeling and the circumstances, then follow with a question that focuses on the client's behavior.
C. It's hard to be good when others are being bad.
   • This general observation about life may be true, but it is not an accurate summary of what the client has said.
D. Your classmates aren't doing what they're supposed to, and it frustrates your teacher.
   • Like your client, you are changing the topic to the behavior of others.

6. Sometimes I act up and get wild. But when I need to, I just tell myself to chill out. I know that if I go on yelling and stuff, I'll get in trouble, which I'm not going to do.
   A. Your goal is to keep out of trouble, and one thing you've tried is telling yourself to stay calm.
   B. It seems that thinking to yourself "chill out" is not working very well for you.
   C. So you have experience with using calming self-statements.
   D. There are times when you yell and act up, but you believe you are able to calm down and control yourself.

Discussion of options.

A. Your goal is to keep out of trouble, and one thing you've tried is telling yourself to stay calm.
   • You have reflected the objective expressed by the client, and effectively moved the interaction into the alternatives phase of problem solving.
B. It seems that thinking to yourself "chill out" is not working very well for you.
   • Your response is overly negative. Rather than discounting what the young person has tried, it is better to build on those efforts.
C. So you have experience with using calming self-statements.
   • Although there are mental health professionals who commonly use the term "self-statements," most young people do not know what it means. Consequently, it is best to use less technical language or to explain such terms when you employ them.
D. There are times when you yell and act up, but you believe you are able to calm down and control yourself.
   • Your comment provides a factual reflection of what has been communicated.

The next five items relate to a client who is being seen in an office that screens applicants for rental assistance.

7. (You are meeting Mrs. Patrice Williams for the first time.)
   A. Offering your right hand, you say, "Hello Mrs. Williams, I'm Ms. Crawford. Thank you for coming in today."

B. Offering your right hand, you say, "Hello Patrice, I'm Ms. Crawford. Thank you for coming in today."

C. Offering your right hand, you say, "Hello Patrice, I'm Laura. Thank you for coming in today."

D. Upon seeing Patrice Williams, you say, "Hello, I'm Ms. Crawford. You must be my 4:00 appointment."

Discussion of options.

A. Offering your right hand, you say, "Hello Mrs. Williams, I'm Ms. Crawford. Thank you for coming in today."
- You demonstrate respect by offering to shake hands and by addressing the client by her last name.

B. Offering your right hand, you say, "Hello Patrice, I'm Ms. Crawford. Thank you for coming in today."
- Offering to shake hands suggests respect, but it is canceled out when you address the client by her first name while introducing yourself by your last name.

C. Offering your right hand, you say, "Hello Patrice, I'm Laura. Thank you for coming in today."
- The handshake shows respect, but the use of first names may suggest a degree of intimacy that really does not exist.

D. Upon seeing Patrice Williams, you say, "Hello, I'm Ms. Crawford. You must be my 4:00 appointment."
- You depersonalize your client by simply referring to her as an appointment time.

8. (Now that the introductions and other pleasantries are over, it is time for you to begin the body of your interview with Mrs. Williams.)

A. How are things going?

B. In order to determine your eligibility for rental assistance, I must gather information from you on a number of topics, including your employment situation. Do you work outside the home?

C. In order to determine your eligibility for rental assistance, I must gather information from you on a number of topics, including your employment situation. Tell me about your work for which you are paid.

D. In order to determine your eligibility for rental assistance, I must gather information from you on a number of topics, including your employment situation. What is the name of your current employer?

Discussion of options.

A. How are things going?
  • Your open question may be puzzling to the client, and it is not very likely to generate productive information.
B. In order to determine your eligibility for rental assistance, I must gather information from you on a number of topics, including your employment situation. Do you work outside the home?
  • After explaining the purpose of the meeting, you ask a closed question. By doing so, you are setting a tone that suggests you will be asking questions and expecting brief replies. If that is how you want the interaction to proceed, this is an appropriate response.
C. In order to determine your eligibility for rental assistance, I must gather information from you on a number of topics, including your employment situation. Tell me about your work for which you are paid.
  • You explain the interaction's purpose, and then use an open probe to request relevant information. This response allows the client some leeway in formulating a reply, and you are likely to receive a fair amount of descriptive information.
D. In order to determine your eligibility for rental assistance, I must gather information from you on a number of topics, including your employment situation. What is the name of your current employer?
  • Once explaining the purpose of the interaction, you ask for a small bit of information, suggesting that you will be precisely specifying topics Mrs. Williams is expected to address. This is the correct tone to set if you desire a complete but limited response from the client.

9. I work two jobs. During the week I'm a packer on the first shift at Cranston Tile, and on the weekends I'm a crew member with Wilson Janitorial Services. At both places I make minimum wage

plus a dollar. But last month when I was working at Wilson, my eight-year-old ran away. Luckily they found him, and he was home by the time I got there. But I don't want to have to leave my kids anymore on the weekends. That's why I'm applying for rental assistance, so I can quit the weekend job.

A. Your child running away is what led you to apply for assistance.

B. It was scary to think about what might have happened to your son. In the future, you wish to be able to provide more supervision.

C. In addition to applying for rental assistance today, what other options have you considered to give you more time with your children?

D. How come you moved into a place you knew you really couldn't afford?

Discussion of options.

A. Your child running away is what led you to apply for assistance.
- You have accurately reflected objective information, making this an effective "range" response.

B. It was scary to think about what might have happened to your son. In the future, you wish to be able to provide more supervision.
- Since you recognize both an emotion and the circumstances, this reflection is deeper than option A. It encourages the client to elaborate further on her fears and desires regarding her child.

C. In addition to applying for rental assistance today, what other options have you considered to give you more time with your children?
- Unless pursuing other options is relative to receiving rental assistance, this response may lead the client away from the task at hand.

D. How come you moved into a place you knew you really couldn't afford?
- This open question has a judgmental tone. It could start you toward an adversarial relationship with Mrs. Williams.

10. It's tough being a single parent. No matter how many hours I work, it's not enough. And working all of those hours means I'm gone from home a lot. I always worry when I'm away from my kids, but the weekends are especially bad because I'm gone all day with them on their own. If I could get this rental assistance, at least they wouldn't have those long stretches without me on Saturdays and Sundays.

   A. I know about a parenting group for single mothers that you might be interested in joining. It meets at 9:00 in the morning on Mondays, Wednesdays, and Fridays.

   B. Having your weekends free to spend with the kids would take away a good deal of anxiety for you. Tell me about the weekend your son ran away.

   C. Although you still would have many of the pressures of being a single mom, you believe not having to work on the weekends would be a big help.

   D. Handling these things on your own is a challenge. The financial pressure and concerns for the children are weighing heavily on you.

Discussion of options.

   A. I know about a parenting group for single mothers that you might be interested in joining. It meets at 9:00 in the morning on Mondays, Wednesdays, and Fridays.
      • Your suggestion sidetracks the interaction away from the reason for the meeting. Rather than focusing on rental assistance, you have introduced a resource that could not be used by any client who works first shift.

   B. Having your weekends free to spend with the kids would take away a good deal of anxiety for you. Tell me about the weekend your son ran away.
      • That is on target for a problem solving interview. The aim of this interaction, however, is to screen Mrs. Williams to see if she qualifies for rental assistance. The open probe that ends this response does not move you toward that end.

   C. Although you still would have many of the pressures of being a single mom, you believe not having to work on the weekends would be a big help.
      • After recognizing that some of the client's stressful circum-

stances are likely to continue, you focus on the concrete outcome that the person is seeking.
D. Handling these things on your own is a challenge. The financial pressure and concerns for the children are weighing heavily on you.
   • Though your reflections are accurate and appropriate, they don't keep the client directed toward the task at hand. There is an even more time-efficient response option that not only reflects the client's remarks, but also brings the interview closer to its objective.

11. That's why I'm here. I want to do whatever it takes to become eligible for rental assistance. Having that extra help will make a big difference in the kind of mother I can be for my children.
   A. Let's continue evaluating your eligibility by taking a look at your income.
   B. Applying for rental assistance is one option for easing the stress on your family. What else have you thought about trying?
   C. Then your goal here today is to apply for assistance in order to spend more time with your children.
   D. Working two jobs is hard, and you believe being with your kids on the weekends would be a significant improvement.

Discussion of options.

   A. Let's continue evaluating your eligibility by taking a look at your income.
      • Your comment focuses the interaction on a concrete task related to achieving the client's objective.
   B. Applying for rental assistance is one option for easing the stress on your family. What else have you thought about trying?
      • The aim of this interview is to establish the client's eligibility for rental assistance. Generating alternatives is beyond the scope of this interaction and may confuse the client.
   C. Then your goal here today is to apply for assistance in order to spend more time with your children.
      • The client described this goal in her opening remarks. Returning to that topic at this point is repetitive.
   D. Working two jobs is hard, and you believe being with your kids on the weekends would be a significant improvement.

- This reflection is accurate, but you are cycling back into material you already have addressed.

The next five items involve a problem-solving interaction with a 75-year-old man who had a stroke 10 months ago and remains paralyzed on his right side. He sits in his wheelchair as you talk with him.

12. I've been pretty much depressed lately. I had a stroke last fall, and this is my fourth nursing home since then. They tell me I may never walk again, and that really depresses me. My whole right side is paralyzed. I just don't want to accept what has happened to me. When they said that I may never be able to walk again, that really shook me up. But now that I'm here in this nursing home, my new physical therapist has me exercising again. Other places I've been gave up on me. They said, "We hate to tell you, but since no strength has come back to your arm or leg by now, it's not likely to ever come back, and you probably never will be able to walk."
    A. It's depressing to receive such a bleak report.
    B. But as you said, your physical therapist has you moving again, and this place hasn't given up on having you walk. It seems as though walking again may be something that actually will happen.
    C. The news about your physical losses has been really discouraging, and though you carry a great deal of sadness, you're glad to have resumed physical therapy sessions.
    D. You really didn't want to hear that gloomy prognosis.

Discussion of options.

A. It's depressing to receive such a bleak report.
    - Your comment uses the word "depressing," which can be taken as a strong clinical term.
B. But as you said, your physical therapist has you moving again, and this place hasn't given up on having you walk. It seems as though walking again may be something that actually will happen.
    - Your response steers the client toward a goal of walking again, which, according to many of the health professionals involved in his case, is highly unlikely. Though taking a pos-

itive approach is important, it is essential to focus on targets that are within the client's grasp.

C. The news about your physical losses has been really discouraging, and though you carry a great deal of sadness, you're glad to have resumed physical therapy sessions.
   • Your response recognizes the client's grief, and then focuses on a bright spot within his control: participating in physical therapy sessions.

D. You really didn't want to hear that gloomy prognosis.
   • Your reflection gets at the heart of the person's concern, which is the loss of a physical ability that is not likely to be regained.

13. I've also fallen out of my wheelchair twice. And I have constant back pain from arthritis which I've had for some time. So it's just a combination of everything.
   A. What medicine do you take for your arthritis?
   B. In addition to the loss of function on your right side, you've had setbacks caused by arthritis and by two falls.
   C. There are multiple factors affecting your physical condition, and at times you have felt quite disheartened. What would you say is your biggest stressor right now?
   D. With the paralysis, the falls, and your arthritis, you've had a lot of trouble lately.

Discussion of options.

A. What medicine do you take for your arthritis?
   • Because discovering this information is not related to the purpose of your meeting, asking such a question sidetracks the interaction away from the current topic. If you were a nurse doing an assessment, this question probably would be relevant and necessary.

B. In addition to the loss of function on your right side, you've had setbacks caused by arthritis and by two falls.
   • This factual reflection recognizes the information provided. It is a good "range" response if you desire to pursue a broad discussion, especially since in your previous remarks you have already recognized the client's reported feelings

C. There are multiple factors affecting your physical condition, and at times you have felt quite disheartened. What would you say is your biggest stressor right now?
  • After a surface-feeling reflection, you have directed the client toward a single topic to discuss at a deeper level. This is an effective "depth" response.
D. With the paralysis, the falls, and your arthritis, you've had a lot of trouble lately.
  • You accurately summarize what the client has told you.

14. I had been visiting my son quite a lot, and then he sold the home he had been living in. I don't like his new house. My wheelchair sinks down into the carpet, and I can't move around. He has to push me. And it's difficult to get through some of the doors. I feel uneasy when I'm there, like it's not a place where I should be.
  A. Some people I've talked to who are confined to a wheelchair have found a motorized chair to be quite helpful. What would you think about getting one to assist your mobility at your son's house?
  B. You feel disowned and abandoned by your son moving to a house that clearly was not meant for you.
  C. When with your son at his new residence, you feel awkward while you're there.
  D. You don't feel comfortable visiting your son at the new house. What have you tried in terms of coping with this new challenge?

Discussion of options.

  A. Some people I've talked to who are confined to a wheelchair have found a motorized chair to be quite helpful. What would you think about getting one to assist your mobility at your son's house?
    • Although such a response could be appropriate later in the interview, it is premature here because you have just begun to explore this topic.
  B. You feel disowned and abandoned by your son moving to a house that clearly was not meant for you.
    • Your underlying feeling reflection is dangerous. It may be inaccurate, and even if true, the client may not be ready to admit such thoughts and emotions.

C. When with your son at his new residence, you feel awkward while you're there.
  • This reflection acknowledges what the client has said.
D. You don't feel comfortable visiting your son at the new house. What have you tried in terms of coping with this new challenge?
  • Your first comment is appropriate to this phase of the session, but your open question moves the interaction too quickly into considering alternatives.

15. (After your last comment, the client does not say anything and there is a 10-second silence.)
  A. Did you hear what I just said?
  B. There's nothing else you have on your mind that you would like to discuss?
  C. (You say nothing.)
  D. So right now, you're pretty discouraged.

Discussion of options.

A. Did you hear what I just said?
  • This closed question addresses the silence, but your response is not likely to foster rapport.
B. There's nothing else you have on your mind that you would like to discuss?
  • Asking such a question is unnecessarily confrontational.
C. (You say nothing.)
  • By simply continuing the silence, you may help to create uneasy feelings in the interaction. Although a slower pace might be appropriate, you do not want to be too passive. Since your last comment was not a question, there is no need to give the client additional time before you say something else.
D. So right now, you're pretty discouraged.
  • This reflection recognizes a feeling that has pervaded all of the individual's comments. By making such an empathic response, you may help the person to continue talking.

16. Client: Yes. I would just like some peace of mind.
  Worker: What would you like to be more at ease about?

Client:Pardon?

A. Earlier you talked about not enjoying the visits with your son anymore. Tell me more about the relationship between the two of you.

B. You would like to be more at ease about something. What is it that you would like to be more at ease about?

C. What would you like to be more at ease about?

D. It doesn't seem to me that you are focused on what we are doing here. You need to do a better job of paying attention when I am talking.

Discussion of options.

A. Earlier you talked about not enjoying the visits with your son anymore. Tell me more about the relationship between the two of you.
   - Although your comments could be appropriate for facilitating exploration, the client has asked you what you just said. A more respectful answer is needed here.

B. You would like to be more at ease about something. What is it that you would like to be more at ease about?
   - Since the person did not understand or did not hear you, it is appropriate to repeat and to clarify your remarks. By offering this combination of a reflection and an open question, you increase the likelihood that the individual will provide a meaningful response.

C. What would you like to be more at ease about?
   - Simply repeating your question might be appropriate, but there is a more helpful option in this group.

D. It doesn't seem to me that you are focused on what we are doing here. You need to do a better job of paying attention when I am talking.
   - Your analysis and advice constitute a strong put-down of the client. Consequently, open communication may become less likely.

In the following four items, the client is a patient on the psychiatric unit of a hospital. Since arriving at the facility a week ago, the person has received a diagnosis of Schizophrenia, Paranoid Type. You are meeting with the individual after the two of you walked to the interviewing room from the cafeteria, where the patient had just finished lunch.

17. What do you want? I wasn't bothering anyone. All I was doing was eating lunch. I have a right to do that. I have a right to do that. I have a right to do that.

    A. Yes, patients have rights. And staff members also have rights. One of my rights is that I can go to the cafeteria and recall a patient to the ward when it is time for that person to talk with me.

    B. You seem worried about maintaining your rights. So the idea of justice is important to you.

    C. Yes, you do have a right to eat lunch in the cafeteria. When I asked if you were finished, you said, "Yes." So I thought we might talk a bit. What did you have for lunch?

    D. You're very angry about being here, and you really don't want to talk with me.

Discussion of options.

    A. Yes, patients have rights. And staff members also have rights. One of my rights is that I can go to the cafeteria and recall a patient to the ward when it is time for that person to talk with me.
       • Although true, your response is needlessly confrontational. By taking an authoritarian stance, you risk escalating the patient's hostility.

    B. You seem worried about maintaining your rights. So the idea of justice is important to you.
       • Since you are interacting with a person who has a thought disorder, your invitation to discuss an abstract topic is not likely to be productive (unless your purpose is to elicit examples of psychotic thinking).

    C. Yes, you do have a right to eat lunch in the cafeteria. When I asked if you were finished, you said "Yes." So I thought we might talk a bit. What did you have for lunch?
       • Defusing the patient's anger is your objective in making these comments. You begin by agreeing with the person;

you recall the facts of a recent interaction; you express your desires in a low-key way; and you end with an easily answered open question.

D. You're very angry about being here, and you really don't want to talk with me.

- Although your statement may be correct, the comment sets you up for two undesirable results: an affirmative response from the patient and increased difficulty in trying to establish a working relationship.

18. You're playing a game with me. You're playing a game with me. You know what I had for lunch. You know what I had for lunch. You're playing a game with me.

A. Some staff members know what you had to eat. But I don't know what you chose. How did you like what you had?

B. You're right. I have X-ray vision, and I can see through five sets of walls from here to the cafeteria. So I know exactly what you had for lunch.

C. I'm not intending to play a game with you, but I am trying to get to know you a little bit better. What did you think of lunch?

D. What game do you think I'm playing?

Discussion of options.

A. Some staff members know what you had to eat. But I don't know what you chose. How did you like what you had?

- By calmly stating your point of view and by asking an easily answered open question, you are attempting to lessen the patient's anger and to focus the interaction on a concrete, nonthreatening topic.

B. You're right. I have X-ray vision, and I can see through five sets of walls from here to the cafeteria. So I know exactly what you had for lunch.

- Your satirical response is likely to be disturbing to a patient who is having difficulty sorting out the real from the unreal.

C. I'm not intending to play a game with you, but I am trying to get to know you a little bit better. What did you think of lunch?

• In a low-key manner you state your intentions, and then ask an open question that focuses on the client's opinions regarding a recent event. Your efforts may result in a productive response.

D. What game do you think I'm playing?

• Unless you are doing so for diagnostic purposes, it is best not to play into the patient's delusional thinking.

19. Lunch was good. The food here is pretty good most of the time. I get to eat what I want. I like the cafeteria. It's the best part of being in the hospital.

A. You enjoy your meals here. I also like the cafeteria.

B. What else is good about being here?

C. Yes, food is something we all need. What is something else that you think we all need?

D. So, you look forward to mealtime.

Discussion of options.

A. You enjoy your meals here. I also like the cafeteria.

• By reflecting the client's remarks and then agreeing with them, you have identified a concrete reality on which you share a common opinion.

B. What else is good about being here?

• Before moving to another topic, first acknowledge what the patient has said.

C. Yes, food is something we all need. What is something else that you think we all need?

• Your combination response ends with a question that is likely to tax a person who has a thought disorder.

D. So, you look forward to mealtime.

• This brief reflection focuses on a positive emotion experienced by the patient.

20. Yeah. You get to pick what you want, and you can take your time to eat. The food is good, and it's hot.

A. Mealtimes are the highlights of your day here at the hospital. You really enjoy going to the cafeteria and eating there.

B. Meals here are something you enjoy. In addition to eating tasty food, what are some other things you like to do?

C. It looks to me like you've been enjoying the food too much. How many pounds have you gained since you got here last week?

D. It sounds to me like there were times in your life when you did not have hot, well-prepared meals.

Discussion of options.

A. Mealtimes are the highlights of your day here at the hospital. You really enjoy going to the cafeteria and eating there.
   • You make an accurate comment, but it adds little to the material you reflected in item 19.
B. Meals here are something you enjoy. In addition to eating tasty food, what are some other things you like to do?
   • Following your second reflection of the patient's satisfaction with the facility's food, you use that enjoyment as a bridge to a new topic. Whether or not the individual crosses your bridge, you have made a good effort.
C. It looks to me like you've been enjoying the food too much. How many pounds have you gained since you got here last week?
   • Your observation and question are provocative rather than being supportive.
D. It sounds to me like there were times in your life when you did not have hot, well-prepared meals.
   • Unless the purpose of the interaction is to gather historical information, you are better off concentrating on present thoughts and feelings rather than shifting the focus to the past.

The next four multiple-choice items focus on a student who is worried about being dismissed from college because of having failing grades for two semesters. The person has expressed regret regarding her academic failure and is beginning to explore how it came about.

21. I know that part of the reason I can't do well on exams is because I miss a lot of classes. My friends always want to go to parties at night, and we stay out late. In the morning I'm often too tired to go to class.
    A. How much do you drink at the parties?

B. You're thinking that the difficulty with exams might have something to do with attending parties in the evenings.

C. How could you go about telling your friends that you need to be spending more time studying instead of going to quite so many parties?

D. Too much partying is a common problem on college campuses. I'm guessing you know quite a few people who go to a lot of parties.

Discussion of options.

A. How much do you drink at the parties?
  • Although drinking may be an important issue, the client has not yet mentioned it. Consequently the question is premature and may elicit defensiveness from her.

B. You're thinking that the difficulty with exams might have something to do with attending parties in the evenings.
  • This reflection highlights the person's recognition that partying may be a problem and encourages further exploration of the issue.

C. How could you go about telling your friends that you need to be spending more time studying instead of going to quite so many parties?
  • The client has not yet expressed interest in decreasing the partying, so this question may demonstrate a lack of empathy. It also indirectly offers advice, which might help to generate an authoritarian atmosphere, as well as defensiveness from the client.

D. Too much partying is a common problem on college campuses. I'm guessing you know quite a few people who go to a lot of parties.
  • Although your statement may be accurate, it moves the focus away from the client and might even provide a way for her to justify the partying.

22. Yes. Some days I have such a bad hangover that I can't even make it to my afternoon classes.
A. Do you think you're drinking too much?
B. Drinking too much at parties has been affecting your health.

C. The sort of situation you are describing is pretty serious. It sounds like your low grades may be a result of an alcohol problem.

D. You sometimes feel sick late in the day, so you're thinking the partying has been affecting more than just your morning classes.

Discussion of options.

A. Do you think you're drinking too much?
- Although the client probably is drinking too much, this closed-ended question may result in the person becoming defensive. The response might also set the stage for an argument.

B. Drinking too much at parties has been affecting your health.
- This reflection is accurate, but it moves away from the client's focus on poor grades.

C. The sort of situation you are describing is pretty serious. It sounds like your low grades may be a result of an alcohol problem.
- You do not have enough information to determine whether there is an "alcohol problem," and the confrontation may lead the client to minimize any existing difficulties.

D. You sometimes feel sick until late in the day, so you're thinking the partying has been affecting more than just your morning classes.
- This reflection highlights the person's recognition of a problem and encourages further exploration.

23. I don't know. It's true that I'm having trouble with all my classes. But I like to party, and I think a social life should be part of the college experience.
　　A. It seems, though, that your partying may be getting out of hand. You just said that you often are still sick in the afternoon after you go to a party.
　　B. You have fun at the parties, and you want your time at college to involve more than just studying.
　　C. Although your academics aren't where you want them to be, you believe partying is one of the reasons for going to college.
　　D. What could you do to improve your grades?

Discussion of options.

A. It seems, though, that your partying may be getting out of hand. You just said that you often are still sick in the afternoon after you go to a party.
  • Your attempt to argue that the client is partying too much may encourage her to take a stand for the opposite opinion, which would interfere with developing a positive working relationship and would move the client further away from considering the need for change. "Rolling with resistance" and allowing clients to come to their own conclusions about the need for change is likely to result in a stronger commitment to adaptive action.

B. You have fun at the parties, and you want your time at college to involve more than just studying.
  • This reflection expresses your understanding of her perspective. In addition, though, it may move the client away from thinking about the need for change.

C. Although your academics aren't where you want them to be, you believe partying is one of the reasons for going to college.
  • Your reflection expresses empathy and involves rolling with resistance, while also maintaining a focus on low academic performance.

D. What could you do to improve your grades?
  • Taking action to improve her academics could be an important target for the client. But she has begun to focus on her partying, and your question might move her away from that subject.

24. Well yes. I like to party and have fun, and everyone else is doing it. But sometimes I think I'm drinking too much. I just don't know.

A. You're afraid your drinking might be excessive. One possibility for us would be to think about some ways to determine whether you are overdoing it.

B. You're beginning to think that your use of alcohol is a problem. What could you do to try to decrease your drinking?

C. You're unsure about whether your drinking is a problem.

D. Well, you said that your hangovers are keeping you from going to classes. So it sounds like your drinking is causing problems for you.

Discussion of options.

A. You're afraid your drinking might be excessive. One possibility for us would be to think about some ways to determine whether you are overdoing it.
   • Your response reflects the client's worry about alcohol use and gives her an opportunity to move toward information gathering. Such efforts are helpful for clients in the precontemplation stage.

B. You're beginning to think that your use of alcohol is a problem. What could you do to try to decrease your drinking?
   • The client is in the precontemplation stage. Even if she "goes along with you" and considers alternatives, she is unlikely to be committed to any of the ideas she generates.

C. You're unsure about whether your drinking is a problem.
   • Although your reflection expresses accurate empathy, it does not encourage any further movement in the stages of change. There is a better option.

D. Well, you said that your hangovers are keeping you from going to classes. So it sounds like your drinking is causing problems for you.
   • Your analysis is probably accurate. However, you risk the client becoming defensive and starting to argue with you. Her recognition of the problem is likely to be stronger if she develops the conclusion herself.

The client in the remaining multiple-choice items has been gambling heavily for five years. In his interaction with you, he has been expressing remorse and is beginning to discuss the consequences of his gambling.

25. I've lost a lot of money from gambling over the years, and I've built up a lot of debts. Just this year the bank foreclosed on my home. I used to have family and friends who tried to help me financially, but they all seem to be pulling away.
    A. Other than asking for help from family and friends, what other steps have you taken to pay off the money you owe?
    B. You've experienced some very unpleasant consequences related to gambling.
    C. It's been sad for you to lose both your home and your friends.

D. It sounds like you've been engaging in pathological gambling.

Discussion of options.

A. Other than asking for help from family and friends, what other steps have you taken to pay off the money you owe?
   - This question moves the focus away from the need to change the gambling.
B. You've experienced some very unpleasant consequences related to gambling.
   - Your reflection highlights the client's recognition of a problem.
C. It's been sad for you to lose both your home and your friends.
   - This reflection expresses empathy, but it doesn't include recognition of the client's awareness of a gambling problem.
D. It sounds like you've been engaging in pathological gambling.
   - Providing a label does not do anything to move the client forward in the stages of change.

26. Yes. And the worst one is that my wife left me when the bank took our house. I miss her so much. I really need to quit gambling.
    A. What types of things have you done to try to stop gambling?
    B. You even lost your wife because of the gambling.
    C. Do you think your wife will come back if you stop gambling?
    D. You're regretting the loss of someone who is very important to you, and you're feeling ready to find alternatives to gambling.

Discussion of options.

A. What types of things have you done to try to stop gambling?
   - This question recognizes his desire to change and encourages him to begin generating alternatives.
B. You even lost your wife because of the gambling.
   - Although this is an accurate surface reflection, it is simply an extension of the last reflection. The client has moved to the preparation stage, so it is important to move with him and reflect his desire for change.
C. Do you think your wife will come back if you stop gambling?
   - Although this question may result in identifying an advan-

tage to changing his behavior, it focuses on a side issue rather than on highlighting his recognition of a need for change. In addition, it is more effective to identify advantages to change that don't rely on the decisions of other people.

D. You're regretting the loss of someone who is very important to you, and you're feeling ready to find alternatives to gambling.
   • This reflection highlights the client's regrets regarding gambling and also acknowledges his movement to the preparation stage.

27. I *am* ready, and I feel like I can do it. I think my wife will come back if I stop gambling. But I know that staying away from gambling is going to be hard.
    A. Gambling has been a part of your life for so long that you believe it will be difficult to give it up.
    B. Stopping something you've been doing for so long won't be easy, but you're feeling motivated and optimistic.
    C. You're afraid you won't be able to stop gambling.
    D. There have been times in the past when you tried to stop gambling. What types of things did you do on those occasions?

Discussion of options.

A. Gambling has been a part of your life for so long that you believe it will be difficult to give it up.
   • This reflection is accurate, but it expresses pessimism rather than supporting self-confidence.
B. Stopping something you've been doing for so long won't be easy, but you're feeling motivated and optimistic.
   • This reflection recognizes the client's realistic outlook, while also supporting his growing self-confidence.
C. You're afraid you won't be able to stop gambling.
   • This reflection is inaccurate and may move the client away from the preparation stage.
D. There have been times in the past when you tried to stop gambling. What types of things did you do on those occasions?
   • Your question probably will get the client to begin thinking about alternative courses of action, which will encourage his

preparation for change. Unfortunately, though, you missed an opportunity to support his growing optimism.

28. I'm really motivated, but it's going to be difficult to stop because gambling was my release. It was a way to escape when I was feeling down or stressed.
    A. There seems to be a part of you that really doesn't want to give up the gambling because it was an effective escape when you were having rough times.
    B. Although you're motivated, you know it will be difficult to stop gambling.
    C. But you've decided that you need to stop a habit that has cost you both your wife and your home. What approaches have you considered to keep yourself from gambling?
    D. You'll miss gambling because it has given you a way to deal with uncomfortable emotions. What else have you done to cope with distressing feelings?

Discussion of options.

A. There seems to be a part of you that really doesn't want to give up the gambling because it was an effective escape when you were having rough times.
   • Although it can be helpful to reflect ambivalence, the client was explaining potential challenges to his desire for change rather than expressing uncertainty. Consequently, this reflection is inaccurate.
B. Although you're motivated, you know it will be difficult to stop gambling.
   • This reflection uses many of the client's own words and has a pessimistic focus.
C. But you've decided that you need to stop a habit that has cost you both your wife and your home. What approaches have you considered to keep yourself from gambling?
   • The client has identified an important disadvantage to changing his gambling behavior. Your combination response fails to recognize that disadvantage.
D. You'll miss gambling because it has given you a way to deal with uncomfortable emotions. What else have you done to cope with distressing feelings?

• Your reflection expresses empathy regarding a loss the client will experience if he gives up gambling. The open question encourages him to prepare for action by exploring ways to offset a disadvantage associated with changing.

SHORT-ANSWER QUESTIONS

Write your answer for each of the following questions.

1. Provide a statement you might say to a young client upon first meeting the child.
2. (Questions 2, 3, and 4 involve the same child.) Imagine you are working with a young person who has been referred to you because of missing a lot of school days. The mother is the person who initiated the referral. You are now in a one-to-one interaction with the child, and you want to describe the purpose of the session. What might you say?
3. Give an example of what you could say to the child in order to begin the process of gathering information.
4. Since the interaction has been progressing nicely, you have not prevented your young client from walking over to the bookcase and examining the titles. But now the child asks if it is OK to pull out a yearbook and look at it. You believe that would be too disruptive. Provide an example of what you might say.
5. You are working with a lower-class client and you ask to see the person next week. The individual says, however, that it will be extremely difficult to arrange child care until two weeks from now. What do you do?
6. You are in your third session with a lower-class individual, and in your opinion, the person is in a bad relationship at home. But the reason she is seeing you is because of the disruptive behavior displayed by her 7-year-old son. You have brought up your beliefs regarding the relationship between the two adults, but the client has indicated a preference to keep your work focused on her son. What do you do?
7. An 80-year-old client spends the first ten minutes of an initial interaction complaining about the difficulty of coming to your

office. Nevertheless, the person eventually is cooperative. At the end of the meeting, the client asks if it would be possible for you to visit the nursing home where he lives. How do you respond?

8. You are conducting a 45-minute interview with a 78-year-old person, but 20 minutes into the interaction the individual seems to become very tired. What do you do?

9. You are interacting with a person who has schizophrenia, and you want to find out how he likes the sheltered workshop he has been attending for the last week. You ask, "How do you like the workshop?" and he says "It's snowy outside. Spaghetti and tuna fish for lunch." (In fact, it is 85° outside, and he had a turkey sandwich for lunch.) How do you respond?

10. In the psychiatric unit of a hospital, you are interacting with a person who has schizophrenia. You want to discuss where she might go after being discharged. In response to your question, "Where would you like to live after you leave the hospital?" she launches into a discussion of cancer cures via hypnosis. What do you say next?

11. You have been interacting with a person who has been placed on probation at work due to poor attendance. Although she has begun missing at least one day of work a week because of hangovers, she does not believe that her drinking is a problem. How do you respond?

12. A client says, "I want to stop drinking, but my friends pressure me to continue. I don't want to lose my friends." How would you respond?

POSSIBLE ANSWERS FOR SHORT-ANSWER QUESTIONS

The answer-checking procedures remain the same as before.

- For each item, compare your answer to the one we provide.
- If you believe your answer is correct, you are done with that item.
- With any question for which you believe your answer is incorrect, consider our answer and, if needed, review relevant portions of the chapter. Keep your original answer that you now think is incorrect, but add to it a response that you believe would be correct.

1. "Hi. I'm Mrs. Martin. Let's go to my office. It's the first door on the right." This statement provides an introduction, a positive invitation to the interviewing room, and directions on how to get there.

2. "Your mother is worried about the number of times you have been absent from school. She asked that you and I talk about that." In a straightforward way, you have described the reason for the meeting.

3. "I want you to think about the last time you were absent. Tell me the reason you didn't go to school that day." This request identifies a specific event and calls for the young person to describe a particular aspect of the episode. Such structuring increases your chances of getting a productive response.

4. "Right now, I would like us to continue talking together, rather than for you to look at the yearbook. But if we continue to have a good session, I will save three minutes at the end for you to look at any book you like." In a positive way, you state your expectations (which deny the child's request), then you give the young person an opportunity to engage in the desired activity (dependent upon you first getting what you want).

5. If the consequences of waiting are not too negative, arrange an appointment for two weeks from now. But if there are strong reasons for meeting next week, engage the client in problem-solving with child care as the focus.

6. For now, concentrate on the topic your client wants help with—her son. As your work progresses, there may be opportunities to address the adult relationship when it relates to issues regarding the child.

7. If it is realistic for you to visit the nursing home, agree to do it. But if that is out of the realm of possibility, consider seeking some other type of contact, such as a telephone interaction.

8. Terminate the interaction. Provide any assistance that might be appropriate and necessary. Consider scheduling subsequent interactions for briefer time periods.

9. Try to keep the sheltered workshop as your topic. You might attempt a more focused statement such as, "Instead of talking about the weather or food, let's talk about the workshop. Tell me what you did at your station this morning."

10. Attempt to return the interaction to the topic of discharge planning. One possible response would be, "Today you are thinking a

lot about cancer and hypnosis, but we also need to think about where you are going to live after you leave the hospital. Before you came into the hospital, you were living with your parents. What do you think about living with them again?"

11. Roll with the resistance and don't argue. Express empathy, but avoid supporting her impression that the drinking is not a problem. A possible reflection would be, "You're missing more work than used to be the case, but you don't think your drinking has played a part in that change."

12. The client has identified a disadvantage of decreasing the use of alcohol. It is important to address that disadvantage. A possible response would be, "Changing will involve finding ways to cope with what your friends think."

FILL-IN-THE-RESPONSE QUESTIONS

Listed below are a series of client statements. For each one, write a worker response that you believe would be appropriate.

1. (The client is a child.) When I stay up late at night I get sleepy, so I don't really mind when mom sends me to bed early. If I do go to bed early and sleep a lot, I can study faster, and I can do my other work faster.

2. (The client is a child.) When I get in the big world, I'll have to control my temper. If somebody bumps into my back and says, "Excuse me," I'll have to accept their apology because it's not always their fault.

3. (The client is a lower-class individual.) Someone stole my car. I reported it to the police. My insurance company says that I have to get the police to send them a copy of the police report. I went to the police station and asked for them to send a copy of the report to my insurance company, but the police said I have to send them a request in writing. But I don't write too good. Will you help me write a letter to the police?

4. (The client is a lower-class individual you are meeting with for the first time. Your organization already has reported the situation to the child abuse authorities.) My doctor said I should come see you. She thinks I need to discipline my child in a different way.

I've been using an ironing cord on him when he is bad. And he is bad a lot of the time.

5. (The client is a 76-year-old person who is a resident at the nursing home where you work.) I know everybody seems to be sick with a cough or the flu or something. But I hate this quarantine you have us under. I have to eat in my room. I can't go to the chapel. The chaplain set up a video camera so you can see the service on television, but the picture is all wobbly and I can hardly make it out.

6. (The client is an 83-year-old individual who is a resident at the nursing home where you work.) At the home where I was before, I had my own television, but it won't fit in my room here. The space is too small. So I've tried listening to recorded books. But they put the player in the second drawer down from the top, and I can barely reach it or look down to see how to change it or how to start it and stop it.

7. (The client is a person who has schizophrenia and is refusing to take his medication for glaucoma. The purpose of the interaction is to encourage him to use his eye drops. If he continues his current practice of not using them, he will lose his sight.) I am Christ. And in five years I will have the second coming. At that time, you will be one of my disciples. Together, we will change the world forever. Nothing will be as it was. Amen. Amen. And Amen.

8. (The client is a person who has schizophrenia.) I've been eating rolls and jumping poles. And you know what that can do to you.

9. I don't want to give up smoking, but the doctor told me that my lungs look pretty bad. My mother got lung cancer and my uncle died of emphysema—both because of smoking.

10. I'm really ready to try again to stop drinking. I know that until I quit, I'm not going to get my life back on track and find a good job.

POSSIBLE ANSWERS FOR
FILL-IN-THE-RESPONSE QUESTIONS

For each response opportunity, there are many possible correct answers. We list two, and, as in previous chapters, we suggest you use them in the following manner.

- Look at our two answers and think about them.
- Consider relevant material covered in the chapter.
- Read the client statement again, then immediately read your answer and the two options listed here.
- Write another response that you believe might be an improvement on your first effort.
- Repeat this procedure for each of the remaining items.

1. • So there are some advantages of having an early bed time.
   • You feel OK about having an earlier time for going to sleep.
2. • You're looking ahead, and you know that it will be important to be able to control your anger.
   • You believe it will be a good idea to respond to others in polite ways rather than in angry ways.
3. • Yes.
   • Yes. We can do it together. It does sound like you've been having a very frustrating time, not only having your car stolen, but then also having to deal with the rules of the insurance company and the police.
4. • It seems that what you have been doing has not been working as well as you would like. One thing we can do together is talk about some other ways of disciplining children.
   • You have been using a lot of physical punishment, but your son still acts up. If you decide to work with me, we could take a look at some other kinds of discipline you might want to try with him.
5. • The quarantine restrictions are irritating.
   • You miss eating in the dining room and attending the chapel services.
6. • You had hoped to start listening to some recorded books, but it's hard to operate your player where it is now.
   • Listening to recorded books would be more enjoyable if it were easier to get to your player. Where would you prefer it to be?
7. • What will happen five years from now is important to you. In order to see what is happening then, you must use your eye drops now. If you continue refusing to use them, you will become blind.
   • You believe the world needs what you have to offer. If you want to see how others react to you, using your eye drops is something you must do. Otherwise, you will become unable to see.

8. • No, I'm afraid I don't understand about the rolls and the poles.
   • No, I'm really not following what you're saying.
9. • You're afraid you might develop a life-threatening illness if you continue smoking.
   • The doctor's report on the condition of your lungs has you worried.
10. • You're looking forward to the positive opportunities that could develop after you give up alcohol.
    • A future without alcohol has a lot of advantages. You have discovered, though, that there a number of issues you will have to deal with if you are to succeed in staying away from it. Based on your previous attempts to abstain, what are some things you know you will have to cope with this time?

SUMMARY

When working with children, use an understandable vocabulary, but keep the demeanor of an adult professional. Since most young people do not refer themselves, you should give attention to three areas: establishing yourself as a caring adult who is not taking sides against the child, clarifying the purpose of the interaction, and addressing confidentiality issues in a straightforward manner. Because of the child's developing mental abilities, you may need to provide a fair amount of structure with regard to two issues: gathering information and fostering appropriate behavior.

Compared to middle-class persons who are accustomed to delayed gratification and feel a strong degree of control over their lives, individuals in lower socioeconomic classes may have somewhat different values. For example, there tends to be more emphasis on immediate gratification and on factors outside of one's control. Consequently, with lower-class clients, it often is appropriate to focus on the present and on the short-term future and to recognize the harsh realities that may be confronting the person. Specific considerations to keep in mind include the following: demonstrating respect, maintaining a professional demeanor, and providing appropriate direction.

Older clients may have a tendency to be more open in expressing their criticisms and complaints. But despite such bluntness, they may highly value the fact that someone is talking with them. When interacting with an older individual, you should keep in mind the impact of any physical difficulties, especially as they relate to hearing ability and energy level.

Supportive helping can play a role in services offered to psychotic individuals. If you work with such persons, practices to keep in mind include the following: speaking in a calm voice, focusing on realities that are easily agreed upon, offering guidance while attempting to avoid confrontation, and, rather than encouraging psychotic thinking, admitting when you do not understand something the person has said.

Long-standing maladaptive behavior, such as the misuse of alcohol or other substances, is sometimes a reason for clients seeing you. With such persons, you can encourage motivation to change by expressing empathy, highlighting differences between current behavior and future desires, rolling with resistance, and supporting self-confidence. Productive efforts are further enhanced when you recognize an individual's current stage of change: precontemplation, contemplation, preparation, action, maintenance, or termination. Knowing the client's stage of change enables you to use approaches that are particularly helpful for that stage.

Congratulations! You've now made it through scores of practice items and—hopefully—several recorded role plays. Having worked hard to develop your helping skills, you need to continue using those talents in order to maintain and enhance your abilities. If you are an undergraduate or graduate student, arrange an internship or get a job that involves supportive helping. And if you are out of school, look for career or volunteer opportunities that will allow you to apply what you have learned. We hope your endeavors are rewarding, and we wish you the best.

Appendix A

INTRODUCTIONS EXERCISE

The following exercise works well with 16 participants, but adjustments can be made so that it can be used with almost any number. For a group of 16, the activity takes about 45 minutes.

PHASE 1

Participants form teams of two. As much as possible, class members should select partners they do not already know. After the teams are created, they spread themselves throughout the room.

The first roles are listener and talker, and eventually the roles switch so that everyone has a chance to do both. Each team decides who will listen first and who will talk first. The task of the listener is to listen without saying anything. (It is OK to have "Mmhmms" and head nods.) The task of the talker is to spend two minutes introducing yourself.

The leader starts the groups, stops them two minutes later, then gives the following instruction. "Listeners, you may ask any questions that came to mind. And talkers, you may respond to those questions." After a minute or so, have the team members switch roles and repeat the process.

PHASE 2

Teams form groups of four. The task is to introduce your partner to the new team. After you have made your introduction, your partner may make any additions or corrections to the information. The leader starts the groups and monitors their progress but does not start and stop individual introductions.

343

PHASE 3

Each group of four joins another to form groups of eight. The task is to introduce someone from the team you just met—*not* your original partner. Other aspects are the same as in Phase 2.

PHASE 4

The groups of eight join to form a group of sixteen. The task is to introduce someone from the group of four you just met. It is easiest to sit in a circle and for one person to do an introduction, then for subsequent introductions to consistently move to that person's right (or left). At the beginning of an introduction the leader can indicate for the individual being introduced to raise a hand. And at the end of the introduction, the leader can ask if the introduced person has any additions or corrections. When the leader was not a member of a group, some brief self-disclosing comments are appropriate after the last introduction.

PROCESSING

The leader begins the processing by stating that the exercise had two purposes. One is that of an icebreaker. It is a way of getting to know one another, which is important because of the trust that is necessary in order to provide and accept feedback on the use of helping skills. The second purpose is to consider a variety of issues associated with listening. The leader can ask the group to discuss the following topics. In parentheses are typical comments that occur.

Again, don't read this section prior to participating in the exercise.

- How did you feel when you were the original talker?
  (I felt uneasy talking about myself. I wasn't sure what to say. I wanted some response from my partner.)
- How did you feel when you were the original listener?
  (I wanted to ask questions. It was tough just to listen.)
- How did you feel as you were being introduced to the subsequent groups?
  (It was nice to be the center of attention. It felt good to know that the person had listened to the information about me.)

- How did you feel as you were making introductions to subsequent groups?
(It was hard. I realized I had forgotten a lot. I wanted to get it right.)
- What did you notice about the length of the introductions as the exercise progressed?
(They got shorter.)

At the end of the processing the leader can review the comments and can make the following points.

- Listening is hard work.
- Listening is selective. You never recall everything the person said.
- There is a natural urge to ask questions, but it is possible for you to resist that urge.

While the participants are still seated in the circle, the leader can begin the task of learning names by using the following exercise. Start with the person on the immediate right or left of the leader and have that individual provide his or her first name. Proceed in the same direction to the next participant. Have that person give his or her first name and then have that individual say the name of the first participant. Move to the third person. That individual says his or her name, the name of the second person, then the name of the first person. Continue in this manner. If a participant forgets a name, have the previously introduced person say his or her name again. At the end, the leader does a complete circuit.

Appendix B

MODES OF RESPONSE EXERCISE

Interviewer: How are things going?

Client: I'm really worried about my father. He's having surgery tomorrow, and he will be receiving a general anesthetic. I've heard of people being put to sleep and not waking up. And I'm not even sure he needs this operation.

What might you say next? For each of the ten possibilities listed below, indicate your opinion of the reply by putting a vertical mark somewhere on the hindering/helpful line. If you like the response your mark should be to the right, and if you don't like the response your mark should be to the left.

A. I'm sure there's nothing to worry about.
   hindering _____ helpful

B. You should try thinking about something besides his operation.
   hindering _____ helpful

C. You're probably feeling this way because you haven't had a chance to talk with his doctor.
   hindering _____ helpful

D. I 'm sorry you're troubled, but everything will be OK.
   hindering _____ helpful

E. How have you tried to deal with your fears?
   hindering _____ helpful

F. Will you be with him tomorrow?
   hindering _____ helpful

G. You don't really want him to go without the surgery, do you?
   hindering _____ helpful

H. Are you going to talk with your father? Can you tell him how you really feel?
   hindering _____ helpful

I. Why did you wait until now to voice your concerns?
   hindering _____ helpful

J. It's scary to think about what might happen tomorrow.
   hindering _____ helpful

Appendix C

FEEDBACK SHEET

Feedback

Interviewer: _____ Date: _____ Client: _____

Helpful Behavior	Hindering Behavior	Alternative Behavior
Nonverbal		
Verbal		

Appendix D

COURSE STRUCTURE

The group or class needs to be structured in a way that encourages practice. With a group of sixteen participants and a single instructor, here is one possibility for using class time.

There are four groups (A, B, C, D) of four. During lecture-discussion days all four groups meet together. On the first day that involves role playing, groups A and B meet with the instructor, group C meets separately, and group D meets separately. During each of the three role-playing meetings there are four video-recorded role plays. If available, a trainer (an individual who has previously completed the course) leads each four-person group by setting up the role plays and by supervising the feedback. On the second day that involves role playing, groups C and D meet with the instructor, group A meets separately, and group B meets separately.

Specific meeting possibilities include the following.

165-minute night class
Day 1

	4:45	Group C (location #2)
	6:30	Lecture-discussion
	7:30	Groups A and B (location #1)
		Group D (location #2)

Day 2

	4:45	Group A (location #2)
	6:30	Lecture-discussion
	7:30	Groups C and D (location #1)
		Group B (location #2)

180-minute morning class
Day 1

	9:00	Lecture-discussion

10:00   Groups A and B (location #1)
        Group C (location #2)
        Group D (location #3)
11:45   Discussion

Day 2

9:00   Lecture-discussion
10:00   Groups C and D (location #1)
        Group A (location #2)
        Group B (location #3)
11:45   Discussion

Twice-a-week class

Day 1 Single 50-minute period
3:00   Lecture-discussion

Day 2 Double period (110 minutes)
1:00   Group C (locátion #2)
3:00   Groups A and B (location #1)
        Group D (location #2)

Day 3 Single period
3:00   Lecture-discussion

Day 4 Double period
1:00   Group A (location #2)
3:00   Groups C and D (location #1)
        Group B (location #2)

The performance and processing of a single role play interaction can take place in the following manner.

The instructor (or trainer) asks for a volunteer to be the worker. That person steps outside. Next, an individual volunteers to be the client. (In the large group, participants experience greater variety if the client is not a member of the worker's small group.) The leader gives the client a card with two or three sentences describing the role to be done. The client takes a seat and, in his or her own words, describes the circumstances and related feelings. The leader asks the worker to return, then signals the role play to begin.

During the role play the leader writes down (as much as possible) on a feedback sheet what the worker says and does. After three to five minutes, the leader stops the role play immediately following a worker comment.

Processing begins by the worker saying what he or she liked or didn't like about the performance. Next, the client gives feedback to the worker. Then each of the remaining participants gives feedback to the worker, followed by the leader providing feedback. Finally, the leader gives the worker a chance to make comments or ask questions regarding the feedback. The group then watches the recording of the role play. After the recording is over, the leader asks if there are any issues that participants would like to discuss. (This is the time when "should haves," "would haves," and "could haves" are addressed.)

The preceding activity generally takes 20 to 30 minutes. Consequently, there is time for four role plays during each role playing meeting.

If the four-person groups do not have trainers or videographers, there are four student roles for each interaction: worker, client, videographer, and leader (who completes a feedback sheet).

After each four-person group, the trainer or one of the members gives the recording and completed feedback sheets to the instructor. The instructor watches the recording and puts his or her own comments on the feedback sheets, then returns the sheets at the next class. If students wish, they can have their role plays recorded on their own personal media; otherwise, all four role plays are on the same recording.

Appendix E

CONSENT FORMS

CONSENT FOR PSYCHOLOGICAL ASSESSMENT AND TREATMENT

for

_____

(name of person under the age of 18)

with

Kenneth France, Ph.D.
Licensed Psychologist

The purpose of providing psychological services to children and adolescents is to help them cope with the demands of growing into adulthood. With the young person, the psychologist discusses situations the individual is encountering and how the person feels about them.

If the young person chooses to work with the psychologist, they also consider ways of responding to demanding circumstances. In order to develop a clear understanding of the individual's thoughts and expectations, the psychologist may ask the person to participate in assessment activities such as responding to items on a personality questionnaire, completing a student skills checklist, or using a goal-setting procedure. (Any materials or tests used during these sessions are available for inspection by the parents or guardians of the young person.) After each session, the psychologist writes a progress note, which will be kept in the psychologist's file for 5 years.

In Pennsylvania, outpatient psychotherapy for persons under the age of 18 requires the consent of a legal guardian. Parents or legal guardians also control access to the treatment records of children 13 and under. But from age 14 through age 17, adolescents control access to their own outpatient treatment records. Regardless of the client's age, psychotherapists are required by law to act in ways that will preserve life and will protect persons from harm in cases of child abuse and in situations involving immediate danger. In both of those instances, the law requires that confidentiality be violated when it is necessary to do so in order to protect the welfare of clients or others.

The psychologist is a resource, but progress will be the result of the young person's own effort. There is no guarantee of success.

The legal guardians of the individual are (please print):

_____

I agree for my child to receive psychological services.

_____   _____
Parent/Guardian's Signature   Date

_____   _____
Parent/Guardian's Signature   Date

_____   _____
Witness   Date

CONSENT FOR PSYCHOLOGICAL ASSESSMENT AND TREATMENT

for

(name of person under the age of 18)

with

Kenneth France, Ph.D.
Licensed Psychologist

Having had part of a session with me, you know what it is like for us to talk together. This form will tell you what we will do if we continue to meet.

We will be working together to help you cope with the demands of being a young person in today's world. We will discuss things that happen to you and how you feel about them.

If you choose to continue working with me, we will also consider ways of responding to circumstances you face. In order to help us develop an understanding of your thoughts and hopes for the future, I may ask you questions or give you tests. After each session, I will write a progress note, which will be kept in my file for 5 years.

In Pennsylvania, outpatient psychotherapy (such as the counseling we do here) for persons under the age of 18 requires the permission of a legal guardian, such as one of your parents. Parents or legal guardians also decide who can see the counseling records of children 13 and under. But from age 14 through age 17, adolescents control access to their own outpatient therapy records. Regardless of the client's age, psychotherapists are required by law to act in ways that will preserve life and will protect persons from harm in cases of child abuse and in situations involving immediate danger. In both of those instances, the law requires that I talk to others about you when it is necessary to do so in order to protect your welfare or the welfare of others.

I am here to help you, but any progress you make depends on your own effort. I may not be able to help you get what you want.

Please check one of the following.

_____ I agree to work with you.

_____ I do not agree to work with you.

_____ _____
Young Person's Signature   Date

_____ _____
Witness   Date

REFERENCES

Bandura, A.: *Self-efficacy: The exercise of control.* New York: Freeman, 1997.

Bandura, A., and Locke, E.A.: Negative self-efficacy and goal effects revisited. *Journal of Applied Psychology, 88*: 87-99, 2003.

Barlow, D.H., Allen, L.B., and Choate, M.L.: Toward a unified treatment for emotional disorders. *Behavior Therapy, 35*: 205-230, 2004.

Berry, D.S., and Pennebaker, J.W.: Nonverbal and verbal emotional expression and health. *Psychotherapy and Psychosomatics, 59*: 11-19, 1993.

Beutler, L.E., Malik, M., Alimohamed, S., Harwood, T.M., Talebi, H., Noble, S., et al.: Therapist variables. In M. J. Lambert (Ed.): *Bergin and Garfield's handbook of psychotherapy and behavior change,* 5th Edition. New York: Wiley, 2004.

Bohart, A. C., Elliott, R., Greenberg, L. S., and Watson, J. C.: Empathy. In J. C. Norcross (Ed.): *Psychotherapy relationships that work: Therapist contributions and responsiveness to patients.* New York: Oxford University Press, 2002.

Bohart, A.C., Magallanes, M., Guzman, R., Smiljanich, K., Aguallo, S., and Humphrey, A.: Emphasizing the future in empathy responses. *Journal of Humanistic Psychology, 33* (2): 12-29, 1993.

Cameron, S., and Turtle-Song, I.: Learning to write case notes using the SOAP format. *Journal of Counseling & Development, 80*: 286-292, 2002.

Cardillo, J.E.: Goal setting, follow-up, and goal monitoring. In T.J. Kiresuk, A. Smith, and J.E. Cardillo (Eds.): *Goal Attainment Scaling: Applications, theory, and measurement.* Hillsdale, NJ: Lawrence Erlbaum Associates, 1994.

Cardillo, J.E., and Smith, A.: Reliability of goal attainment scores. In T.J. Kiresuk, A. Smith, and J.E. Cardillo (Eds.): *Goal Attainment Scaling: Applications, theory, and measurement.* Hillsdale, NJ: Lawrence Erlbaum Associates, 1994.

Daniels, J.A., and Larson, L.M.: The impact of performance feedback on counseling self-efficacy and counselor anxiety. *Counselor Education & Supervision, 41*: 120-130, 2001.

Deci, E.L., and Ryan, R.M.: The support of autonomy and the control of behavior. *Journal of Personality and Social Psychology, 53*: 1024-1037, 1987.

Elliot, A.J., and Church, M.A.: Client-articulated avoidance goals in the therapy context. *Journal of Counseling Psychology, 49*: 243-254, 2002.

Elliot, A.J., and Sheldon, K.M.: Avoidance personal goals and the personality-illness relationship. *Journal of Personality and Social Psychology, 75*: 1282-1299, 1998.

Elliot, A.J., Sheldon, K., and Church, M.: Avoidance personal goals and subjective well-being. *Personality and Social Psychology Bulletin, 23*: 915-927, 1997.

Elliott, R., James, E., Reimschuessel, C., Cislo, D., and Sack, N.: Significant events and the analysis of immediate therapeutic impacts. *Psychotherapy, 22*: 620-630, 1985.

Evon, D.M., and Burns, J.W.: Process and outcome in cardiac rehabilitation: An examination of cross-lagged effects. *Journal of Consulting and Clinical Psychology, 72*: 605-616, 2004.

Farber, B.A., and Lane, J.S.: In J. C. Norcross (Ed.): *Psychotherapy relationships that work: Therapist contributions and responsiveness to patients.* New York: Oxford University Press, 2002.

Friedlander, M.L., Thibodeau, J.R., and Ward, L.G.: Discriminating the "good" from the "bad" therapy hour: A study of dyadic interaction. *Psychotherapy, 22*: 631-642, 1985.

Gallagher, M.S., and Hargie, O.D.W.: Evaluation of a microskills programme with field-based counsellors: Effects on core attitudes and counselling skills. *Counselling Psychology Quarterly, 2*: 405-417, 1989.

Geller, J.D., Lehman, A.K., and Farber, B.A.: Psychotherapists' representations of their patients. *Journal of Clinical Psychology, 58*: 733-745, 2002.

Gollwitzer, P.M.: Implementation intentions: Strong effects of simple plans. *American Psychologist, 54*: 493-503, 1999.

Greenberg, L.S., Elliot, R., Watson, J.C., and Bohart, A.C.: Empathy. *Psychotherapy: Theory, Research, Practice, Training, 38*: 380-384, 2001.

Hall, M.H.: A conversation with the father of Rogerian therapy. *Psychology Today*: 19-21, 62-66, 1967, December.

Hargie, O.D.W.: Training teachers in counselling skills: The effects of microcounselling. *British Journal of Educational Psychology, 54*: 214-220, 1984.

Hartley, J.: Notetaking in non-academic settings: A review. *Applied Cognitive Psychology, 16*: 559-574, 2002.

Hill, C.E., Helms, J.E., Spiegel, S.B., and Tichenor, V.: Development of a system for categorizing client reactions to therapist interventions. *Journal of Counseling Psychology, 35*: 27-36, 1988.

Horvath, A.O., and Bedi, R.P.: The alliance. In J. C. Norcross (Ed.): *Psychotherapy relationships that work: Therapist contributions and responsiveness to patients.* New York: Oxford University Press, 2002.

Johnson, D.W.: *Reaching out: Interpersonal effectiveness and self-actualization,* 8th Edition. Englewood Cliffs, NJ: Prentice-Hall, 2003.

Kiresuk, T.J., and Choate, R.O.: Applications of Goal Attainment Scaling. In T.J. Kiresuk, A. Smith, and J.E. Cardillo (Eds.): *Goal Attainment Scaling: Applications, theory, and measurement.* Hillsdale, NJ: Lawrence Erlbaum Associates, 1994.

Kiresuk, T.J., Smith, A., and Cardillo, J.E. (Eds.): *Goal Attainment Scaling: Applications, theory, and measurement.* Hillsdale, NJ: Lawrence Erlbaum Associates, 1994.

Kivlighan, D.M., Jr.: Changes in counselor intentions and response modes and in client reactions and session evaluation after training. *Journal of Counseling Psychology, 36*: 471-476, 1989.

Klein, M. H., Kolden, G. G., Michels, J. L., and Chisholm-Stockard, S.: In J. C. Norcross (Ed.): *Psychotherapy relationships that work: Therapist contributions and responsiveness to patients.* New York: Oxford University Press, 2002.

Koestner, R., Lekes, N., Powers, T.A., and Chicoine, E.: Attaining personal goals: Self-concordance plus implementation intentions equals success. *Journal of Personality and Social Psychology, 83*: 231-244, 2002.

Lambert, M.J., and Barley, D.E.: Research summary on the therapeutic relationship and psychotherapy outcome. In J. C. Norcross (Ed.): *Psychotherapy relationships that work: Therapist contributions and responsiveness to patients*. New York: Oxford University Press, 2002.

Lambert, M. J., and Ogles, B. M.: The efficacy and effectiveness of psychotherapy. In M. J. Lambert (Ed.): *Bergin and Garfield's handbook of psychotherapy and behavior change*, 5th Edition. New York: Wiley, 2004.

Levitt, D.H.: Active listening and counselor self-efficacy: Emphasis on one microskill in beginning counselor training. *The Clinical Supervisor, 20*: 101-115, 2001.

Lewis, T.F., and Osborn, C.J.: Solution-focused counseling and motivational interviewing: A consideration of confluence. *Journal of Counseling & Development, 82*: 38-48, 2004.

Martin, D.J., Garske, J.P., and Davis, M.D.: Relation of the therapeutic alliance with outcome and other variables: A meta-analytic review. *Journal of Consulting and Clinical Psychology, 68*: 438-450, 2000.

McNeil-Haber, F.M.: Ethical considerations in the use of nonerotic touch in psychotherapy with children. *Ethics & Behavior, 14*: 123-140, 2004.

Miller, W. R., and Rollnick, S.: *Motivational interviewing: Preparing people for change*, 2nd Edition. New York: Guilford Press, 2002.

Nezu, A.M.: Problem solving and behavior therapy revisited. *Behavior Therapy, 35*: 1-33, 2004.

Nezu, A.M., Nezu, C.M., Felgoise, S.H., McClure, K.S., and Houts, P.S.: Project genesis: Assessing the efficacy of problem-solving therapy for distressed adult cancer patients. *Journal of Consulting and Clinical Psychology, 71*: 1036-1048, 2003.

Norcross, J.C. (Ed.): *Psychotherapy relationships that work: Therapist contributions and responsiveness to patients*. New York: Oxford University Press, 2002.

Orlinsky, D.E., Ronnestad, M.H., and Willutzki, U.: In M. J. Lambert (Ed.): *Bergin and Garfield's handbook of psychotherapy and behavior change*, 5th Edition. New York: Wiley, 2004.

Pichot, T.: Co-creating solutions for substance abuse. *Journal of Systemic Therapies, 20*: 1-23, 2001.

Prieto, L.R., and Scheel, K.R.: Using case documentation to strengthen counselor trainees' case conceptualization skills. *Journal of Counseling & Development, 80*: 11-21, 2002.

Prochaska, J.O., and Norcross, J.C.: Stages of change. In J.C. Norcross (Ed.): *Psychotherapy relationships that work: Therapist contributions and responsiveness to patients*. New York: Oxford University Press, 2002.

Prochaska, J.O., and Prochaska, J.M.: Why don't continents move? Why don't people change? *Journal of Psychotherapy Integration, 9*: 83-102, 1999.

Prochaska, J.O., Norcross, J.C., DiClemente, C.C.: *Changing for good*. New York: Morrow, 1994.

Rejeski, W.J., Brawley, L.R., Ambrisius, W.T, Brubaker, P.H., Focht, B.C., Foy, C.G., et al.: Older adults with chronic disease: Benefits of group-mediated counseling in the promotion of physically active lifestyles. *Health Psychology, 22*: 414-423, 2003.

Richard, J.T.: Ideas on fostering creative problem solving in executive coaching. *Consulting Psychology Journal: Practice and Research, 55*: 249-256, 2003.

Rogers, C.R.: The necessary and sufficient conditions of therapeutic personality change. *Journal of Consulting Psychology, 21*: 95-103, 1957.

Rogers, C.R. (Ed.): *The therapeutic relationship and its impact, A study of psychotherapy with schizophrenics.* Madison, WI: University of Wisconsin Press, 1967.

Safran, J.D., Muran, J.C., Samstag, L.W., and Stevens, C.: Repairing alliance ruptures. In J. C. Norcross (Ed.): *Psychotherapy relationships that work: Therapist contributions and responsiveness to patients.* New York: Oxford University Press, 2002.

Schlosser, R.W.: Goal Attainment Scaling as a clinical measurement technique in communication disorders: A critical review. *Journal of Communication Disorders, 37*: 217-239, 2004.

Senecal, C., Nouwen, A., and White, D.: Motivation and dietary self-care in adults with diabetes: Are self-efficacy and autonmous self-regulation complementary or competing constructs? *Health Psychology, 19*: 452-457, 2000.

Sharpley, C.F., Fairnie, E., Tabary-Collins, E., Bates, R., and Lee, P.: The use of counsellor verbal response modes and client-perceived rapport. *Counselling Psychology Quarterly, 13*: 99-116, 2000.

Sheldon, K.M., and Elliot, A.J.: Not all personal goals are personal: Comparing autonomous and controlled reasons for goals and predictors of effort and attainment. *Personality and Social Psychology Bulletin, 24*: 546-557, 1998.

Sheldon, K.M., and Elliot, A.J.: Goal striving, need satisfaction, and longitudinal well-being: The self-concordance model. *Journal of Personality and Social Psychology, 76*: 482-497, 1999.

Sheldon, K.M., and Houser-Marko, L.: Self-concordance, goal attainment, and the pursuit of happiness: Can there be an upward spiral? *Journal of Personality and Social Psychology, 80:* 152-165, 2001.

Sheldon, K.M., and Kasser, T.: Pursuing personal goals: Skills enable progress but not progress is beneficial. *Personality and Social Psychology Bulletin, 24*: 1319-1331, 1998.

Smith, A.: Introduction and overview. In T.J. Kiresuk, A. Smith, and J.E. Cardillo (Eds.): *Goal Attainment Scaling: Applications, theory, and measurement.* Hillsdale, NJ: Lawrence Erlbaum Associates, 1994.

Smith, E.W.L., Clance, P.R., Imes, S. (Eds.): *Touch in psychotherapy: Theory, research, and practice.* New York: Guilford, 1998.

Spence, S.H., Sheffied, J.K., and Donovan, C.L.: Preventing adolescent depression: An evaluation of the problem solving for life program. *Journal of Consulting and Clinical Psychology, 71*: 3-13, 2003.

Tryon, G.S., and Winograd, G.: Goal consensus and collaboration. In J. C. Norcross (Ed.): *Psychotherapy relationships that work: Therapist contributions and responsiveness to patients.* New York: Oxford University Press, 2002.

Vansteenkiste, M., Simons, J., Sheldon, K.M., Lens, W., and Deci, E.: Motivating learning, performance, and persistence: The synergistic effects of intrinsic goal contents and autonomy-supportive contexts. *Journal of Personality and Social Psychology, 87*: 246-260, 2004.

Whiston, S.C., and Sexton, T.L.: An overview of psychotherapy outcome research: Implications for practice. *Professional Psychology: Research and Practice, 24*: 43-51, 1993.

Wierzbicki, M., and Pekarik, G.: A meta-analysis of psychotherapy dropout. *Professional Psychology: Research and Practice, 24*: 190-195, 1993.

INDEX